The reputation of philanthropy since 1750

MANCHESTER
1824

Manchester University Press

THE REPUTATION OF PHILANTHROPY SINCE 1750

Britain and beyond

Hugh Cunningham

Manchester University Press

The right of Hugh Cunningham to be identified as the author of this work has been asserted by him in accordance with the Copyright, Designs and Patents Act 1988.

Published by Manchester University Press
Altrincham Street, Manchester M1 7JA
www.manchesteruniversitypress.co.uk

British Library Cataloguing-in-Publication Data
A catalogue record for this book is available from the British Library

ISBN 978 1 5261 4638 0 hardback

First published 2020

The publisher has no responsibility for the persistence or accuracy of URLs for any external or third-party internet websites referred to in this book, and does not guarantee that any content on such websites is, or will remain, accurate or appropriate.

Typeset by Newgen Publishing UK
Printed in Great Britain
by TJ International Ltd, Padstow, Cornwall

Contents

Figures

Tables

Acknowledgements

My thanks to Malcolm Andrews, Beth Breeze, Grayson Ditchfield, David Turley and to the anonymous readers for Manchester University Press for their help and comments.

Introduction

In May 1914 a leading article in *The Times* claimed that 'Philanthropist is about as much a term of abuse as of praise'.[1] This one sentence introduces a key element in public discourse on philanthropy in Britain, that it was criticised as much as it was praised. Philanthropy is a word of Greek origin meaning love of humankind. It became widely used in Britain only from 1750. How was it that many people from the end of the eighteenth century onwards could come to dislike philanthropy and philanthropists with a passion that can shock? This book seeks to find out.

A second issue was prompted by a White Paper on Giving issued by the Coalition government in 2011. It contained a page headed 'Philanthropy Advice' and was addressed to people who 'give substantial sums'. There were going to be 'local portals, channeling philanthropists to a range of donor models and proactively connecting mass affluent and high net worth individuals to the best help and support for their charitable giving'.[2] Cutting through the jargon, why was 'philanthropy', distinguished from other forms of giving, promoted as exclusively for the rich? A love of humankind does not, in itself, have anything to do with money. How did philanthropy become associated with wealth, how did it become monetised?

Historians of philanthropy tend to assume that it is self-evident what their subject matter will be. They look to the past for evidence of private individuals giving money to beneficial public causes; they write histories of giving and gifting. They are then able to make some assessment as to whether the early seventeenth century did or did not outshine the Victorian period as a golden age of philanthropy. Or, as some argue, perhaps the golden age lay in the eighteenth century.[3] No one claimed that it lay in the twentieth century, except perhaps towards its close and reaching into the twenty-first century when a 'new philanthropy' was proclaimed.

An alternative approach, and one to which a number of historians have made valuable contributions, is to turn the focus on what contemporaries made of philanthropy. This study of the reputation of philanthropy falls into this category. Its starting point is a study of the words 'philanthropy' and 'philanthropist' and of the contexts in which they were used. 'Philanthropy' had little purchase in English until the mid-eighteenth century. 'Philanthropist' emerged a little later. People in the seventeenth century or before who are now described as 'philanthropists' were not so-called by their contemporaries. They were most likely 'benefactors'. The history of these words – and the importance of it – is well illustrated in a remark of John Dryden in 1693. Seeing 'philanthropy' 'every where manifest' in the writings of Polybius, he commented that 'we have not a proper word in *English* to express' it. But it was not only that there was no currency to the word 'philanthropy'. Perhaps more surprising was that Polybius's philanthropy was displayed not in giving money but in writing history 'Wherein he has left a perpetual Monument of his publick Love to all the World'.[4] For better or worse, it is difficult to imagine a modern historian being credited with philanthropy.

Philanthropy as it emerged in the second half of the eighteenth century was wrought out of an amalgam of the Enlightenment and Romanticism. It was a feeling of love for all humans, experienced physically – and inclining those who felt it to express this in verse. It might entail, but did not require, giving money. It could have potentially huge implications. The slave trade and slavery jarred implacably with any feeling of love for all humans. Love of humankind implied that all humans had rights, rights that were universal and not country-specific as were the 'rights of the free-born Englishman'. Even criminals fell within the compass of philanthropy. The first person to win the accolade of 'philanthropist' was John Howard, the prison reformer, who counted the miles he travelled across Europe, not the money he gave.

This first phase of philanthropy began to be sharply challenged with the outbreak of war against revolutionary France in 1793. Could you, should you, love the enemy you were fighting, who was trying to invade your country? Many answered no. 'Universal philanthropy', a philanthropy that knew no borders, became much more rarely invoked. To add to the problems for philanthropy, radicals and those seen as revolutionaries began to proclaim philanthropy, seeing it as a potent weapon against those who would deny them rights. The followers of Thomas Spence, the radical land reformer, called themselves the 'Spencean Philanthropists'.

It was, ironically, the opponents of philanthropy who did most to define the next phase in its history. Campaigners for the abolition of the slave trade (achieved in 1807) and of slavery (achieved in 1833) rarely spoke or thought of themselves as philanthropists. Their opponents, however, criticised what they saw as their ill-judged philanthropy. Evangelicals played a prominent part in the campaigns against slavery – and those campaigns in time came to be thought of as an achievement in which the nation could take great pride. So it was that there grew up an association between evangelicalism and philanthropy. Enlightenment and Romantic philanthropy was followed by evangelical philanthropy, a phase that was dominant in the period up to the mid-nineteenth century. Evangelicals were prominent in innumerable organisations and institutions that could be described as philanthropic and themselves proclaimed the merits of 'Christian philanthropy' – and decried any other kind. But what gave most specificity to this phase was the virulence of the criticism of this evangelical philanthropy. Expressed volubly in *The Times*, it reached an apogee in the mid-century fulminations of Thomas Carlyle against prison reform and anti-slavery, the two causes with which evangelical philanthropy was most closely associated.

Evangelical philanthropy became less controversial, less central to public discourse, in the second half of the nineteenth century. A new phase, marked by the relationship between capitalism and philanthropy, began to dominate discussion. That relationship, with different sub-phases, has characterised philanthropy ever since.

From its outset philanthropy had an uneasy relationship with political economy, which, like philanthropy, came to the fore in the later eighteenth century. Political economy put a premium on the free workings of the labour market. Its advocates railed against those who sought in any way to supplement wages or to give help to those who were deemed to be undeserving. Some argued that philanthropy might work in harness with political economy to bring order and rationality to charitable giving. Others came increasingly to feel that philanthropy was no better in this respect than charity. Both, it was often said, did more harm than good. The relief of poverty had been at the heart of charitable giving and activity since the fifteenth century. In the nineteenth century those who sought to contribute to this cause found themselves looking over their shoulders in case a political economist was bearing down upon them. Would-be philanthropists turned their attention to other causes that would avoid the censure of political economy.

Three in particular marked the second half of the nineteenth century, each of them, now for the first time, associated with the giving, expenditure or investment of money. The first consisted of donations of land and money by local capitalists for the provision of cultural and social facilities in towns and cities. Libraries, public parks, museums, art galleries, hospitals and universities became part of the urban landscape, some of them aided by money from the rates, many of them outright donations. Second, there was a marriage of philanthropy and capitalism in attempts to ease urban housing problems. Five per cent philanthropy, as it was called, offered a return on capital, set below market rates, for those who put up money to build new tenements for the working classes. Third, some employers, the Quaker chocolate makers most prominently, began to build model villages and provide leisure facilities for their employees in a policy that was part good industrial relations and part a genuine desire to improve lives.

Many philanthropists themselves, however, doubted whether these three forms of philanthropy, even if they escaped the criticisms of political economists, did much to solve deep-rooted urban problems. Towards the end of the nineteenth century there came a call for a 'new philanthropy', to be marked not by money giving, but by 'service'. Toynbee Hall in Whitechapel was the headquarters of this new movement, a place where the young middle classes could spend time living in the midst of poverty and seeking to raise the aspirations and standards of living of the poor. A more radical response was to argue that philanthropy had failed and to call upon the state to intervene in the resolution of social and economic problems.

By the early twentieth century philanthropy was dropping out of public discourse, seen as a thing of the past. Building on the work of volunteers, most of them women, there evolved a new profession, 'social work', for tackling intractable problems. Some argued in the inter-war period that yet another 'new philanthropy' could work in harmony with the professionals, and to some extent this happened, but philanthropy was slipping into a role that David Owen described as being the 'junior partner in the welfare firm'.[5]

In the late twentieth century the welfare state came under attack from those who, like the political economists of the nineteenth century, argued that welfare, like charity before it, created a dependency class. This facilitated the rise of another 'new philanthropy'. Buoyed by accumulated wealth, its advocates asserted its claims to be able to use methods honed in business practice to do what the state had tried and failed to do. The *Economist* bluntly asserted what enabled such a new philanthropy to flourish: 'inequality is a friend of philanthropy, and large fortunes encourage individual generosity'. Another 'golden age', it hoped, 'may be about to dawn'.[6]

Histories of gifting or giving provide invaluable data and often allow insight into motivation. They are not in themselves, however, histories of philanthropy. The history of 'philanthropy' and 'philanthropist' as words reveals big changes in their meaning and reputation. A close attention to context alone can both demonstrate and explain these changes. Such an approach shows that philanthropy existed in a public and political domain. The Enlightenment, Romanticism, evangelicalism and capitalism provide essential context. They open gateways into topics without which understanding of philanthropy is diminished: poverty and the Poor Laws; slavery and anti-slavery; political radicalism; mutualism; civil society; national identity; gender; poetry and fiction; empire; voluntary societies and volunteering; citizenship; the welfare state.

Philanthropy occupied for a time a prominent place in public discourse. Well-known people – perhaps they could be called 'public intellectuals' – assessed its merits and demerits. They included Adam Smith, William Godwin, William Wordsworth, Samuel Taylor Coleridge, Thomas Chalmers, John Stuart Mill, Thomas Carlyle, George Bernard Shaw and William Beveridge. This book is more about them and about the novelists, Charles Dickens, George Eliot, John Galsworthy, Virginia Woolf and others, who dissected philanthropy than it is about those who were called philanthropists. I am interested in who the label was attached to and why – and to that extent in what they did or gave. But this is not the book for those who want to find out more about Angela Burdett-Coutts or George Peabody or Dr Barnardo, or about those who were sometimes called 'philanthropists in humble life' of whom three stood out in the publications of the day: John Pounds (1766–1839), disabled Portsmouth cobbler, who taught the poorest children, Sarah Martin (1791–1843) who was a prison visitor in Great Yarmouth, and Kitty Wilkinson (1786–1860), famous in Liverpool for her work in the cholera epidemic of 1832.

Philanthropy was frequently seen as an articulation and embodiment of national identity. The language in which this was expressed poses problems. Philanthropy was seen variously as 'English' or 'British', rarely 'Scottish' or 'Welsh'. The English often wrote of 'England' when they meant 'Britain'. As Lord Rosebery, a Scot, put it, England's wealth, power and population 'make her feel herself to be Great Britain'. There were certainly articulations of Englishness that were specific to England. That was the case in much writing about the landscape. It was also true of popular Conservatism in the later nineteenth century, which could be overtly anti-Scottish or, less strongly, anti-Welsh.[7] With philanthropy, however, at least for the English, England and Britain were interchangeable. Scottish philanthropy did have distinctive features. In providing an entry into the public sphere for women in the later nineteenth century, for example, there was in Scotland an emphasis in discourse and action on the temperance issue that was much stronger than in England.[8] Olive Checkland, however, concluded from her study of the motivations and achievements of Scottish philanthropy that 'the Scots, though they achieved much, did so largely on an imitative and emulative basis, rather than by invention and innovation. Time and again the story is one of borrowing ideas from the larger world, especially England'.[9] That perhaps does less than justice to some of her own evidence: Scots were, for example, in the forefront of the ragged schools movement, and in the formation of the YMCA and the Boys' Brigade. Nevertheless, the point remains that the English and Scots broadly thought in the same way about philanthropy and created institutions that bear a remarkable similarity. Moreover, Scottish writing about philanthropy, for example that of Adam Smith and Thomas Chalmers, was influential in England, suggesting that at this level, too, there was considerable common ground between the two countries. Welsh philanthropy has received less attention than English or Scottish. It had its own distinctive features, largely dependent on environment. In Cardiff, for example, growing from small beginnings and heavily influenced by the ownership of much of its land by the Scottish Marquis of Bute, philanthropy was highly dependent on donations from the Bute Estate and there was less evidence of the strong middle-class influence that was to be found in a city such as Bristol, the two separated only by the mouth of the Severn river.[10] There is nothing, however, to suggest that the Welsh had a substantially different view of and attitude towards philanthropy than the English or Scots. This book, then, encompasses Britain, even though, if we give literal credence to contemporary writings, some of it seems to be about England alone.

British philanthropy reached out beyond the shores of Great Britain. The British saw themselves as the most philanthropic nation in the world and an important element in their sense of themselves was their global role. Take three examples. First, missionary societies established themselves overseas from the 1790s. By 1900 there were about 10,000 British missionaries at work in the world, the largest number of them in the China Inland Mission.[11] Second, solutions to what was seen as a problem of surplus children from the 1820s onwards were often thought to lie in transporting the children to supposedly healthier environments in South Africa, Canada and later Australia, a policy continued into the 1960s.[12] Third, anti-slavery campaigns ensured that philanthropy remained in the public eye for decades after the abolition of slavery in British possessions in 1833. All these forms of philanthropy had their cheerleaders, but also critics. In all three philanthropy's reputation was at stake.

Less contentious were the connections that British philanthropists established and maintained with their counterparts in other countries. In the eighteenth century strong links between British and American philanthropists survived the trauma of the American Revolution. In opposition to the British Empire, an 'empire of humanity', Enlightenment-inspired, and sustained by correspondence, publications and visits, was made up of a network of like-minded reformers on both sides of the Atlantic. Prison reform was an abiding common concern.[13] These international links were taken a step further after the Napoleonic Wars when 'philanthropic tourism' spread: philanthropists crossed national borders to visit institutions for reform that seemed to promise a solution to pervasive social problems, particularly those for children. Agrarian colonies, for example, originating in the Netherlands and Switzerland, spread to Germany and Belgium, to find their most famous exemplar, Mettray, in France in 1839. Matthew Davenport-Hill described how 'No Mahommedan ... believes more devoutly in the efficacy of a pilgrimage to Mecca, than I do in one to Mettray'.[14]

Links of this kind were sustained and grew throughout the nineteenth century. In the late 1880s Jane Addams visited Toynbee Hall and took from it inspiration for Hull House in Chicago, as well as establishing a lifelong friendship with Henrietta Barnett, a prominent British philanthropist. In association with the World's Fair in Chicago in 1893 'thousands of philanthropists from the United States and Europe convened for a weeklong International Congress of Charities, Correction, and Philanthropy', some of its proceedings published in *Women's Mission*, edited by Angela Burdett-Coutts.[15]

These international links suggest the possibility of a history of philanthropy that includes within its ambit both Europe and North America. Within such a broad framework there were, however, distinct national variations. French philanthropy, for example, like British, was Enlightenment and secular in origin; unlike British philanthropy, it maintained this emphasis through and beyond the years of revolution, the period when in Britain philanthropy was becoming associated with evangelicalism. Philanthropy, argues Arthur Gautier, is a 'historically contested concept' within nations; it is also one between them.[16]

Chapter 1 analyses the way the history of philanthropy has been written, highlighting the fact that making definitions at the outset of what philanthropy is, or is not, shapes the narratives that follow. This is followed in Chapter 2 by a profile of philanthropy in public discourse, using data on mentions of philanthropy in periodicals and newspapers. Philanthropy on these measurements came into existence in the second half of the eighteenth century, rose sharply in the 1830s and 1840s and fell equally sharply in the very late nineteenth and first half of the twentieth centuries. It has then grown again since the late twentieth century. This data and other sources are then probed for content in chronological chapters, starting, in Chapter 3, with the genesis of a discourse relating to philanthropy in the second half of the eighteenth century. In Chapter 4 the focus is on John Howard, the eighteenth-century prototype of what a philanthropist should be. This is followed in Chapter 5 by examination of Howard's legacy through the nineteenth century, both as a philanthropist who could not be equalled and for the linkage that his life established between philanthropy and prison reform. Chapter 6 analyses the deep impact on philanthropy of the French Revolution and the conservative reaction to it in Britain. Chapter 7 covers the period from the end of the Napoleonic Wars up to mid-century, a period marked by a dominant association between philanthropy and evangelicalism, with many lauding philanthropy and others equally strongly opposed to it, not least for the alleged neglect of the poor at home in favour of slaves and others overseas. In the mid-Victorian period from 1850 to 1880, surveyed in Chapter 8, philanthropy took new forms in association with capitalism; it was praised as part of the identity of the nation, but continued to be subject to heavy criticism by political economists, by those who saw it as 'effeminate' and by others who disliked the 'professionalism' that seemed to provide jobs and salaries for those who worked for the voluntary organisations that made up the philanthropic world. The volume of criticism rose in the period 1880–1914 that is analysed in Chapter 9. Radical alternatives to philanthropy as it had been understood took shape, at Toynbee Hall and other settlements, and in the arguments of socialists and New Liberals that an increased role for the state was essential. In the century since the First World War, the subject of Chapter 10, philanthropy was first in danger of being overtaken by a new language centered on citizenship, democracy and volunteering, and then made an unanticipated revival in the shape of a 'new philanthropy' built on new wealth. The Conclusion stresses the extent to which the philanthropy of the Victorian age was unashamedly political in the causes it adopted and was consequently deeply implicated in the public discourse of the age. For most of the twentieth century it carried too much baggage to be resuscitated and quietly dropped out of public discourse and concern. Its revival was closely linked to the rise of neoliberalism. The book closes by considering the implications of the findings, particularly the level of criticism, and pointing to how the world leadership of philanthropy passed from Britain to the United States in the late nineteenth century. Philanthropy there in the twenty-first century raises controversial issues, some of which are equally evident in Britain.

Notes

1 *The Times*, 12 May 1914.
2 White Paper on Giving, 2011, CM. 8084, p. 20.
3 D. Owen, *English Philanthropy 1660–1960* (London: Oxford University Press, 1965), p. 469. For the eighteenth-century, B. Rodgers, *Cloak of Charity: Studies in Eighteenth-Century Philanthropy* (London: Methuen, 1949), p. 3.
4 *The Works of John Dryden*, Vol. XX (Berkeley, Los Angeles and London: University of California Press, 1989), p. 21.
5 Owen, *English Philanthropy*, pp. 527–53.
6 *The Economist*, 29 July 2014.
7 A. Howkins, 'The discovery of rural England', and H. Cunningham, 'The Conservative party and patriotism', in R. Colls and P. Dodd (eds), *Englishness: Politics and Culture 1880–1920* (London: Croom Helm, 1986), pp. 62–88, 283–307, quoting Rosebery, p. 294; D. Matless, *Landscape and Englishness* (London: Reaktion, 1998).
8 M. Smitley, *The Feminine Public Sphere: Middle-Class Women in Civic Life in Scotland, c. 1870–1914* (Manchester: Manchester University Press, 2009).
9 O. Checkland, *Philanthropy in Victorian Scotland: Social Welfare and the Voluntary Principle* (Edinburgh: John Donald, 1980), p. 332.
10 N. Evans, 'Urbanisation, elite attitudes and philanthropy: Cardiff, 1850–1914', *International Review of Social History*, 27 (1982), 290–323.
11 A. Porter, 'Religion, missionary enthusiasm, and empire', in A. Porter (ed.), *The Oxford History of the British Empire*, Vol. III (Oxford: Oxford University Press, 1999), pp. 222–46.
12 J. Parr, *Labouring Children: British Immigrant Apprentices to Canada, 1879–1924* (London: Croom Helm, 1980); P. Bean and J. Melville, *Lost Children of the Empire: The Untold Story of Britain's Child Migrants* (London: Hyman, 1989).
13 A. B. Moniz, *From Empire to Humanity: The American Revolution and the Origins of Humanitarianism* (New York: Oxford University Press, 2016); K. Lloyd and C. Burgoyne, 'The evolution of a transatlantic debate on penal reform, 1780–1830', in H. Cunningham and J. Innes (eds), *Charity, Philanthropy and Reform: From the 1690s to 1850* (Basingstoke: Macmillan, 1998), pp. 208–27.
14 J. J. H. Dekker, 'Transforming the nation and the child: Philanthropy in the Netherlands, Belgium, France and England, c. 1780–c. 1850', in Cunningham and Innes (eds), *Charity, Philanthropy and Reform*, pp. 130–47.
15 S. R. Robbins, 'Sustaining gendered philanthropy through transatlantic friendship: Jane Addams, Henrietta Barnett, and writing for reciprocal mentoring', pp. 211–35, and F. Q. Christianson and L. Thorne-Murphy, 'Introduction: Writing philanthropy in the United States and Britain', in F. Q. Christianson, and L. Thorne-Murphy (eds), *Philanthropic Discourse in Anglo-American Literature, 1850–1920* (Bloomington: Indiana University Press, 2017), pp. 1–3.
16 A. Gautier, 'Historically contested concepts: A conceptual history of philanthropy in France, 1712–1914', *Theory & Society*, 48 (2019), 95–129.

1

Writing the history of philanthropy

The historiography of philanthropy is sparse. Compared to other contingent areas of social history, for example the history of poverty and the Poor Laws, it is extremely thin. In this chapter I analyse the approaches taken in the main books that have informed views of how the history of philanthropy should be written.

B. Kirkman Gray, W. K. Jordan and David Owen

One marker of the poverty of the historiography is that students coming new to the subject are routinely directed to three books, B. Kirkman Gray's *A History of English Philanthropy from the Dissolution of the Monasteries to the First Census* (1905), W. K. Jordan's *Philanthropy in England 1480–1660: A Study of the Changing Pattern of English Social Aspirations* (1959) and David Owen's *English Philanthropy 1660–1960* (1965). One of these is over a century old, the other two over half a century. In no other field of history have books written so long ago failed to be superseded. There have been significant additions to our understanding of philanthropy in Britain since the publication of the three bedrocks but for a long-run chronology they remain in place. From my perspective one of the points of interest in them is that they all employ the word 'philanthropy' in their titles even though in two of them (Gray and Jordan) the word was hardly ever used by contemporaries and in Owen not for the first of his three centuries. This suggests (and it is hardly surprising) that the authors' forays into the past were an attempt to make sense of the present.

Gray was the most explicit about this. 'If we retrace this history [of philanthropy]', he wrote, 'we ought to be able to throw some light on its present meaning and problems'. 'What is the meaning and worth of philanthropy?' was the fundamental question he addressed.[1] Born in 1862, the son of a Congregational minister, Gray had a wide experience of teaching and had drifted towards Unitarianism before in 1897 taking up social work in London. A nervous breakdown in 1902 brought this to an end and he turned to trying to make sense of his experience. 'I had become aware, in the course of several years' work among the unfortunate subjects of philanthropic activity, of what is, of course, a matter of common knowledge, viz., that philanthropy does not entirely fulfil its aim, since the evils which it seeks to allay still continue, and many of them in an increasing degree.' It is curious that with this agenda he chose to close his book with the first census of 1801. He argued that the census marked the point at which government and the state first began to become aware of the condition of the population and that from it followed, not immediately, but with some effect from the 1830s, a period when philanthropy started to lose ground to the state in tackling social problems. Continuing into the nineteenth century, Gray argued, 'would have involved matters of present-day controversy'. His conclusion, however, was clear: philanthropy in the centuries he studied had failed in the sense that 'the amount of want was far greater than the efforts made to relieve it'.[2]

The books by Jordan and Owen can in some respects be considered alongside each other. Most obviously, Owen began in 1660, Jordan's end date. Less obviously, both were funded by the Ford Foundation. Owen described how the origin of his book 'lies in the decision of the Ford Foundation in 1955 to sponsor a series of studies of modern philanthropy'. He 'was asked to undertake a survey, rather general in scope, of English philanthropy, which might serve as a background for more detailed investigations of the American experience'. Jordan's research began 'many years' before publication, benefitting from a variety of funding sources, but his work was 'brought to completion with the help of a generous grant from the Ford Foundation'.[3] What prompted the Ford Foundation to fund historical work on philanthropy? Philanthropy was becoming a subject that was attracting interest in the United States through the 1950s. F. Emerson Andrews's *Philanthropic Giving* was supported and published by the Russell Sage Foundation in 1950, and rapidly reprinted. 'Informed, witty, and sensible', it provided useful advice to donors as well as a brief 'glance at history'.[4] The University of Wisconsin hosted the 'History of American Philanthropy Project', one important output from which was Robert H. Bremner's *American Philanthropy* (1960), published as a contribution to the Chicago History of American Civilization. The moment was perhaps ripe for further study and funding. Established in 1936 in Michigan, the Ford Foundation in the post-war world began to separate itself from the Ford Motor Company, to broaden the scope of its activities and to move its headquarters to New York. Much of this was prompted by recommendations of a committee set up to chart the Foundation's future under the chairmanship of H. Rowan Gaither in the late 1940s. From 1953 to 1956, in the years when the decision was made to fund studies of philanthropy, Gaither was President of the Foundation.[5] There is evidence that one of Gaither's prime concerns (and he was of course not alone in this) was the Cold War. It is at least not impossible that a motive for financing studies of philanthropy was that they might highlight the contributions that philanthropy had made, and could make, to what Jordan was to describe as 'liberal society'. One of the distinctions being made at the time by political scientists was that between 'totalitarianism' and political democracy, the latter marked by the plethora of voluntary organisations that mediated between the state and the mass of the people. Philanthropy was a safeguard against totalitarianism.

If there was a Cold War agenda behind the Ford Foundation's funding of studies of philanthropy Jordan's work must have delighted his sponsors. Based primarily on a study of wills, he argued that there was an outpouring of philanthropy directed away from the religious foundations of the medieval period towards what he called secular objectives, poverty relief, almshouses, schools, municipal improvement. Headed by merchants and gentry, over half the amount given emanating from London, Jordan celebrated a shift in men's aspirations that created and grew out of a culture that made it a norm to leave an endowment at death to support a worthy cause in perpetuity. Here is Jordan in typical vein on the contribution made by private charity to poor relief between 1600 and 1660:

> A truly magnificent effort was undertaken by private charity in the six decades with which our period closes to raise up and endow institutions which would at last bring endemic poverty under control by effective relief and achieve its cure by an immense expansion of the area of social responsibility for all classes of men. The state stood poised for intervention after 1597, if the need should arise, but because of the prodigal generosity of private men who had assumed for themselves an heroic burden of social responsibility that intervention was in fact to be long delayed; delayed, it is fair to say, in its ultimately complete sense, until our own century.

Jordan clearly preferred a society where such 'incredible charitable generosity' rendered the role of the state distinctly secondary.[6] In contrast to Gray, far from failing, philanthropy became what we would now call an integral and successful element in civil society.

Jordan's research, based on painstaking work on individual wills, was widely praised, but the conclusions he drew from it were immediately challenged. He had, knowingly, failed to take account of inflation and of rising population in tracing long-term trends. His critics argued that if these were factored in, Jordan's rapid growth turned into a decline in the real value of charitable giving.[7] Jordan was also criticised for his assertion that 'in no year prior to 1660 was more than 7 per cent of all the vast sums expended on the care of the poor derived from taxation'. J. F. Hadwin concluded that Jordan's downplaying of the significance of the Poor Law 'now seems incredible'. Paul Slack endorsed this judgement; Jordan's calculation 'was deficient in almost every respect'. Local studies in the sixteenth and seventeenth centuries suggest that half or more of such relief was from poor rates.[8] This covered only charity given through wills; gifts given to the poor from living donors, Jordan thought, were one-third of the total. They were probably considerably more, certainly if casual giving to beggars is included. Slack concluded that they 'may well have been more substantial in aggregate than those contained in wills'. If these conjectures about lifetime giving are right, then, on the one hand, the role of charity assumes greater importance but, on the other, Jordan's focus on wills looks as though it distorts the reality of what was happening on the ground.[9]

The attempt to draw a sharp line in the relief of poverty between charity and taxation, as Jordan did, was misguided. Many endowments, probably over one-third of them on Jordan's own reckoning, arranged for the distribution of relief to be carried out by parish or municipal officials. Much giving was in response to briefs, calls at national or local level for assistance in response to emergencies such as fire damage.[10]

The concentration by critics of Jordan on his failure to build into his figures anything for inflation and population rise, and his exaggeration of the contribution by charity as opposed to poor rates, has distracted attention from his wider claims about the significance of the changes in charitable giving. Jordan's subtitle, 'A Study of the Changing Pattern of English Social Aspirations', was in many ways a better clue to the argument he was making than his main title; the 'philanthropy' of his title may have been a word he felt obliged to use. The Reformation was for Jordan the key factor in changing 'social aspirations'. Whereas in pre-Reformation England, he argued, the main motive to giving was a concern for one's own soul, post-Reformation it was for the good of society. Protestantism provided the 'impulse' for change, its impact 'revolutionary'.[11] Since Jordan wrote, pre-Reformation charity has been reassessed more positively and scholars of Catholic Europe have documented changes on a scale and chronology comparable to those in Protestant England.[12] To put it at its mildest, Jordan's emphasis on the degree and uniqueness of England's changing aspirations looks overstated.

There is also a problem with Jordan's emphasis on the shift to the secular. Jordan was well aware that most of his donors 'were deeply pious men'. The almshouses and schools they founded, the bequests they made for the relief of poverty, nearly always had a profoundly religious element to them, at the very least an expectation of religious behaviour and observance in the beneficiaries. In what sense, then, were they 'secular'? Only that they attended to needs and aspirations in this world which were seen as part of the make-up of a godly society. Jordan's perception of them as 'militantly and aggressively secular in temper and in purpose' raised challenging questions. Many historians doubt whether it makes sense to try to draw a firm line between the religious and the secular in Jordan's centuries. As Paul Slack put it, 'Gifts to the poor and for education were no less pious in intent, no less directed towards saving the souls of donors and recipients, than gifts to churches or religious orders'.[13] Jordan made the further claim that charitable giving, particularly outwards from London, contributed to the process whereby 'England becomes a nation'.[14] In short, 'philanthropy' was accorded a level of significance in bringing about change, and as evidence of that change, that few other historians find plausible.

David Owen, while acknowledging that his book 'deals with a similar theme (and begins nominally at his concluding date)', was adamant that it 'is not designed as a sequel to Jordan's monumental study'. Its scope was 'wider and the evidence leads to no such precise conclusions as he is able to draw'. Moreover, the sections dealing with the 1660s to the 1780s and from 1914 onwards 'are hardly more than prologue and epilogue to the main sections' on the late eighteenth and nineteenth centuries.[15] Equally significant was the difference in tone. Where Jordan was forthright and assertive, Owen was reflective and measured. As John Clive wrote after Owen's death in 1968, 'his historical sympathies rarely remained untempered by irony ... he possessed empathy and skepticism in more or less equal proportions'.[16] If there was a narrative thrust running through his book it was that, admirable and extensive though charitable giving was in his centuries, it was never going to be sufficient to meet need. An increasing role for the state was more or less inevitable. In some ways, though less assertively, it reinforced the message that Kirkman Gray had first outlined.

Jordan and Owen, however, have this in common, that their instinct was to measure philanthropy by the amount of money given. Jordan's choice of sources made this almost inevitable – he argued that some two-thirds of giving was through wills. Owen was at pains to point out how difficult it was to chart developments in amount given when the pattern of giving changed so radically after 1660; the proliferation of subscription societies in the eighteenth century make wills a much less suitable source than they were for Jordan and there was no ready replacement. Nevertheless Owen did not disguise that for inclusion in his work 'a primary test applied here is pecuniary. This study has little to do with good works, personal service, or labors in the public interest, save as these were accompanied by substantial contributions of money from individuals and groups'.[17] This meant that individuals and activities normally regarded as falling within the compass of philanthropy were excluded. Thus 'The movement for prison reform as a whole lies outside, or at least on the periphery, of philanthropy as understood in this study'. John Howard was mentioned, but as a source of information and data not as a philanthropist. And again, 'the anti-slavery crusade raises questions about the boundary between philanthropy and politico-social reform ... [It] was more an exercise in reform agitation than an example of the voluntary effort that we customarily think of as philanthropic'. It nevertheless merited four pages for there was in it 'pecuniary sacrifice and sensitiveness to human suffering', suggested by Owen as 'earmarks of a philanthropic movement'.[18] Further, 'personal service', which many argued in the nineteenth century should be central to philanthropy, was left out of account by Owen.

Pose the question, 'What are the earmarks of a philanthropic movement' or indeed, simply, of philanthropy, and my argument in this book will be that the answer will change and that you might, legitimately, get different answers at any one point in time. If we are to understand the history of philanthropy we have to listen to what contemporaries said and thought about it. That means, since they said very little before the mid-eighteenth century, that the history of philanthropy starts then.

The books by Jordan and Owen, covering the period from 1480 to 1960, might appear to provide a narrative framework. If they do, it is a curious one. If Jordan's evidence is taken at face value the highpoint of philanthropy was in the first sixty years of the seventeenth century. The Charity Commissioners in 1895 thought that 'the latter half of the 19th century will stand second in respect of the greatness and variety of the Charities created within its duration to no other half-century since the Reformation'. But as Owen admitted after quoting this, 'In the light of Professor Jordan's evidence it may be doubted whether the late Victorians were investing in charity as large a proportion of the national income as did their Tudor-Stuart ancestors'.[19] The Victorian age may have been in some respects, as often claimed, a golden age of philanthropy but after Jordan's work it did not appear to match up to the seventeenth century. To further complicate any simple narrative, Betsy Rodgers in *Cloak of Charity: Studies in Eighteenth-Century Philanthropy* (1949) had claimed that 'The eighteenth century was the golden age of philanthropy. Charity blossomed so fully at this point in history because the economic and social condition of the poor demanded immediate notice, and because the sentimental and moral temper of the times ensured a quick response to this demand'.[20] With chapters on a familiar cast, Thomas Coram, Jonas Hanway, John Howard, Robert Raikes, Mrs Trimmer, Hannah More and the abolition of the slave trade, by no means uncritical of what was thought and said, Rodgers nevertheless made a strong case for the eighteenth century. The one century that no one was claiming was a golden age was the twentieth, Rodgers indeed wondering 'whether philanthropists will become an extinct species'.[21]

The eighteenth and nineteenth centuries

If it has become difficult from the historiography to pinpoint the highpoints of philanthropy, there has, since the time of Kirkman Gray, been broad agreement on a significant change in the methods of philanthropy located in the late seventeenth century. Gray gave it a name that has stuck, though contemporaries never used it: 'associated philanthropy'. Gray saw this as both copying and paralleling the development of joint stock companies, 'A feeling for the power of association'.[22] What this meant was that people came together to form societies that raised money on a regular basis from subscribers to support projects, notably charity schools and in the eighteenth century hospitals. Ben-Amos has questioned the novelty of this, seeing it as building on the traditions of guilds with their elected officers and subscriptions and reminding us that there was regular giving at church festivals – as there was also in distribution of doles at Christmas.[23]

Ben-Amos's emphasis for the seventeenth century was that 'gift giving multiplied and forms of support became more robust and diverse throughout'.[24] Donna T. Andrew in *Philanthropy and Police: London Charity in the Eighteenth Century*, by contrast, was alert to change. There was, she accepted, much continuity from the past: up to mid-century 'clerics continued to insist that almsgiving, directed by the spirit of sacrifice, was essentially a self-regarding religious act'. But charity was increasingly linked to what were perceived as the needs of the nation. Moderation and discrimination in charitable giving were urged, the provision of employment preferable to cash handouts. Anything that would lead to an increase in population and employment and an encouragement of virtue received support. It was in this context that the Foundling Hospital, the Marine Society and Lying-in Hospitals were born and thrived in mid-century. But by the end of the century that moment had passed. Far from fearing a decline of population, the worry became that it would increase too fast. Further, political economy was gaining dominance in discussions of employment and the call for moral regeneration, articulated and organised by evangelicals, was loud. Charity, insisted the leaders of the influential Society for Bettering the Condition of the Poor, had to become a 'science'.[25]

Andrew fleshes out and adds new elements to Owen's 'prologue' on the eighteenth century. She ends in the early nineteenth century. Thereafter Owen remains the authority but, as we have seen, his compass was narrow. In an extended critique of Owen's book in *Victorian Studies* in 1966 Brian Harrison highlighted that narrowness and at the same time drew attention to negative aspects of Victorian philanthropy: 'the quarrels and vendettas endemic in the philanthropic world', the duplication of effort, the social climbing, the lack of attention to need, the fierce resentment of philanthropy and charity by many contemporaries, the conservatism and lack of imagination.[26] Harrison returned to the topic under the same title, 'Philanthropy and the Victorians', in 1982, omitting much of the earlier article, adding 'a great deal of new material' and completely rewriting it. For Harrison 'Philanthropy extends through a wide range of social behaviour – from the informal expression of kindness to a dependent at one end to legislative campaigning for social justice at the other'. With this broad remit he then discussed the motives of philanthropists and the criticism to which they were subjected. It was certainly not what might be described as 'a golden age' analysis, though it ended on an upbeat note, calling for an acknowledgement of 'the substantial and continuing contribution made by volunteers and philanthropists to our history'.[27]

Harrison gave space to gender in his critique, but the issue was only put centre stage in F. K. Prochaska's *Women and Philanthropy in Nineteenth-Century*

England.[28] Prochaska followed this up with a chapter on 'Philanthropy' in
The Cambridge Social History of Britain 1750–1950. Here, as with Owen,
the emphasis was on the nineteenth century, the half-centuries with which
he might have been expected to commence and finish receiving hardly any
attention. On the nineteenth century itself Prochaska's approach was always
interesting, sometimes challenging, but distinctly idiosyncratic. His starting
point was 'to think of the history of philanthropy broadly as the history of
kindness'. On the positive side this allowed him to describe how kindness was
taught and fostered within families of all social classes and to give full weight
to the charity of the poor to the poor. Alert, as was Harrison, to some of the
absurdities and dysfunctional aspects of Victorian philanthropy, he nevertheless saw them as outweighed by the neighbourliness and social cohesion that
philanthropic action both encouraged and exemplified. Christianity, especially in its evangelical form, was, he argues, at the root of such philanthropy,
chapels, churches and their offshoots often the organising agents. For him
'the relatively prosperous mid-Victorian period was a philanthropic golden
age. What would be the repercussions for charity and welfare in a time of
Christian decline?'[29]

Prochaska gave his answer in a number of short books that, while rooted
in the nineteenth century, took his story forward into the twentieth century.
In *The Voluntary Impulse: Philanthropy in Modern Britain*, pre-dating his
chapter in *The Cambridge Social History of Britain 1750–1950*, he confessed
'that the commonplace has interested me rather more than the exceptional,
and thus I have consciously given much of my attention to local institutions
and humble labours which I believe typify British philanthropy'.[30] Thus
the chapter that started 'If the first half of the nineteenth century saw philanthropy ascendant, the second half witnessed its triumph' was entitled
'Parochial service in practice' and highlighted district visiting, mothers'
meetings and the role played by women.[31] This parish life, he argued, was
fractured by the challenges posed by the First World War, not least the con-
current decline in Christian belief, and the consequent secularisation of philanthropic bodies. Nonetheless, he distanced himself from Owen's conclusion
that philanthropy became after the Second World War a 'junior partner in
the welfare firm'. Writing in the late 1980s he saw continuities from the
past in small-scale practices, coupled with disillusionment with state welfare
practices and achievements. Britain's 'seven million philanthropists' in the
1980s (volunteers who participated in the provision of charitable services)
provided evidence of the continuing strength of the 'voluntary impulse'.[32]
The problem for the historian of philanthropy is that very few if any of the
seven million would have thought of themselves as 'philanthropists'.

In *Schools of Citizenship: Charity and Civic Virtue* Prochaska picked
up another theme, the way that participation in the work of charitable
organisations was both exemplary of democracy and a training in democratic practices. For him the passage of the Third Reform Act in 1884 that
enfranchised most men marked the moment when democracy began to

decline: 'The triumph of universal suffrage did not promote local democratic forms, rather the reverse.' If voluntary organisations provided a buffer
between state and people, sharply reducing the danger of the spread of
totalitarianism, their heyday was in the mid-nineteenth rather than the mid-
twentieth century.[33]

Finally, in *Christianity and Social Service in Modern Britain: The
Disinherited Spirit*, the title itself was an indication of the argument. The
decline of Christianity, he argued, was linked to a decline in voluntary action
and a growing role for the state, trends that he deplored, not least for their
impact on democracy.[34]

The downside of defining philanthropy as kindness was that social reform
movements (which Harrison had been keen to see included within the remit
of philanthropy) were excluded, as was any sustained consideration of the
power dimension in giving. More surprising was the omission in Prochaska's
analysis of the great names of Victorian philanthropy: Elizabeth Fry, Baroness
Burdett-Coutts, Lord Shaftesbury, Thomas Barnardo, George Peabody and
others make no or only fleeting appearance, yet if we are to understand how
the Victorians themselves viewed their philanthropy these were the names
that were paraded as evidence of a golden age.

Surveying the field of philanthropy in Britain in the nineteenth century,
and trying to bring new thinking to how it might be studied, Alan Kidd in
1996 acknowledged that 'Owen, Harrison and Prochaska remain required
reading'.[35] Nearly quarter of a century later that remains the case. What
needs emphasis is that their approaches were very different and they differed
precisely because they disagreed about what constitutes 'philanthropy'.
For Owen 'the pecuniary element' was central. For Harrison social reform
movements required to be given a prominent role in any analysis. Prochaska
had little time for either the pecuniary element (though he was insightful on
the mechanics of fund-raising) or for reform movements: his emphasis was
on the innumerable ways through which 'kindness' was operative at all levels
of society but perhaps above all below the aristocracy and upper middle
classes. Anyone reading these three authors in succession would be bound
to conclude that historians differ widely in what they understand by 'philanthropy', and that therefore any history of it will depend on the definitions
that writers start out with. An alternative approach, the one pursued in this
book, is to see what contemporaries understood by philanthropy. Like the
historians, they came up with many different notions.

Civil society and philanthropy

The history of philanthropy in the twentieth century has attracted little
attention. If it has appeared anywhere it has normally been incorporated in
studies of the rise of the welfare state, the theme its inadequacies in dealing
with social problems and its consequent diminishing role. Prochaska has

emphasised the spike in philanthropic activity generated by the two world wars, but most see these, if they acknowledge them at all, as exceptions to an inexorable trend. True, it is often argued that philanthropy continued to have a role in the welfare state, in particular as an innovator in dealing with social problems. But for most of the century it was regarded largely as a thing of the past – and, it was argued, rightly so.

Two factors towards the end of the twentieth century and into the twenty-first have shifted that analysis. First, since the end of the Cold War in the late 1980s the concept of 'civil society' has attracted enormous interest. Voluntary organisations, many of them explicitly philanthropic, positioned between the state, the family and the market, are often taken to epitomise civil society – and they are seen positively. Britain, in this literature, was a pioneer, 'civil society' there burgeoning in and after the eighteenth century. This view does scant justice either to the changes in meaning of 'civil society' over time or to the extent to which the positive history is borne out by in-depth his-torical study.[36] Nevertheless, the idea of 'civil society' has helped to focus attention on many aspects of philanthropy. Geoffrey Finlayson's *Citizen, State and Social Welfare in Britain 1830–1990* (1994), was an early, and excel-lent, product of the thinking that underlay the concept of civil society; he did not himself use the term, but his focus on citizenship and voluntarism directly contributed to ideas of civil society. In the new century, and more explicitly, Nicholas Deakin explored the changes in the relationship between voluntary organisations, the state and the market, opening with a chapter on the English experience since the eighteenth century.[37] The starting point for any such history is likely to be Gray's 'associated philanthropy', exemplified most prominently in the eighteenth century by the foundation of 'voluntary' hospitals. They were 'voluntary' because their finances were raised by public subscription not by taxes. Similarly, though with less justification as much of their funding in fact came from the state, schools from 1870 onwards that were not rate-funded Board Schools, were described as 'voluntary schools'. Voluntary organisations in the twentieth century increasingly sought funding from the state and in the twenty-first frequently became locked into contracts for the delivery of services. Even so, in their structure and governance they were independent of the state and separate from the market: they were civil society. William Beveridge was confident in the 1940s that 'The practice of making public grants to voluntary agencies without destroying their volun-tary character is well established'. Half a century later Robert Whelan was less confident that this was the case.[38]

Volunteers were the other element in civil society, Prochaska's 'seven million philanthropists'. They need to be considered separately from volun-tary organisations. As was noted in 1945, and has become more so since then, 'many of the most active voluntary organizations are staffed entirely by highly trained and fairly well-paid professional workers'.[39] But there was also recognised to be a place, both in voluntary organisations and in public authorities, for unpaid volunteers. In *The Voluntary Citizen: An Enquiry into the Place of Philanthropy in the Community* (1938) Constance Braithwaite described philanthropy as 'essentially an expression of voluntary citizenship', the route through which the relationship between state and citizen was formed and negotiated.[40] At the very time that the welfare state was coming into being the man regarded as in many ways its founder, William Beveridge, in *Voluntary Action: A Report on Methods of Social Advance* (1948), was loud in praise of action 'outside each citizen's home for improving the condition of life for him and for his fellows'.[41] Perhaps taking its inspiration from Beveridge, a Voluntary Action History Society was formed in 1991.

The problem with histories of civil society is one they share with histories of philanthropy: what people understand by 'civil society' now (and there are many different understandings) differs substantially from how the term was understood in the eighteenth and nineteenth centuries. Whereas now civil society is seen as a sphere of activity separate from the state, often described as 'voluntarism', in the eighteenth century the state and its ability to establish and uphold a legal framework for the protection of property was the key component of civil society. In the words of Jose Harris, 'Voluntarism *per se* ... was never directly equated with civil society by any British commentators before the 1980s'.[42]

The second prompt to rethinking the history of philanthropy in the twentieth century was the proclamation from the beginning of the 1990s of a 'new philanthropy'. Built on new money and assembling around it organisations such as New Philanthropy Capital, founded in 2002, it has been able to make a case for a much more substantial role for philanthropy than there seemed likely to be earlier in the century when the state was shrinking philanthropy's role. New philanthropy has consciously sought to distinguish itself from previous forms of what passed for philanthropy. One consequence is a gulf separating it from the work of volunteers and voluntary organisations that is emphasised in the civil society tradition. Once again we are back in the realm of definitions of philanthropy.

Philanthropy and the gift relationship

In a quite separate development academic historians in the later twentieth century turned to anthropology for deeper understanding of philanthropy. Abandoning the attempt to measure the amount of it, they began to focus on the interactions between donor and recipient. The text that they turned to for inspiration was Marcel Mauss's *The Gift: The Form and Reason for Exchange in Archaic Societies*, published in 1925 and first translated into English in 1954. Mauss described a variety of societies where there was reciprocity in giving, contrasting them briefly with his own society where such reciprocity had in large part been lost but where he could also see some welcome signs of its revival.[43]

Following Mauss, philanthropy could be reimagined as exchange. Peter Mandler in 1990 alerted historians to the challenge: 'Anthropologists', he wrote, 'assume that the poor understand the rich better than the rich understand the poor because for the rich social knowledge is a luxury and for the poor it can be essential to survival'. Historians, on the other hand, assumed the opposite because the sources encouraged them to do so. The gift relationship approach gave equal if not greater emphasis to the recipient.[44] Alan Kidd in 1996 highlighted the gift relationship as central to an understanding of philanthropy. He defined it as 'non-commercial social transfers of wealth, material objects or non-material assistance rendered in forms that are culturally meaningful and that generate moral relationships between individuals or groups such as solidarity, dependence, legitimacy, and reputability'.[45] The history of philanthropy in this perspective became not simply a history of giving, far less of giving only by the rich. It involved examining both sides of the relationship, and that brought it into close engagement with many other branches of history.

Historians of continental Europe have been more alert to this than those in Britain. Marco van Leeuwen has argued that there was a 'logic of charity'. On the part of elites – and the same might also be said of the bourgeoisie – poor relief could help to regulate the labour market, to stabilise the social order, to avert turmoil, to reduce the risk of infection, to civilise the poor, to affirm their own status, to forward a career and a web of patronage, and to promote one's own salvation. Sandra Cavallo has stressed, with special reference to Turin, that giving was often a way of deepening the ties of family and of patronage, and thereby of exercising power. There was nothing new in this. In fifteenth-century Florence 'charity and patronage became almost indistinguishable'. It was no accident that there was increasing emphasis on confining eligibility for charity to those born in a particular city. In the rituals that accompanied giving there was a high quotient of symbolic action that reinforced a particular notion of social order. There was also in giving much rivalry between institutions, social actors and power blocs. Need, in any kind of objective measurement, did not determine the level or direction of charity. On the other side of the equation, the poor had a range of survival strategies, including pawning, migration, begging, prostitution, crime, revolt, formation of mutual societies and accepting poor relief. Turning to charity was by no means the first avenue they explored, nor did it ever enjoy exclusive preference.[46]

A focus on the gift relationship has had the tendency to inject into the history of philanthropy a degree of scepticism about the motives of philanthropists. It cannot be reduced simply to kindness and generosity on the part of the well-to-do. It is an exercise of power. On a different level, it draws attention to the persistence of giving among equals in ways that might have reassured Mauss. Giving by the poor to the poor, it was frequently claimed in the nineteenth century, outweighed that given by the rich to the poor. The major study of the gift relationship in early modern England, however, Ilana Krausman Ben-Amos's *The Culture of Giving: Informal Support and Gift Exchange in Early Modern England* (2008), while briefly acknowledging that there were some negative sides to gift giving, argues positively, in almost Jordanian style, for the 'profusion, expansion and growing vitality of gift exchange and informal support systems over the course of the period'.[47]

Conclusion

Philanthropy is an indeterminate field. It has meant different things to the scholars who have written about it. The approach of most has been to start with a definition, almost always drawn from present-day concerns and, if they have any interest in the past, to trace back in time to see what their definition tells them. Here are two typical definitions. In the first philanthropy is 'the voluntary giving and receiving of time and money aimed (however imperfectly) towards the needs of charity and the interests of all in a better quality of life'. In the second it is 'a social relation governed by a moral obligation that matches a supply of private resources to a demand of unfulfilled needs and desires that are communicated by entreaty'. There is a tendency for the definitions to grow in complexity so that applying them in any society becomes almost an exercise in ticking boxes to see if any particular action qualifies as philanthropy.[48] In the histories we have of philanthropy there is a wide disparity between those that focus entirely on Owen's 'pecuniary element' and those that range more widely to include social and political movements for reform. In this book I adopt a different approach. I look to see what contemporaries had to say about philanthropy.

This survey does scant justice to the many more recent contributions to the history of philanthropy. Their work is incorporated into the chapters that follow. It is a mark of them that they set out to situate philanthropy more firmly within the time frame and the society they are writing about, and to link it to other areas of historiography. The liveliest new work has focused on gender and philanthropy with an emphasis on ways in which philanthropy, despite frequent male opposition, opened up new opportunities and avenues for women.

Notes

1 B. Kirkman Gray, *A History of English Philanthropy From the Dissolution of the Monasteries to the Taking of the First Census* (London: P. S. King & Son, 1905), pp. v–vi.
2 Ibid., pp. vi–vii, 283.
3 D. Owen, *English Philanthropy 1660–1960* (London: Oxford University Press, 1965), pp. vii, 9.

4 F. Emerson Andrews, *Philanthropic Giving* (New York: Russell Sage Foundation, 1950); R. H. Bremner, *American Philanthropy* (Chicago: Chicago University Press, 1960), p. 199.

5 Wikipedia, 'Ford Foundation'.

6 W. K. Jordan, *Philanthropy in England 1480–1660: A Study of the Changing Pattern of English Social Aspirations* (London: Allen & Unwin, 1959), pp. 127, 131.

7 For immediate criticism of Jordan on inflation, see reviews by L. Stone in *History*, 44 (1959), 257–60; *English Historical Review*, 77 (1962), 327–9; D. C. Coleman in *Economic History Review*, 13 (1960), 113–15; A. Everitt in *Economic History Review*, 15 (1962), 376–7. For later critical assessment, see W. G. Bitte and R. T. Lane, 'Inflation and philanthropy in England: A reassessment of W. K. Jordan's data', *Economic History Review*, 29 (1976), 203–10; and D. C. Coleman in *Economic History Review*, 31 (1978), 119. For a partial defence of Jordan, see J. F. Hadwin, 'Deflating philanthropy', *Economic History Review*, 31 (1978), 105–17, and C. Wilson, 'Poverty and philanthropy in early modern England', in T. Riis (ed.), *Aspects of Poverty in Early Modern Europe* (Sijthoff: Alphen aan den Rijn, 1981), pp. 253–79.

8 Jordan, *Philanthropy in England*, p. 140; Hadwin, 'Deflating philanthropy', 110; P. Slack, *Poverty and Policy in Tudor and Stuart England* (London: Longman, 1988), pp. 169–72.

9 Jordan, *Philanthropy in England*, pp. 23–4; Slack, *Poverty and Policy*, p. 166. For further evidence on lifetime giving, see I. W. Archer, 'The charity of early modern Londoners', *Transactions of the Royal Historical Society*, 12 (2002), 238–44; S. Hindle, *On the Parish? The Micro-Politics of Poor Relief in Rural England c. 1550–1750* (Oxford: Clarendon Press, 2004), p. 120.

10 Jordan, *Philanthropy in England*, pp. 121–2; M. K. McIntosh, 'Local responses to the poor in late medieval and Tudor England', *Continuity and Change*, 3 (1988), 212; Slack, *Poverty and Policy*, p. 166; Archer, 'Charity of early modern Londoners', 238–44.

11 Jordan, *Philanthropy in England*, pp. 143–239, 15.

12 See, e.g., B. Pullan, 'Support and redeem: Charity and poor relief in Italian cities from the fourteenth to the seventeenth century', *Continuity and Change*, 3 (1988), 177–208; J. T. Rosenthal, *The Purchase of Paradise* (London: Routledge & Kegan Paul, 1972); M. Rubin, *Charity and Community in Medieval Cambridge* (Cambridge: Cambridge University Press, 1987); O. P. Grell and A. Cunningham (eds), *Health Care and Poor Relief in Protestant Europe 1500–1700* (London: Routledge, 1997) and O. P. Grell and A. Cunningham (eds), *Health Care and Poor Relief in Counter-Reformation Europe* (London: Routledge, 1999).

13 Jordan, *Philanthropy in England*, pp. 20, 247; Slack, *Poverty and Policy*, p. 163.

14 Jordan, *Philanthropy in England*, pp. 362–5.

15 Owen, *English Philanthropy*, p. 2.

16 J. Clive, Foreword, p. xii in D. Owen, *The Government of Victorian London 1855–1889* (Cambridge, MA and London: The Belknap Press, 1982).

17 Owen, *English Philanthropy*, p. 1.

18 Ibid., pp. 61, 129, 132.

19 Ibid., p. 469.
20 B. Rodgers, *Cloak of Charity: Studies in Eighteenth-Century Philanthropy* (London: Methuen, 1949), p. 3.
21 Ibid., p. 1.
22 Gray, *History of English Philanthropy*, p. 80.
23 I. K. Ben-Amos, *The Culture of Giving: Informal Support and Gift-Exchange in Early Modern England* (Cambridge: Cambridge University Press, 2008), pp. 138–40.
24 Ibid., p. 375.
25 D. T. Andrew, *Philanthropy and Police: London Charity in the Eighteenth Century* (Princeton: Princeton University Press, 1989), esp. pp. 15, 174.
26 B. Harrison, 'Philanthropy and the Victorians', *Victorian Studies*, 9 (1966), 353–74, quoting 363.
27 B. Harrison, 'Philanthropy and the Victorians' in B. Harrison, *Peaceable Kingdom: Stability and Change in Modern Britain* (Oxford: Clarendon Press, 1982), pp. 217–59, quoting pp. 220, 259.
28 F. K. Prochaska, *Women and Philanthropy in Nineteenth-Century England* (Oxford: Clarendon Press, 1980).
29 F. K. Prochaska, 'Philanthropy', in F. M. L. Thompson (ed.), *The Cambridge Social History of Britain 1750–1950*, 3 vols (Cambridge: Cambridge University Press, 1990), Vol. 3, pp. 357–393, quoting pp. 360, 378.
30 F. Prochaska, *The Voluntary Impulse: Philanthropy in Modern Britain* (London: Faber & Faber, 1988), p. xiv.
31 Ibid., p. 41.
32 Ibid., pp. xiv, 10.
33 F. Prochaska, *Schools of Citizenship: Charity and Civic Virtue* (London: Institute for the Study of Civil Society, 2002), quoting p. 30.
34 F. Prochaska, *Christianity and Social Service in Modern Britain: The Disinherited Spirit* (Oxford: Oxford University Press, 2006).
35 A. J. Kidd, 'Philanthropy and the "social history paradigm"', *Social History*, 21 (1996), 180.
36 J. Harris (ed.), *Civil Society in British History: Ideas, Identities, Institutions* (Oxford: Oxford University Press, 2003), esp. Harris's own contributions, pp. 1–37.
37 G. Finlayson, *Citizen, State and Social Welfare in Britain 1830–1990* (Oxford: Clarendon Press, 1994); N. Deakin, *In Search of Civil Society* (Basingstoke: Palgrave, 2001).
38 W. Beveridge, *Voluntary Action: A Report on the Methods of Social Advance* (London: George Allen & Unwin, 1948), p. 315; R. Whelan, *Involuntary Action: How Voluntary is the 'Voluntary Sector'?* (London: IEA Health and Welfare Unit, 1999).
39 A. F. C. Bourdillon (ed.), *Voluntary Social Services: Their Place in the Modern State* (London: Methuen, 1945), p. 3.
40 C. Braithwaite, *The Voluntary Citizen: An Enquiry into the Place of Philanthropy in the Community* (London: Methuen, 1938), p. 78.
41 Beveridge, *Voluntary Action*, pp. 8–9.

42 J. Harris, 'Introduction: Civil society in British history: paradigm or peculiarity?' and 'From Richard Hooker to Harold Laski: Changing perceptions of civil society in British political thought, late sixteenth to early twentieth centuries', in Harris (ed.), *Civil Society in British History*, pp. 1–37, quoting p. 9; see also, K. Thomas, *In Pursuit of Civility: Manners and Civilization in Early Modern England* (New Haven and London: Yale University Press, 2018), pp. 120–39, and A. Kidd, 'Civil society or the state: Recent approaches to the history of voluntary welfare', *Journal of Historical Sociology*, 15 (2002), 385–412.

43 M. Mauss, *The Gift: The Form and Reason for Exchange in Archaic Societies* (London: Routledge, 2002).

44 P. Mandler (ed.), *The Uses of Charity: The Poor on Relief in the Nineteenth-Century Metropolis* (Philadelphia: University of Pennsylvania Press, 1990), p. 1.

45 Kidd, 'Philanthropy and the "social history paradigm"', 184.

46 M. H. D. van Leeuwen, 'Logic of charity: Poor relief in preindustrial Europe', *Journal of Interdisciplinary History*, 24 (1994), 589–613; S. Cavallo, 'The motivations of benefactors', in J. Barry and C. Jones (eds), *Medicine and Charity before the Welfare State* (London: Routledge, 1991), pp. 46–62; J. Henderson, *Piety and Charity in Late Medieval Florence* (Oxford: Clarendon Press, 1994), p. 424. For a similar approach in England, see P. Shapely, *Charity and Power in Victorian Manchester* (Manchester: Chetham Society, 2000).

47 Ben-Amos, *Culture of Giving*, pp. 378, 388–9.

48 J. van Til, 1990, and P. Schervish, 1998, quoted in M. Sulek, 'On the modern meaning of philanthropy', *Nonprofit and Voluntary Sector Quarterly*, 39 (2010), 202–3.

2

The profile of philanthropy

The internet has made possible the research that underlies this project. Databases make it possible to trace the use of key words such as 'philanthropy'. The method I have adopted is to trace the history and usage of the word 'philanthropy' based mainly on a search of use of it and of cognate words such as 'philanthropist', in print – in newspapers and periodicals primarily but also in books, both non-fiction and fiction, and other forms of print. A major research tool has been the on-line collections of British newspapers and periodicals.[1] The aim is to establish a chronological profile of philanthropy in public discourse. I have supplemented this in places from private correspondence.

First, it is useful to compare the profiles over time of 'charity', 'benevolence' and 'philanthropy', three words that overlapped in meaning and were often used in conjunction with one another. In the eighteenth century 'benevolence' and 'philanthropy' were commonly linked, both seen as rooted in human nature. In some usages from the early nineteenth century onwards 'charity' and 'philanthropy' were used interchangeably as referring to the growing number of voluntary organisations that aimed to be of public benefit. In others, however, they were contrasted with one another in ways that will be elucidated in later chapters: both supporters and opponents of philanthropy sought to distinguish it from charity.

The profiles of the three words in Figures 1, 2 and 3 show strong similarities in trends with the Victorian period standing out from what came before and after it. From 1910 up to 1949 they are all at a low level. What the data also show is that in terms of numbers of mentions 'philanthropy' lagged far behind 'benevolence' and even further behind 'charity'. This could suggest the relative unimportance of philanthropy.

Many of the mentions of charity were uncontroversial reports of the fund-raising and achievements of innumerable charitable organisations that existed in any community. Others, however, were heavily critical of charitable trusts. From 1818 to 1837, a Commission of Inquiry into Charities examined these in detail. Critics, on the radical side of politics, claimed that funds were misused. In Bristol, for example, in the 1820s and 1830s charitable trusts were central to local politics. For the second half of the century W. L. Burn concluded that 'from the almost innumerable criticisms of their administration and from the attacks on individual trustees one could construct a theory that the mid-Victorians were interested in nothing else'. That, of course, as Burn quickly acknowledged, was not the case, but there was no escaping the fact that many charities, hamstrung by their foundation deeds, were no longer, as we would say, 'fit for purpose'.[2] Charity, too, had a legal definition set out in the Charitable Uses Act of 1601 that gave it a statutory status and defined what could and could not come within its compass. All these factors help to explain its numerical dominance over benevolence and philanthropy.

Benevolence had no such encumbrances as charity. It was used to describe a disposition to do good and a feeling of affection, whether for an individual or for humanity. It was personified in literature in the Cheeryble brothers in Charles Dickens's *Nicholas Nickleby*, men whose goodness knew no bounds. The benevolent might be taken advantage of, they might be simple in their goodness, but few doubted that benevolence was something to praise, whether it was the benevolence of an individual or of a nation – the British were portrayed as exceeding other nations in their benevolence. It was at its peak in the 1850s, declining quite sharply from the 1870s, whereas philanthropy and charity reached their highpoints in the 1880s and 1890s.

A leading article in *The Times* in 1869 referred in passing to 'private benevolence and public philanthropy'.[3] Philanthropy, not so much in its eighteenth-century origins as in its development in the nineteenth century, became public and political. On a positive view, philanthropy could claim, amongst other things, to have ended the slave trade and slavery and to have reformed prisons. These were political achievements and they had created enemies for philanthropy. If benevolence was largely private, philanthropy was public. For this reason, although it gets fewer mentions, those that it does get, whether celebratory or condemnatory, leave no doubt in the reader's mind of its importance. 'Philanthropists', for example, were often linked with 'statesmen' as the people who might solve what were essentially political problems in Ireland or India, or who might legitimately have a say on Poor Laws or prison reform. Thus, although 'philanthropy' gets fewer mentions, the content of them places philanthropy higher in the pecking order of public discourse.

Turning specifically to philanthropy, Table 1 sets out data from newspapers and periodicals for the eighteenth century.

This table shows how mentions of philanthropy, starting from scratch, began to increase in number, particularly in the last two decades of the century. Philanthropist* (catching both singular and plural forms) gained many

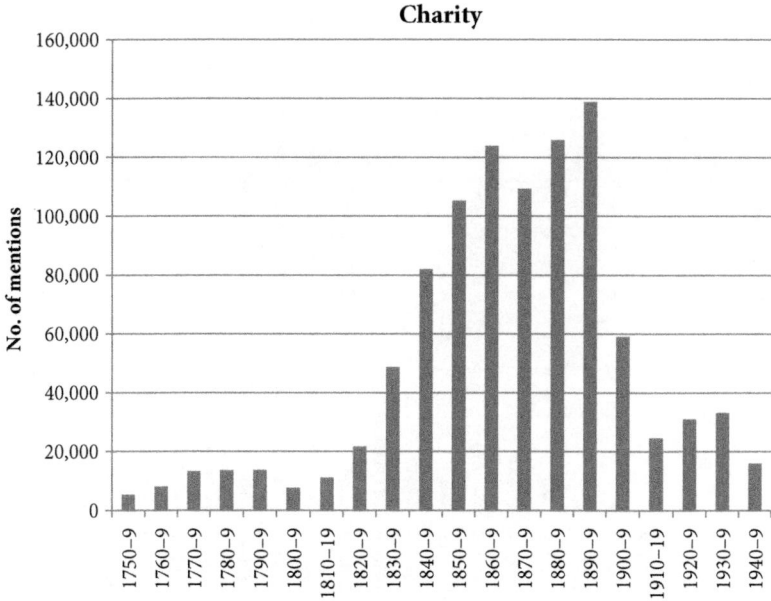

Figure 1 Mentions of 'charity' in British newspapers, 1750–1949

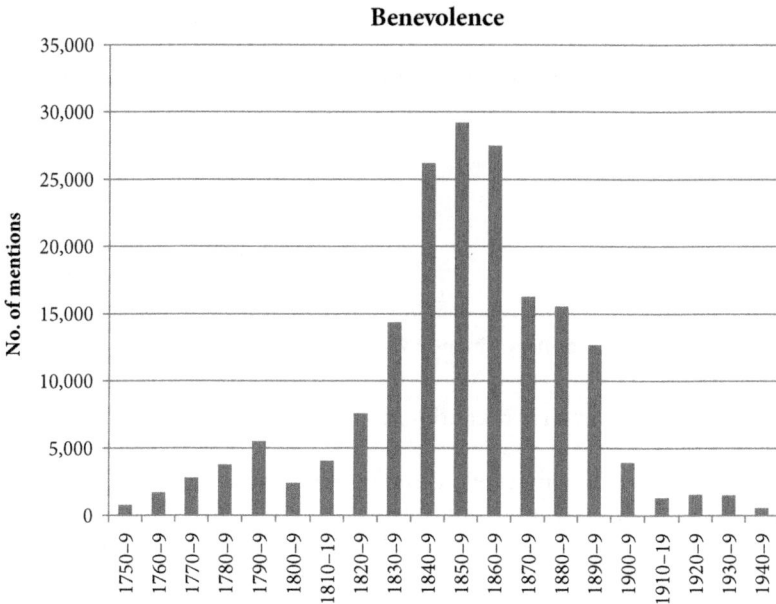

Figure 2 Mentions of 'benevolence' in British newspapers, 1750–1949

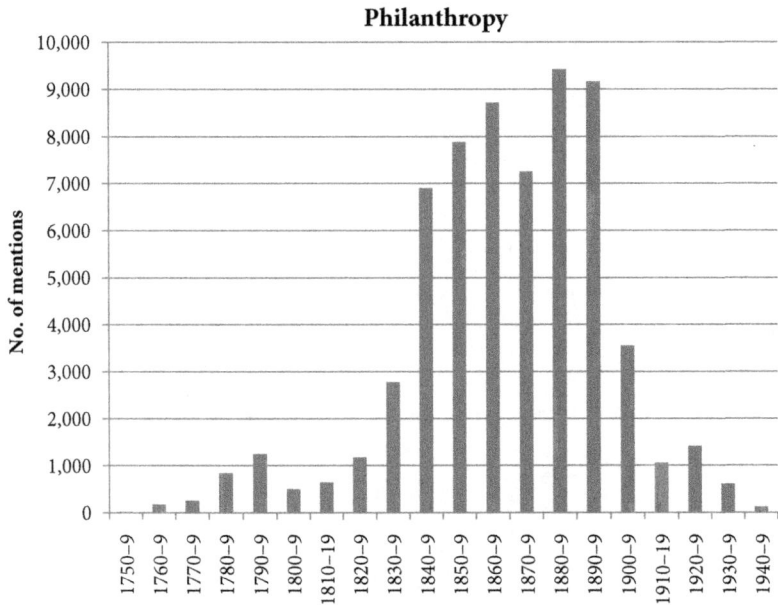

Figure 3 Mentions of 'philanthropy' in British newspapers, 1750–1949

Table 1 Mentions of philanthropy and philanthropist★ in British periodicals and newspapers, 1700–99

Date	Periodicals		Newspapers	
	Philanthropy	Philanthropist★	Philanthropy	Philanthropist★
1700–49	6		9	
1750–9	62		18	
1760–9	151	1	175	8
1770–9	340	16	260	11
1780–9	760	8	841	41
1790–9	1,187	440	1,246	98

Source: 17th-18th Century Burney Collection Newspapers.

of its entries from letter writers describing themselves as 'Philanthropist' or 'A Philanthropist'.

Moving into the nineteenth century, Figures 4 and 5 provide profiles for 'philanthropy' and 'philanthropist★' by decade from 1800 to 1949 for newspapers (Figure 4) and periodicals (Figure 5). For newspapers the figures for the early decades cannot be read straight on from those given in Table 1: the Burney Collection covered a greater number of papers than those in Gale NewsVault. Thus for the 1790s the 1,246 mentions in the Burney Collection are matched by only 200 in Gale NewsVault.

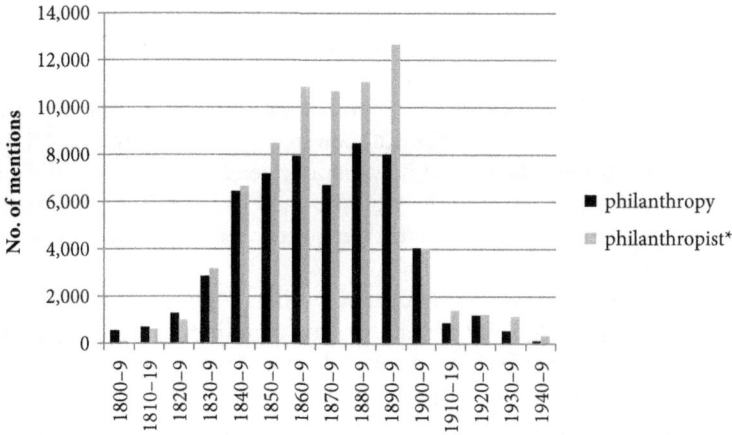

Figure 4 Mentions of 'philanthropy' and 'philanthropist*' in British newspapers, 1800–1949

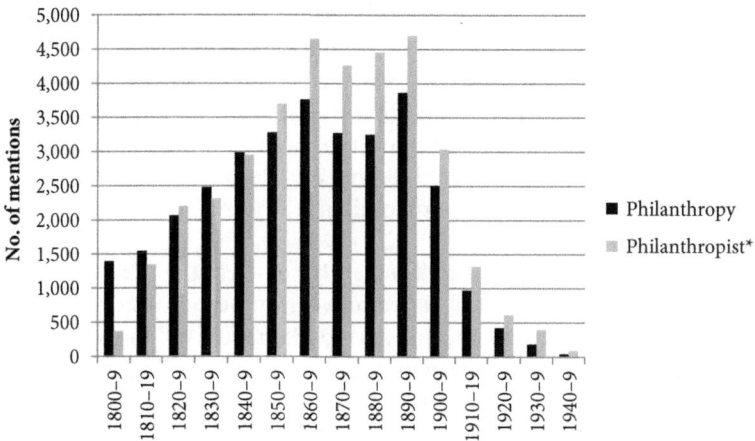

Figure 5 Mentions of 'philanthropy' and 'philanthropist*' in British periodicals, 1800–1949

Looking first at 'philanthropy', growth was particularly sharp in the 1840s and 1850s. Thereafter there is something of a plateau through to the end of the century, followed by a sharp decline. The database changed with the beginning of the twentieth century and the extent of decline in its first decade may be exaggerated, but that cannot account for the further sharp decline in the 1910s, and in a further fall-off after that. By the 1940s there was less mention of philanthropy in newspapers than in the 1760s. For periodicals the rise was steady with a plateau similar to that for newspapers through to the end of the century, followed by sustained decline. As with newspapers, in the 1940s figures were lower than at any point in the second half of the eighteenth century.

Turning to 'philanthropist' or its plural, the numbers become greater than for philanthropy from the 1830s for newspapers and from the 1840s for periodicals. Both periodicals and newspapers peak in the 1890s, the decline thereafter precipitous. The words could be used to describe individuals (but rarely oneself) but also referred to the public role expected generally of philanthropists.

The overall pattern to come out of this data suggests that philanthropy and its cognates had high and generally rising prominence in both periodicals and newspapers from the 1830s through to the 1890s and then underwent a sharp decline, reaching a nadir in the mid-twentieth century.

For further evidence on the profile of philanthropy I have turned to particular newspapers. Special attention has been paid to *The Times*. For the period up to 1850 all usages have been checked, thereafter at ten-year intervals (1859, 1869, 1879, 1889) for all usages and for all years where the words appeared as a keyword. Some of these uses are in leading articles, expressing *The Times*'s opinion, and account must obviously be taken of the bias intrinsic to these, not least because, especially in the 1840s, *The Times* was engaged in a fierce attack on contemporary manifestations of philanthropy. Other uses are in news reports, in letters, in reports of parliamentary proceedings, in extracts from other newspapers and in advertisements. Given the dominance of *The Times* as an organ of public opinion, the views expressed and the news reported at the very least provide parameters in relation to public discourse about philanthropy in the upper and middle classes.

For a comparison with *The Times* I have used the *Observer* and the *Manchester Guardian*, and for the twentieth century the *Daily Mail*, searching for uses of the words 'philanthropy' and 'philanthropist*' in the texts of the papers (this includes advertisements, court case, leading articles, news, obituaries and reports of proceedings in Parliament) and, for *The Times*, isolating leading articles and features in which philanthropy or philanthropists make an appearance. It is a coincidence, but a useful one, that *The Times* commenced publication in 1785, precisely at the time when John Howard was becoming proclaimed as a philanthropist. The *Observer* (Sundays only) is available from 1791, the *Manchester Guardian* from 1821, the *Daily Mail* from 1896. The results are set out by decade to facilitate the establishment of a chronology of philanthropy in public discourse (Figure 6).

It can be objected that the methodology adopted is as likely to be measuring changes in newspaper practice as changes in the profile of philanthropy. The scale of change, however, points firmly to the conclusion that the profile of philanthropy in public discourse underwent transformations. In the decade 1800–09, for example, there were in *The Times* eighty-two mentions

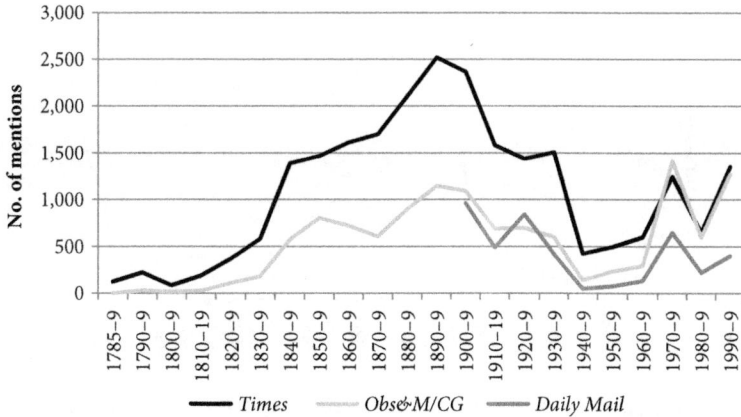

Figure 6 Philanthrop★ in *The Times*, *Observer* and *Manchester Guardian* and *Daily Mail* (all mentions)

Note: 'Philanthrop★' here encompasses both 'philanthropy' and 'philanthropist(s)'.

of philanthropy/philanthropist(s) and only one in a leading article whereas in the decade 1850–59 there were 1,465 mentions including 388 in leading and feature articles. Use of these individual newspapers, all showing a decline from 1900 to 1909, further suggests that the possible bias in newspapers as a whole, mentioned above with respect to Figure 4, did not distort the shape of decline in a significant way, though for all of them decline was sharper between 1910 and 1919.

The pattern that emerges from these figures closely parallels that for periodicals and newspapers as a whole. There was a low profile through to the 1820s, succeeded by a significant rise in the 1830s and an even more prominent one in the 1840s that is sustained through to the end of the century. In terms of overall usage of the words there was a peak for both *The Times* and the *Observer/Manchester Guardian* in the 1890s. Leading and feature articles in *The Times*, however, had been in decline since 1870 (Figure 7). The overall trend of decline running through the first half of the twentieth century reached its nadir in the 1940s, the decade in which the welfare state came into being. Thereafter there was some rise, with a sudden surge of total usage in the 1970s due entirely to a big increase in advertising. Christopher Hampton's play *The Philanthropist*, opening a long run in August 1970, was the cause. There were 839 advertisements in *The Times* in the 1970s compared to sixty-five in the 1980s and the decade was a low point for leading article and feature usage. There was then a significant impact of 'new philanthropy' from the 1980s onwards. The clearest evidence lies in the increase in leading and feature articles in *The Times*.

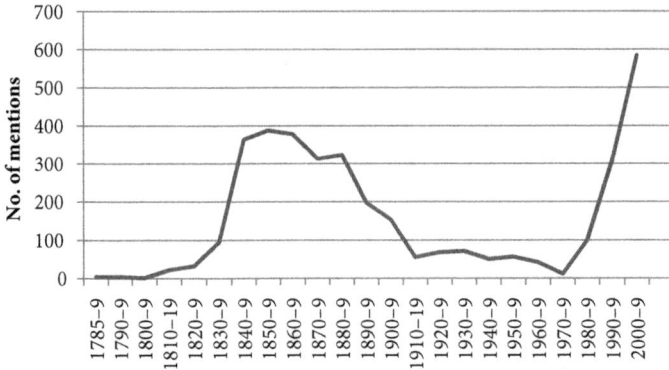

Figure 7 Philanthrop★ in leading and feature articles in *The Times*

Note: 'Philanthrop★' here encompasses both 'philanthropy' and 'philanthropist(s)'.

The data outlined here, coming from different sources, is consistent and clear-cut in what it tells us about the public discourse profile of philanthropy from its inception in the 1750s up to the present. At least in terms of public discourse the Victorian age deserves its reputation as a golden age for philanthropy: the dates for highest profile correspond exactly with her reign. It is also clear that there was a sharp decline in the profile running through the twentieth century up to the 1980s. Since then 'new philanthropy', on the evidence provided by *The Times*, the *Manchester Guardian*, the *Observer* and the *Daily Mail*, has generated a new high level of public discourse.

The level of public discourse provides an essential background to the main purpose of this book, to track and explain the changes in the meanings and reputation of philanthropy. To achieve this, I have quoted extensively from sources, providing space for contemporary voices to be heard. Philanthropy was contentious, its meaning unstable. Only by listening to what was written can there be any understanding of how it came about that philanthropy – a love of humankind – became, by complex routes, associated with giving by the rich. If there was a high level of public discourse about philanthropy and philanthropists in the Victorian era, we need to ask what was the content of that discourse? To put it simply, a high level in public discourse did not necessarily mean a high level of approval of philanthropy.

Notes

1 For newspapers I have used the 17th–18th Century Burney Collection Newspapers, the British Library newspapers available on Gale NewsVault and, for individual newspapers, the British Library Newspaper Archive. For

periodicals I have used the four collections of British Periodicals available through ProQuest. All were accessed on 21 Nov. 2017.

2 R. Tompson, *The Charity Commission and the Age of Reform* (London: Routledge & Kegan Paul, 1979); M. Gorsky, *Patterns of Philanthropy: Charity and Society in Nineteenth-Century Bristol* (Woodbridge: Boydell Press, 1999), pp. 63–85; W. L. Burn, *The Age of Equipoise: A Study of the Mid-Victorian Generation* (London: George Allen & Unwin, 1964), p. 114.

3 *The Times*, 20 Jan. 1869.

3

The genesis of philanthropy

Philanthropy began to become a feature of British public discourse in the mid-eighteenth century. This chapter traces its spread through print, the meaning accorded to it and the feelings it aroused. Mostly these were positive, but there were also critics, notably those who questioned whether mere humans could indeed extend love to all of humanity. It was notable that many of those who preached the universality of philanthropy were nevertheless confident, despite French claims to the contrary, that Britain was especially notable for its philanthropy.

Human nature and philanthropy

Philanthropy as a word in English can be traced back to Francis Bacon's late sixteenth-century essay on 'Of goodness, and goodness of nature'. Bacon recalled the Greek word *philanthropia* as meaning goodness as 'affecting of the weal of men'. Goodness of nature was the inclination to do good, goodness the habit of doing it. The word 'humanity', thought Bacon, was 'a little too light to express' this habit of doing good.[1] Philanthropy through the seventeenth and for much of the eighteenth century continued to be seen as Greek. In 1693 John Dryden, seeing 'philanthropy' 'every where manifest' in the writings of Polybius, commented that 'we have not a proper word in *English* to express' it.[2] In 1720 Richard Fiddes emphasised the strong impulse of 'natural tenderness' in humans 'which ... from the *Greeks*, we very significantly render *Philanthropy*; from the *Latins, Humanity*; and which in the Language of our own Nation, and with a particular respect to the Genius of it, we express by *good Nature*'. Philanthropy was not yet English. Humanity, it was said in 1735, was called 'by Heathens, *Philanthropy*, or *Love* of our *Fellow Creatures*', or, in English, repeating Bacon and Fiddes, '*Good-nature*'.[3] This way of thinking fed through into Samuel Johnson's *A Dictionary of the*

English Language (1755) where philanthropy was defined as 'a love of mankind; good nature'.[4]

It was from these middle years of the eighteenth century that philanthropy began to spread. It is true that letter writers to the periodicals and newspapers in the first half of the century, starting in the *Spectator* in 1712, sometimes signed off as 'Philanthropos' or 'Philanthropus'; there were nineteen in periodicals in both the 1730s and the 1740s. But the content of these letters, often disputatious, did not necessarily betoken any obvious love for the human species and in the first half of the century 'philanthropy' received only six mentions in British periodicals and only nine in British newspapers. By contrast, in the second half of the century there were 2,500 mentions in the periodicals and 2,540 in the newspapers. 'Philanthropist' had no existence at all until the 1760s and from then until the end of the century there were 465 mentions in periodicals and 158 in newspapers, the vast majority of them, 440 and 98 respectively, in the last decade of the century.

The growth in the use of the words 'philanthropy' and 'philanthropist' was in part a reflection of the growth of a print culture in the eighteenth century. Philanthropy spread through the written word, and there were many more words in print in the late eighteenth century than in the earlier decades. In London in the 1780s there were at least nine daily newspapers, eight tri-weekly and nine weekly, or, to put it another way, 25,000 papers published every day, reaching a readership ten times that number, a substantial increase over the situation some ten years previously. The number of provincial newspapers rose steadily, reaching fifty by 1779 and seventy before the end of the century.[5] The growth rate of 'philanthropy', however, was much greater than the growth rate of print culture. Compare 'philanthropy' and 'misanthropy'. 'Misanthropy' first appeared in a British periodical in 1760 and from then until the end of the century there were only thirty-six mentions, less than one a year on average, and thirteen of these thirty-six were in the last two years of the century. 'Misanthrope', the nearest equivalent to 'philanthropist', first appeared in 1732, then again in 1750, but in total there were only twenty-six mentions in the century. The trajectories of 'philanthropy' and 'misanthropy' differed sharply, both growing, but the latter at a snail's pace compared to that of 'philanthropy'. In short, there was something about philanthropy that drew to it those engaged in writing for late eighteenth-century readers.

The reason for this lay in changing views on human nature. In the eighteenth century the word most commonly used to describe the doing of good to or for others was 'benevolence'. Its origins go back to the later seventeenth century. In his *Treatise on the Laws of Nature* of 1672 Richard Cumberland, criticising Hobbes and his bleak view of human nature, gave a preeminent place to what he called 'universal benevolence'. God, Cumberland argued, was essentially benevolent, and humankind inherited this disposition. Cumberland's way of thinking filtered through to inform Latitudinarianism in the Church of England in the later seventeenth and eighteenth centuries: playing down doctrinal differences and favouring toleration of Protestant Dissent, Latitudinarians placed a high value on benevolence.[6] Francis Hutcheson, Professor of Moral Philosophy at the University of Glasgow 1730–46, was the leading proponent in the first half of the eighteenth century of the view that humans had a disposition towards benevolence across the globe, and that consequently virtue consisted in the exercise of benevolence. As Adam Smith, who studied under Hutcheson, summarised, 'The most virtuous of all affections … was that which embraced as its object the happiness of all intelligent beings'.[7]

What were the springs of benevolence? Within human nature, it was thought, there was an instinctive quality of sympathy. The nerves, as Newton and Locke argued, acted as conduits of sensation, including sympathy and sensibility. To the five senses was added a sixth, the 'moral sense'. People were endowed with differing amounts of sympathy and sensibility, women on the whole having more than men, but everyone had some element of them, and it was these innate feelings that inclined people to virtuous action on behalf of others.[8] David Hume was by no means consistent in what he wrote about benevolence, but by the time he wrote *Enquiries Concerning Human Understanding and Concerning the Principles of Morals* in the mid-eighteenth century (1748, 1751), he seems to have accepted that there was 'a general benevolence in human nature', a 'natural philanthropy', something which was 'real, from general experience, without any other proof'. Moreover, 'nothing can bestow more merit on any human creature than the sentiment of benevolence in an eminent degree', for, amongst other things, it promoted 'the interests of our species, and bestow[ed] happiness on human society'. It was the premier virtue.[9]

Hume's linkage of 'a general benevolence' and 'a natural philanthropy' suggested, as was the case, that there was very little to distinguish the two. Samuel Johnson had distinguished between benevolence as a 'disposition to do good; kindness' and 'beneficence', which was 'kindness … exerted in action'.[10] 'Action' might follow from benevolence but it was not central to it, nor was it to philanthropy.

Benevolence and philanthropy were frequently linked. The *Gentleman's Magazine* in 1751 praised the recently deceased Prince of Wales for having had 'a source of benevolence and philanthropy that seemed inexhaustible'. In very similar terms in 1766 the *Monthly Review* wrote of Edward Watkinson, author of *Frugality and Diligence Recommended and Enforced by Scripture*, that his 'benevolence and philanthropy seem to be inexhaustible'.[11] *Sermons on Humanity and Beneficence*, claimed the *Critical Review* in 1768, 'contain some excellent sentiments of philanthropy and benevolence'. 'A spirit of philanthropy and benevolence characterizes the present age', wrote Philanthropos in the *Monthly Ledger* in 1774. In a critical review of G. Gregory's *Essays Historical and Moral* in the *English Review* in 1785, the writer conceded that Gregory's 'heart swells with an extensive philanthropy and benevolence'.[12]

Philanthropy, as some of the above examples show, was frequently seen as a characteristic of authors and their works. A review of Sterne's sermons was pleased to find in them 'so large a share of philanthropy'. Adam Ferguson's *Essay on the History of Civil Society* was praised, amongst other qualities, for 'the sentiments of philanthropy with which this essay abounds'. The verses in *The Atheist. A Poem* were partially redeemed by 'the spirit of philanthropy in which they appear to have been written'.[13] 'Amiable philanthropy' characterised James Harris, author of *Philological Inquiries*. 'A spirit of pure philanthropy breathes' through John Fuller's *Some New Hints* concerning the recovery of those apparently dead from drowning – though the critic had no time for the substance of the work.[14] Philanthropy expressed itself not so much in deeds as in words. It was a sentiment – and a powerful one. As The Idler put it in 1759, on reading the bible, 'I felt my heart expanded by warm philanthropy, and exalted to dignity of sentiment'. He immediately sat down to write 'an Essay on Benevolence'.[15]

Experiencing this 'warm philanthropy' Christians felt that they were in their own small way replicating the 'divine philanthropy' of God. If God loved the world and its human inhabitants, it was incumbent on humans to do likewise to the best of their ability. As Philaretes from Berwick-on-Tweed put it in 1771, 'Humanity and benevolence are virtues which demonstrate the true grandeur and elevation of the *rational* nature. The compassionate, sympathizing, charitable mind, is the noblest image of Deity in this lower world'. It was said of Brigadier General Oglethorpe that he was 'with divine philanthropy inspir'd'.[16] Preaching before the Royal Humane Society, set up to rescue people from drowning, Colin Milne in 1778 declared that in saving life, 'You were above yourselves. You were superior to mere humanity. Ye were angelic. Ye were godlike and divine: for the source of excellence, and standard of perfection, we never so completely resemble, as when like him, we are benevolent, compassionate and merciful'.[17] Acting benevolently, you became godlike.

Divine philanthropy was universal in scope. Human philanthropy aimed to replicate this universality. In 1761 'Philanthropos', in response to an attack on Deism by 'Evangelicus', replied:

You will not allow the Deist to profess Philanthropy; on the contrary, I think, he *must* be a *Philanthropist*. As he ascribes all excellence to the Creator, *benevolence* must rise first in his view; not limited and partial, but extensive and universally diffused. This presents the Supreme Being the common father of all his rational creatures; which naturally induces him to consider every individual of the human species as brother or sister.[18]

This was easier said than done, but the desirability of so doing was reiterated. 'Humanity! Philanthropy! Thou charming virtue, why cannot I raise an altar to thee in all hearts?' asked a writer 'On Humanity' in the *Universal Magazine of Knowledge and Pleasure* in 1772: 'let us pass out of ourselves', it was urged;

'let us widen, I do not say the circle of our ideas, but that of our sentiments, and happiness will reign every-where'. Let us cherish 'the gentle affections of philanthropy and universal benevolence'.[19] Publication after publication preached the same message. The *Lady's Magazine* advised those of its readers who might be seeking a husband to be on the lookout for a man whose heart was 'warmed by the noble principle of universal philanthropy'. *Four Sermons on the Good Samaritan* were 'admirably calculated to inspire the reader with sentiments of universal benevolence and philanthropy'. Universality at its highest level demanded that in addition to feeling boundless philanthropy the philanthropist must recognise that those often denominated as 'barbarians' could have the same feelings.[20]

A poet in the *Town and Country Magazine* for October 1774 perhaps best captured this widespread sentiment in favour of universality:

Urg'd with a warm benevolence of soul,
Man should not feel for parts, but for the whole:
By no contracted, sordid views confin'd,
His boundless love should take in all mankind.
Those do most honour to the human race
In whom no selfish sentiments we trace,
Who, from all local prejudices free,
Breathe the pure spirit of philanthropy.[21]

In the history of philanthropy this was the age of poetry. It lasted through to the early nineteenth century. Odes to philanthropy filled the printed page. As a character in Henry Mackenzie's *The Man of Feeling* (1771) put it, 'There is at least ... one advantage in the poetical inclination, that it is an incentive to philanthropy. There is a certain poetic ground, on which a man cannot tread without feelings that enlarge the heart'.[22] The age of prose that succeeded it was much more down to earth.

Universality was closely linked to philanthropy that was 'pure'. As early as 1740 a writer in the *Champion* was thankful that ancestors were infused with 'such a Profusion of Humanity and Benevolence ... [with] the purest and warmest Philanthropy'. *Five Letters on Important Subjects* about easing the burdens of the poor, releasing prisoners for debt and regulating private madhouses, were 'written from motives of pure philanthropy'. The Humane Society, it was said, erected 'on the broad basis of humanity ... originates from the purest philanthropy'.[23]

The rewards of philanthropy and benevolence were widely attested to. James Thomson in *The Seasons* (1726–30) wrote of 'the inward rapture' inspired by true benevolence. For Archbishop Tillotson in 1728, 'There is no sensual Pleasure in the World comparable to the Delight and Satisfaction that a good Man takes in doing good'. The exercise of benevolence, said the *Gentleman's Magazine* in 1732, gave 'the most lasting, valuable and exquisite pleasure'.[24] Henry Fielding in *The History of Tom Jones* (1749) described how 'In Friendship, in parental and filial affection, and indeed in general Philanthropy, there is a great and exquisite Delight' and Tom rhapsodised about 'the warm, solid content, the swelling satisfaction, the thrilling transports, and the exulting triumphs, which a good mind enjoys in the contemplation of a generous, virtuous, noble, benevolent action'.[25] The *Universal Magazine* in 1754 printed an extract from Stackhouse's *Body of Divinity* in which it was claimed that we may 'prove the divine philanthropy from what we feel in ourselves, or perceive in others. We find in our own breasts a desire and readiness to do good, and to be beneficial to our fellow-creatures, and, when we relieve their wants, we seem to relieve our own bowels'. 'What satisfaction' there was, echoed David Hume, 'in relieving the distressed, in comforting the afflicted'.[26] Children's books in the late eighteenth century taught children how to give, 'perhaps the most prevalent of all themes in children's literature', and emphasised the happiness that came from giving.[27]

Critics of philanthropy

The broad swell of opinion in favour of philanthropy among writers for and readers of the periodical press was challenged from a number of quarters. First, there were those who argued that human motivations, passions and behaviour fell equally as often under the misanthropic as the philanthropic label. In the first half of the century Bertrand Mandeville in *The Fable of the Bees: Or, Private Vices, Publick Benefits* had argued that self-love and pride lay at the core of much that counted as charity. In language designed to offend, he described how a rich and selfish miser, wanting posthumous fame, might 'leave his Estate to some famous University: they are the best Markets to buy Immortality at with little Merit … There Men are profoundly skill'd in Human Nature, and know what it is their Benefactors want'.[28] Human nature, for Mandeville, was not as the new language of philanthropy imagined. In similar vein, 'The Misanthropist' in Henry Mackenzie's *The Man of Feeling* (1771) asserted that there are those who 'boast of generosity and feeling. They tell us (perhaps they tell us in rhime) that the sensations of an honest heart, of a mind universally benevolent, make up the quiet bliss which they enjoy; but they would not, by this, be exempted from the charge of selfishness'. Their pleasure came from the knowledge they were safe and secure while others were not. 'With vanity', went on the Misanthropist, 'your best virtues are grossly tainted: your benevolence, which ye deduce immediately from the natural impulse of the heart, squints to it for its reward'.[29] Percival Stockdale in 'An essay on misanthropy' made the case for 'rational and just Misanthropy'. An adjective often applied to philanthropy and philanthropists was 'amiable' in a positive sense. John Duncan's *An Essay on Happiness* in 1773 was 'strongly marked by this amiable philanthropy'. 'Amiable philanthropy', wrote the author of 'On social virtue', 'is the source of every social virtue'. Jonas Hanway was frequently praised for his philanthropy. He was not a good writer, wrote one critic, but 'The effusions of his philanthropy are ... so amiable'. Stockdale launched an attack on those 'seduced with the delusive epithet *amiable*'.[30] To face the world armed only with amiable philanthropy was to court disaster.

A generation earlier, in 1750, a writer had introduced to his readers 'Philanthropy ... this Word of Greek Derivation'. He saw it as the equivalent of the English 'good nature', but the latter, he thought, had come to be equated with 'Weakness of the Head'. Philanthropy, he confidently (but mistakenly) proclaimed, 'cannot be so perverted': it 'does not exclude Courage, Fortitude, Greatness of Sentiment, from the same Breast. On the contrary, we find that some of the most renowned Princes, Generals, and Philosophers, both in ancient and modern Story, were the most distinguished Philanthropists'. In the *Monthly Review* for January 1753 this was taken further, not discounting courage, but demanding that it be linked to philanthropy: 'Where philanthropy and universal benevolence are wanting, *courage* is only brutality, and *power* a curse upon the earth.'[31] But by the 1770s the association of philanthropy with amiability suggested to critics that far from being linked to courage and fortitude, philanthropy had become dangerously close to 'Weakness of the Head'.

Philanthropy's claims to universality were also under scrutiny. Was it really possible to love humankind? It had long been questioned how far imperfect humans could or should hope to act out the principles of 'Universal benevolence'. Was it the case that 'our good-will is circumscribed by no boundary, but may embrace the immensity of the universe'? That was the question posed by Adam Smith in *The Theory of Moral Sentiments* (1759). Rejecting the arguments of Francis Hutcheson, his conclusion was that only 'the great Director of the universe', 'this benevolent and all-wise Being', had the capacity for universal benevolence and the power to act on it, to maintain in the universe 'at all times, the greatest possible quantity of happiness'. Suppose, wrote Smith, that 'the great empire of China, with all its myriads of inhabitants, was suddenly swallowed up by an earthquake', how would 'a man of humanity in Europe' be affected? Not very much, was Smith's reply, less than if he lost his little finger. In the sixth edition of *The Theory of Moral Sentiments* (1790) Smith added a new section on 'Of universal Benevolence', stressing again that

> The administration of the great system of the universe ... the care of the universal happiness of all rational and sensible beings, is the business of God and not of man. To man is allotted a much humbler department, but one much more suitable to the weakness of his powers, and to the narrowness of his comprehension; the care of his own happiness, of that of his family, his friends, his country.

Neither 'the soft power of humanity', wrote Smith, nor 'that feeble spark of benevolence which Nature has lighted up in the human heart' was 'capable of counteracting the strongest impulses of self-love'. Self-love could work outwards through the power of 'habitual sympathy' to encompass family, friends, neighbours and country. Beyond that its influence was minuscule. 'Man', he wrote, 'must not be satisfied with indolent benevolence, nor fancy himself the friend of mankind because in his heart he wishes well to the prosperity of the world'.[32]

From a different angle, James Ramsay, the evangelical campaigner against slavery and the slave trade, reached similar conclusions. Criticising 'the theoretical, lifeless notions of universal benevolence that can never be reduced to practice because the objects of them … can never be within their reach', he argued that 'family, friends, and country' should be the focus of attention.[33]

Granville Sharp, also active in the campaign against slavery and the slave trade, had no time for such reservations. Neglect of the opportunity to act benevolently, he wrote, was 'as great an offence before God as if we had denied assistance to *Christ himself*'. Christ, Sharp argued, taught that 'all *mankind*, even our *professed enemies* … must necessarily be esteemed our neighbours … so that the same benevolence … is indisputably due, *under the Gospel*, to *our brethren of the universe*'. Josiah Wedgwood wrote to Sharp in 1773, welcoming his 'disinterested love of mankind' at a time when 'universal benevolence seems to be discouraged'. Sharp remained, as his biographer put it, 'in charity a universalist'.[34] Others did, too. When Rev. Rice Hughes preached in 1789 on 'Social Union and Benevolence' before the Ancient and Honorable Order of Bucks, he saw in mankind a 'beneficent disposition [which] is actuated by a diffusive principle of liberty, and universal kindness. It knows no partial distinctions, and is confined to no bounds … it incloses in the embrace of love and charity, all ranks and communities of men, to the utmost boundaries of the peopled globe'.[35]

Universal benevolence easily translated into an assertion of a language of rights. Sharp himself wrote of 'the natural rights of mankind'. David Hartley in the House of Commons in the aftermath of American independence urged that 'the only contention henceforward between Great Britain and America be, which shall exceed the other in zeal for establishing the fundamental rights to liberty of all mankind'.[36]

Critics were sceptical. Perhaps contrary to the expectations of readers, in the *Sentimental Magazine* in 1773 'The sentimental philosopher' argued that 'national opposition is … essential to preserve the virtues and talents of mankind, and consequently, that they, whose benevolence of heart would introduce universal philanthropy, would enfeeble the human character'. This desirability of competition and opposition between nations was, however, anathema to most who praised philanthropy. As the author of 'The fatal separation: A moral tale' put it in 1779, 'That peace is a blessing of inestimable value, and that war is a calamity deeply to be deplored, every man who feels the slightest emotions of philanthropy in his bosom must readily allow'. Leave aside war, even trade and navigation could endanger the spread of philanthropy.[37] Philanthropy had its critics but their arguments were met head on.

Philanthropy and national identity

Benevolence and philanthropy might be in theory universal, but they were also claimed to be peculiarly British. A print of the Foundling Hospital of 1749 was accompanied by verses that acknowledged that the French (and, it might have been admitted, most other nations) had foundling hospitals before Britain, but

> Tho Frenchmen sneer, Their boasted first Design,
> British benevolence shall far outshine.[38]

English travellers to Italy in the sixteenth and seventeenth centuries had been deeply impressed by the hospitals and other charitable institutions there, acknowledging that their own were inferior.[39] On the other hand, post-Reformation, the British played up the superiority of Protestant charity over Catholic. Now, in the mid-eighteenth century, there was a more confident assertion of charity as a national virtue. Charity, wrote Henry Fielding in 1752, was 'the very characteristic of this Nation at this Time', and it was even more evident in 1755 when the British contributed £100,000 to the relief of victims of the Lisbon earthquake. The 'virtues of benevolence', reflected Smollett, 'are always springing up to an extraordinary growth in the British soil'.[40] At the end of the century it was confidently asserted that 'British liberality, generosity, and charity, are themes of praise in every clime'.[41] The annual service for charity school children in St Paul's elicited similar reflections. For Sarah Trimmer, it was 'a spectacle for Britons to exult in, for no nation but their own can furnish the like'. *The Times* declared that it was 'a sight which foreigners must behold with wonder, but which Englishmen must feel with pride, when they reflect that no nation upon the face of the earth can produce its parallel'.[42]

It was difficult to deny, however, that philanthropy also had roots in the Enlightenment in Europe and especially in France.[43] Like the revolution to come, it reflected a powerful strand of anti-clericalism in French society, a strong critique of existing charities and an optimistic belief that in a well-ordered society human beings would throw off the chains, both physical and psychical, that restricted them. The background to it was a collapse in donations through wills to existing charities, and increasing socio-economic pressures.[44] The foundation of the Société Philanthropique de Paris in 1780, though it had little impact in its first five years, was a landmark. It was 'an association of several persons who, inspired by benevolence, work to assist, through uniting their fortune and their understanding, suffering and indigent virtue'. By early 1789 it had 744 subscribers, half of them nobles, and directly assisted 1,500 of the poor in Paris as well as providing funds for other charities. Its novelty lay in its independence of both church and government, in its emphasis on charitable activity, and in its optimism, its hope that poverty might be eliminated by teaching the poor to help themselves. Beyond this, it linked philanthropic action closely with the wellbeing of the nation; in a 1787 manifesto it declared that philanthropic activity was the main duty of a citizen. Hitherto charitable giving had been incited by the belief that it was a duty incumbent on Christians. Now it became, as it remains, the mark of true citizenship. Philanthropy was in these ways a product of the Enlightenment. Indeed it has been claimed that 'philanthropy was central to the Enlightenment's definition of itself'.[45] That is perhaps to overstate the case. The Société Philanthropique was not a total break with the past, far from it, and it became in the nineteenth century the repository of conservative attitudes. Nevertheless its impact was considerable. There were soon Sociétés Philanthropiques in French provincial towns. And, as we shall see in Chapter 7, in 1788 there was a Philanthropic Society founded in London. Philanthropy in the 1780s was making its mark.

In Britain philanthropy in the 1780s began to be seen as in tune with the enlightened spirit of the age. *The Times* in 1785 wrote of 'The spirit of philanthropy and religious tolerance that so peculiarly mark the present age'. In 1786 it hoped that attempts to divide the people of Ireland by reviving religious differences would not work 'in these times, when philanthropy is making such rapid strides, and the film of prejudice is being wiped from the eye of reason'. Later in the same year it referred to 'the enlightened sense and philanthropy of the present age'.[46] Tolerance, reason, enlightenment and philanthropy were bracketed together. On a donation to Belfast Academy *The Times* commented that 'the pure principal of philanthropy and religious toleration which it breathes does the donors much honour as enlightened Christians'. The attempts in various countries to bring relief to the peasantry signalled 'the triumph of reason and philanthropy over that accursed lust of domination, which is too common to the human heart'.[47]

Politically philanthropy positioned itself on the liberal or radical wing, in defence of the liberties of the people. In the farewell edition of the *Remembrancer* in 1751 Mr Cadwallader recalled how three and a half years previously it had started with 'a commission as large, as generous, and as publick-spirited as that superlative degree of philanthropy which constitutes patriotism, could dictate'. His aim had been to induce 'his fellow-subjects … to assert their own rights and claims, against the encroachments of corruption: And to assist in the rescue of the constitution, for the sake of re-establishing their own felicity'.[48] 'Ministerial corruption' was also the target of 'An Inferior Junius' in 1774, praising 'English patriotism' for its stand against it, but lamenting that it had not been sustained enough to prevent 'the eradication and opposition of public spirit and national philanthropy'. The rise of party was deplored. 'With tears of philanthropy', wrote John Brand, 'we have viewed the rapidity of its late devastations'.[49] There were occasionally tories who might be admitted into the world of philanthropy. Of Dr Arbuthnot it was said that 'Though a tory, he breathes philanthropy itself; and even when we consider him as a party-man, he bears a most amiable character'. But in general writers on philanthropy appealed to 'liberal and philosophical readers'.[50]

Such readers constituted a growing number in the middling and upper strata of society. Philanthropy took its place alongside other eighteenth-century words that together constituted a moral and cultural world for its readers – the key ones were 'humanity', 'sensibility', 'sympathy' and 'benevolence'. Women were thought to be more susceptible than men to the appeal of these words. The message readers received about philanthropy was consistent. It was a sentiment experienced in the body, in the breast or the bosom or the bowels; it was exquisite, pure, warm. Charity, by contrast, was often described as 'cold' – 'as cold as charity' as the saying went. In exploring the origins of human rights, Lynn Hunt has argued that these bodily sensations gave rise to the claim, expressed most forcibly in the American Declaration of Independence in 1776 and the French Declaration of the Rights of Man and Citizen in 1789, that all humans are born equal and have certain 'self-evident' and unalienable rights.[51] As Amanda Moniz has shown, these feelings of love of humanity, shared across the north Atlantic, survived the American Revolution to be reconstituted as 'the Empire of Humanity'.[52] As part of this world of thought and feeling, philanthropy extended beyond this to reach the furthest corners of the world. For humans it reflected divine philanthropy and in exercising philanthropy humans came closest to the divine. All that was now required was a human being who could personify philanthropy. To have feelings of philanthropy was one thing. To define oneself as 'a philanthropist' or to be so defined by others was on a different scale. In John Howard, however, contemporaries found such a person.

Conclusion

Histories of philanthropy in the eighteenth century tend to focus on the expansion of voluntary societies that built hospitals, founded charity schools and established the Foundling Hospital and the Marine Society. These achievements were considerable and imposed their presence on urban landscapes and in public consciousness. Yet none of them was proclaimed at the time as a manifestation of philanthropy. It is true that Jonas Hanway, who contributed to many of these developments, was praised in the 1780s, alongside John Howard, for his philanthropy, but it was as a personal attribute rather than being heralded as a public policy.

Philanthropy had its origins in print and in the feelings that were stirred up in reading about it. It was experienced in the body. This makes it difficult to see philanthropy as a product solely of the Enlightenment, for rationality, a separation of mind from body, is a key ingredient of the Enlightenment. The quotations from newspapers and periodicals in this chapter demonstrate that there was something beyond rationality in the ways in which contemporaries wrote about and experienced philanthropy. Philanthropy was a feeling, a sentiment. It was as much part of the Romantic Movement as it was of the Enlightenment.

Notes

1 *The Essayes or Counsels Civill & Morall, of Francis Bacon Lord Verulam* (1597: London: Robert Rivière & Son, n.d.), pp. 37–9.

2 *The Works of John Dryden*, Vol. XX (Berkeley, Los Angeles and London: University of California Press, 1989), p. 21.

3 Quoted in R. S. Crane, 'Suggestions toward a genealogy of the "man of feeling"', *English Literary History*, I (1934), 225–6, 219–20.

4 S. Johnson, *Dictionary of the English Language* (Johnsonsdictionaryonline.com).

5 H. Barker, *Newspapers, Politics and Public Opinion in Late Eighteenth-Century England* (Oxford: Clarendon Press, 1988), pp. 23–7, 111.

6 G. J. Barker-Benfield, *The Culture of Sensibility: Sex and Society in Eighteenth-Century Britain* (Chicago and London: University of Chicago Press, 1992), pp. 67–70; A. R. Humphreys, '"The friend of mankind" (1700–1760): An aspect of eighteenth-century sensibility', *Review of English Studies*, 24 (1948), 204–10.

7 A. Smith, *The Theory of Moral Sentiments*, ed. D. D. Raphael and A. L. Macfie (Oxford: Clarendon Press, 1976), p. 303.

8 Barker-Benfield, *Culture of Sensibility*, pp. 3–5.

9 D. Hume, *Enquiries Concerning Human Understanding and Concerning the Principles of Morals*, ed. L. A. Selby-Bigge, 3rd edn (revised by P. H. Nidditch) (Oxford: Clarendon Press, 1975), pp. xxv, xxvi, 227, 219, 298, 300.

10 Johnson, *Dictionary*.

11 *Gentleman's Magazine*, Mar. 1751, 140; *Monthly Review*, Sept. 1766, 239.

12 *Critical Review*, May 1768, 400; *Monthly Ledger*, Mar. 1774, 127; *English Review*, July 1785, 19. For further linkages of philanthropy and benevolence see *Critical Review*, Jan. 1777, 76; May 1779, 374; Apr. 1786, 316; *European Magazine*, Dec. 1784, 424.

13 *Monthly Review*, Mar. 1766, 207; *Critical Review*, Mar. 1767, 186; Dec. 1770, 481.

14 *Westminster Magazine*, Aug. 1781, 437; *London Magazine*, Oct. 1784, 304.

15 *Universal Chronicle*, 28 July 1759, quoting 'Scholar's Journal' from *The Idler*. Samuel Johnson wrote most of the content of *The Idler*. This piece, however, was probably by Bennet Langton – though it described Johnson's way of working.

16 *Weekly Magazine*, 4 Apr. 1771, 9; *Gentleman's Magazine*, Sept. 1744, 501.

17 Quoted in C. D. Williams, '"The luxury of doing good": Benevolence, sensibility and the Royal Humane Society', in R. Porter and M. M. Roberts (eds), *Pleasure in the Eighteenth Century* (Basingstoke: Macmillan Press, 1996), pp. 98–9.

18 *London Magazine*, Mar. 1761, 133.

19 *Universal Magazine of Knowledge and Pleasure*, Jan. 1772, 14–15.

20 *Lady's Magazine*, 11 (1780), 592–3; *Critical Review*, Jan. 1777, 76; *Weekly Magazine*, 4 Apr. 1771, 9.

21 *Town and Country Magazine*, Sept. 1774, 516.

22 H. Mackenzie, *The Man of Feeling* (1771; Oxford: Oxford University Press, 2001), p. 61.

23 *The Champion*, 3 Jan. 1740, 155; *Monthly Review*, Apr. 1772, 452; *Town & Country Magazine*, Sept. 1775, 473.

24 Thomson quoted in Humphreys, '"The friend of mankind"', 209; Tillotson in Crane, 'Suggestions toward a genealogy', 228; *Gentleman's Magazine* in R. Porter, 'The gift relation: Philanthropy and provincial hospitals in eighteenth-century England', in L. Granshaw and R. Porter (eds), *The Hospital in History* (London: Routledge, 1989), p. 162.

25 *Oxford English Dictionary*, 'Philanthropy'; H. Fielding, *The History of Tom Jones, a Foundling*, 2 vols (London: J. M. Dent & Sons, 1929), Vol. I, p. 133.

26 *Universal Magazine*, Dec. 1754, 266; Hume quoted in Barker-Benfield, *Culture of Sensibility*, p. 135.

27 M. O. Grenby, '"Real charity makes distinctions": Schooling the charitable impulse in early British children's literature', *British Journal for Eighteenth-Century Studies*, 25 (2002), 185, 192, 194.

28 B. Mandeville, *The Fable of the Bees: or, Private Vices, Publick Benefits*, ed. F. B. Kaye, 2 vols (Oxford: Clarendon Press, 1924), Vol. I, p. 265.

29 Mackenzie, *Man of Feeling*, pp. 32–3.

30 Stockdale in *London Magazine*, Jan. 1785, 26–30; for 'amiable philanthropy', *Weekly Miscellany*, 5 June 1775, 233; *London Review*, June 1775, 414.

31 *Old England*, 25 Aug. 1750, 711–12; *Monthly Review*, Jan. 1753, 36.

32 Smith, *Theory of Moral Sentiments*, pp. 106, 136–7, 235–7.

33 D. Turley, *The Culture of English Antislavery, 1780–1860* (London: Routledge, 1991), p. 173; C. L. Brown, *Moral Capital: Foundations of British Abolitionism* (Chapel Hill: University of North Carolina Press, 2006), p. 348.

34 Turley, *Antislavery*, pp. 20, 91; Brown, *Moral Capital*, p. 187.

35 R. Hughes, *Social Union and Benevolence* (London, 1789), p. 6.

36 Brown, *Moral Capital*, pp. 164, 186.

37 *Sentimental Magazine*, Dec. 1773, 486; *Town & Country Magazine*, Mar. 1779, 133; *Universal Magazine*, 2 Jan. 1772, 7.

38 Quoted in D. H. Solkin, *Painting for Money: The Visual Arts and the Public Sphere in Eighteenth-Century England* (New Haven and London: Yale University Press, 1993), p. 161.

39 E. P. de G. Chaney, '"Philanthropy in Italy": English observations on Italian hospitals, 1545–1789', in T. Riis (ed.), *Aspects of Poverty in Early Modern Europe* (Sijthoff: Alphen aan den Rijn, 1981), pp. 183–218.

40 Quotes in Humphreys, '"The friend of mankind"', 216, 218.

41 *Anti-Jacobin Review*, Apr. 1799, quoted in Ford K. Brown, *Fathers of the Victorians: The Age of Wilberforce* (Cambridge: Cambridge University Press, 1961), p. 168.

42 Quoted in H. Cunningham, *The Children of the Poor: Representations of Childhood since the Seventeenth Century* (Oxford: Blackwell, 1991), pp. 40–1.

43 M. Sulek, 'On the modern meaning of philanthropy', *Nonprofit and Voluntary Sector Quarterly*, 39 (2010), 194–5.

44 C. Jones, *Charity and Bienfaisance: The Treatment of the Poor in the Montpellier Region 1740–1815* (Cambridge: Cambridge University Press, 1982).

45 D. Garrioch, '"Making a better world": Enlightenment and philanthropy', in M. Fitzpatrick, P. Jones, C. Knellwolf and I. McCalman (eds), *The*

Enlightenment World (Abingdon: Routledge, 2007), pp. 486–501, quoting pp. 486, 496; C. Duprat, *Le temps des philanthropes: la philanthropie parisienne des lumières à la Monarchie de juillet* (Paris: Éditions du C. T. H. S., 1993).

46 *The Times*, 13 Jul. 1785; 16 Feb. 1786; 6 June 1786.

47 Ibid., 31 Oct. 1785; 30 Aug. 1787.

48 *London Magazine*, June 1751, 270–1.

49 *Sentimental Magazine*, Mar. 1774, 119–20; *Gentleman's Magazine*, Aug. 1777, 383.

50 *Critical Review*, July 1766, 2; July 1773, 77.

51 L. Hunt, *Inventing Human Rights: A History* (New York and London: W. W. Norton and Company, 2007).

52 A. B. Moniz, *From Empire to Humanity: The American Revolution and the Origins of Humanitarianism* (New York: Oxford University Press, 2016).

4

John Howard, the philanthropist

Philanthropy by the 1780s had for thirty years been paraded before the British reading public. Many people had written about philanthropy, many readers had felt it. Letter writers had signed themselves 'Philanthropist' or sometimes 'Philanthropus', but for a named person to be hailed as a 'philanthropist' was something quite new. It was the prison reformer John Howard's fate to be so described. People looked up to him in awe, they saw him as 'god-like'. He had a very different view of his own merits and demerits. That, however, did not prevent him being held up as the model of what a philanthropist should be, a model that was hardly challenged for a good century after his death in 1790. This chapter describes how John Howard became 'the philanthropist' and how that shaped the history of philanthropy.

John Howard

What was it about Howard himself or what he had done that lead to him being acclaimed as a philanthropist? Howard's personality has both intrigued and baffled biographers. He was forty-seven in 1773, the year when he became High Sheriff of Bedfordshire and embarked on the prison visiting that was to make him famous. Born in 1726 to a wealthy Dissenting upholsterer family in London, Howard lost his mother when he was five, failed to do well at Dissenting boarding schools, was apprenticed into the grocery trade, but bought himself out when his father died in 1742. He was left £7,000 and extensive property, enough to live off comfortably. He spent the next few years travelling in Europe and recovering from illness. He married the landlady of his lodgings in Stoke Newington in 1752; she, more than double his age, had nursed Howard through illness, but herself died within three years. Thereafter he based himself at the family estate in Cardington in Bedfordshire where he embarked on extensive improvement to cottages linked to strict rules of behaviour and conduct for the tenants. An intended visit to Lisbon in the aftermath of the earthquake in 1755 was cut short by capture by French privateers and imprisonment in France. Released, he sought help for those still in prison. In 1756 he was elected a Fellow of the Royal Society – his particular interest lay in recording temperatures – and in 1758 of the Royal Society of Arts, suggesting that he had a network of contacts in those worlds. Remarrying in 1758, his wife in 1765 gave birth to a son, John or Jack, but died a few days later. Thereafter Howard resumed a life of European travel combined with lengthy visits to Bath or Bristol to recover his health.[1]

As a Dissenter Howard had a right to refuse to become High Sheriff, as his father had done, but at the cost of having to pay a substantial penalty. Howard at first refused. Samuel Whitbread, the brewer, Howard's relative (there had been a marriage between the families in the 1670s), friend and neighbour in Bedfordshire, interceded on his behalf with the Lord Chancellor, Lord Bathurst. On hearing from Whitbread that Howard was indeed 'a Protestant Dissenter in the strictest sense', Bathurst excused him from having to become High Sheriff. Whitbread, however, was able to persuade Howard to change his mind.[2] One of his duties as High Sheriff was to inspect prisons. He found that prisoners who had been acquitted or released without a charge being brought against them were often being kept in prison because they were unable to pay debts incurred to the gaoler. Howard suggested that the county should pay off these debts, but was asked to investigate practice in other counties. Thus began his prison visiting. Between 1773 and 1783, on his own computation, he travelled 42,033 miles and many more miles after that.[3]

Howard soon had in his head a model of what a prison should be. The gaoler should be paid a salary, debtors should be separated from felons, and both from those awaiting trial. There should be adequate light, ventilation, water, diet and exercise yards. Prisons should aim at reform as much as punishment. To this end prisoners should be put to work and have a separate cell. There should be a chaplain. On entering a prison Howard would check it against these requirements – and nearly always find it wanting. He counted the steps down to dungeons, measured rooms, inquired about the gaoler's means of livelihood, scrutinised the water supply. His book, *The State of the Prisons*, published in 1777, recorded his findings, prison by prison throughout Great Britain and Ireland and extending to the Continent where he was particularly impressed by prisons in the Netherlands.

Howard's precise calculation of the miles travelled hints at an obsessive personality. Punctuality was one of his trademarks. In his last few months at Kherson in Ukraine he used to visit Admiral Priestman: 'he would place his watch upon the table, and pass exactly an hour with him in conversation'. He may, it has been suggested, have suffered from Asperger's Syndrome. Perhaps his constant travelling was an attempt to overcome his sense of loss after the death of his second wife and to distract from a tendency to depression. Isaac Wood told in 1797 how when Howard had visited him in

Shrewsbury in 1788 'He informed me that it was the death of his wife whom he tenderly loved – and when he told me this his gushing tears manifested the pang which the recollection gave him – that induced him to devote himself so entirely to this employment as a relief under so severe a domestic affliction'.[4]

People found Howard odd. When Arthur Young, the agriculturist, staying with Samuel Whitbread in 1772, visited Howard at Cardington, he found him 'rather pragmatical in his speech, very polite, but expressing himself in a manner that seemed to belong to two hundred years ago'.[5] In 1775 Jemima Marchioness Gray, in a letter to her daughter about a party, thought that 'It was no bad addition considering all things to have such a sort of whimsical character as little Mr Howard of Cardington among us'.[6] Little Mr Howard with his whimsical character sounds very different to the celebrated philanthropist; rather, he appears as a socially awkward neighbour who might provide some amusement, if not at the time, at least in retrospect. Howard's diet added to the sense of oddness. Recovering from illness in his early twenties he restricted his diet from then onwards to vegetables, fruit, bread, milk and tea – and in sparing quantities.[7]

Howard described himself as 'a firm Dissenter and anti-Ministerial Man in America and many other Affairs'.[8] Brought up an Independent, moderately Calvinist in belief, he was anything but sectarian. As a young man in Stoke Newington he formed a lasting friendship with Richard Price, one of the leading Unitarians.[9] John Aikin in Warrington, another Unitarian, helped him in preparing his work for publication.

Broad-minded as he was within the world of Dissent and beyond it, Howard seems never to have escaped from an unremitting sense of his own sinfulness. He perhaps doubted that he was one of the elect. He described himself in his diaries as a 'fruitless barren cold dead vile Creature' and lamented 'my corrupt and depraved Nature'.[10] This does not suggest someone confident of his own salvation, in any sense experiencing joy in or through his faith. On the eve of departing on his last journey, 'I now fly to Thee to deliver me from the wrath to come. I come to Thee as my last Refuge to save me from Hell and Damnation which I have so justly deserved throwing myself at thy feet resolving if I perish to perish there; save me O Lord or I perish'. On this last journey he carried with him a covenant with God that his wife had signed in 1748. Howard read and signed it in Moscow on 25 September 1789, on 14 October 1789 and, 'weak and faint', at Kherson on 10 January 1790 (though he dates it 1789). 'Oh! God', he writes at Moscow, 'permit a poor worm to subscribe his unworthy name to this solemn Covenant'.[11]

John Aikin saw Howard every day for months at a time in Warrington, 'being his corrector and reviser and so forth'. 'His labors', Aikin reported to his sister, 'are most amazing, and a wonderful proof of what may be done by one man entirely devoted to a single object. Yet he has not, I think, a very enlarged mind, and will be chiefly useful as a collector of facts for others to reason upon. His narrow education (as he himself often laments) is an eternal and insuperable bar to him. In resolution, firmness, and integrity, he is unequalled'.[12] This was a shrewd judgement, Howard's not very enlarged mind balanced by 'resolution, firmness, and integrity'. Howard's single-mindedness struck others. To Jeremy Bentham, 'His thoughts, his conversation, his writings are confined to this one subject'.[13]

Prison reform

Howard's entry into the world of prisons was well timed for reform was in the air. 'In the twenty years between 1775 and 1795 a wholesale rebuilding of the country gaols and bridewells was accomplished.'[14] There were two factors that go some way towards explaining the timing of the reform of prisons. The first was the prevalence of gaol fever. An outbreak in 1783 exposed the danger, perhaps strongest in Lancashire, but evident elsewhere, in Gloucester, Worcester and Maidstone.[15] The way to eliminate it, it was thought, lay in ventilation and cleanliness. So unhygienic were so many of the old prisons that demolition and rebuilding were a necessity. And this programme was a success – better ventilation and hygiene not only brought purer air, it also reduced the prevalence of the lice that, unknown to contemporaries, spread typhus. By 1789 it could be claimed that 'gaol fever ... is now almost eradicated' – though that assessment was distinctly optimistic: there were further outbreaks in the nineteenth century.[16] The second reason was that with the outbreak of war with the American colonies it became impossible to continue transporting prisoners there. Prisons for most of the eighteenth century were holding pens for debtors, those about to be transported or executed, and those awaiting trial. About half of all prisoners were debtors.[17] With transportation off the agenda until it was resumed from 1787 with the opening of Botany Bay, a new regime for convicted criminals had to be instituted in hulks or in prisons. What kind of discipline and punishment should they be subjected to? Could they be reformed?

Gaol fever and the end of transportation were the two immediate pressures on prisons in the 1770s. There had, in addition, been numerous attempts through the eighteenth century at reform and change. Transportation, the default punishment after an Act of 1718, always had critics, and was in decline before the mid-1770s.[18] Imprisonment with hard labour had prominent supporters, for example the magistrate and author Henry Fielding in 1753. The notion that prisoners might be reformed as well as punished had its advocates in the late seventeenth century, and in 1769 a prominent supporter in Sir William Blackstone in his enormously influential *Commentaries on the Laws of England*. Jonas Hanway advocated solitude and a prominent role for chaplains before Howard did.[19] But the outcome of these ideas and initiatives had been piecemeal at best. Only with the 1770s was there a sustained debate in print about crime and punishment – and Howard was both part of that and an inspirer of it.[20] His intervention was well timed; there was a receptive audience waiting.

News of Howard's accumulation of evidence about the state of prisons gave renewed hopes for more substantial and long-lasting reforms. His work, described by Jeremy Bentham in 1778 as 'a model for method', encouraged further systematic collection of statistics and information about crime and prisons.[21] He was acknowledged as an expert, called to the Bar of the House of Commons in 1774 to be formally thanked.

Howard's ambitions extended beyond making prisons more efficiently run and healthier. He wanted to institute a regime of discipline that would reform prisoners. Deeply impressed by some of the institutions he had seen on the continent, he argued that 'We have too much adopted the gothic mode of correction, viz., by rigorous severity, which often hardens the heart; while many foreigners pursue the more rational plan for softening the mind in order to its amendment'.[22] The 'rational plan' had at its heart solitude for the prisoner. Its most vocal advocate was Jonas Hanway who was often bracketed with Howard for his philanthropy. For Hanway 'There is scarce any wickedness that solitude will not work on it'.[23] Howard was more cautious: he thought that 'solitude and silence are favourable to reflection and may possibly lead [prisoners] to repentance', but felt that complete solitude, day and night, was both impractical and too severe.[24] But even solitude at night entailed a redesign of prisons, with the single-occupied cell as the building block. Linked with a cellular construction was the necessity for separating out different types of prisoners, by sex, age and type of offence. On top of this, a regime of hard work was 'indispensably requisite. *Not one* should be idle, that is not sick … The keeper should be a master of some manufacture … And he should keep his prisoners at work ten hours a day; mealtimes included'.[25] Few existing prisons could be redesigned to meet these requirements.

Howard's plans for reform garnered support across the country. Thomas Bayley in Manchester and Sir George Onesiphorus Paul in Gloucestershire both acknowledged their indebtedness to Howard, the latter describing him as 'the presiding Genius of Reform of these Melancholy Mansions of Oppression and Distress … to him all future reformers are indebted for seeing what they see, and feeling what they feel'.[26]

Howard's visits to prisons gave him an unrivalled status as the foremost expert on prisons and punishment and as the man who had instigated reforms that held out the promise of reformation of prisoners through a humane regime. He had a very clear sense of the reforms he wanted to see put in place, and could not but be aware of the high regard in which he was held across Europe. Lord Carmarthen, secretary of state for foreign affairs, tried (unsuccessfully for Howard had published critical comments on the Bastille) to get him permission to enter France. Ambassadors in The Hague, Vienna, Naples and Constantinople went out of their way to help him. In Vienna in 1785 an Englishman reported how Sir Robert Keith was 'much taken up by … the celebrated Mr. Howard'. On his return through Vienna in 1786 he had an audience of two hours with Emperor Joseph II at the latter's request, the two men evidently standing throughout as Howard refused to kneel on entry (just as he had refused to kneel to the Pope).[27] Nearer home, he was granted the freedom of Edinburgh, Cork and Paisley.[28] And there was an even greater honour proposed for him.

'An *extravagance* of philanthropy': John Howard and the statue

In the *Gentleman's Magazine* in May 1786 Anglus proposed that a subscription be set on foot to raise funds for a statue of John Howard. Anglus had met Howard in Rome two months previously and 'I did all but worship him'. He was, wrote Anglus, 'the most truly glorious of mortal beings', 'the *Consummate Philanthropist*', 'an ornament to human nature in general, and, in particular, to this glorious country which produced him'. John Nichols, editor and printer of the *Gentleman's Magazine*, added his support and undertook to collect subscriptions.[29] John Coakley Lettsom, a wealthy Quaker doctor involved in many good causes, gave strong backing to the proposal. Enclosing ten guineas, 'to commemorate the godlike actions of the *living* Howard', he proposed that the first five people to subscribe ten guineas should be appointed as a committee with power to add to it other subscribers.[30] In the event it was three men, Nichols, Lettsom and Anglus (who turned out to be Dr John Warner, an Anglican clergyman and later a strong supporter of the French Revolution) who carried forward the proposal.[31]

Through the summer of 1786 tributes to Howard filled the pages of the *Gentleman's Magazine*. There was, as John Aikin put it, 'an *extravagance* of philanthropy which could not but appear ridiculous to those whose judgment was not dazzled by the ardour of admiration'.[32] The irascible Philip Thicknesse, writing under the name Polyxena, was moved by an account of Howard's deeds 'so fraught with benevolence, and told with such modesty, humility, and philanthropy', qualities which he himself so rarely displayed.[33] John Call, sheriff of Cornwall in 1771, and helped by Howard in the reform of penal institutions, praised Howard's 'unexampled philanthropy'. B. N. T. thought that Howard, 'our great philanthropist', was on a par in the history of the nation with Shakespeare and Newton. To another correspondent he was 'our unparalleled prodigy of a philanthropist', to yet another he displayed 'the most transcendant philanthropy'. John Nichols himself wrote of Howard's 'exuberant philanthropy', now no longer confined to Europe.[34]

John Howard was not the only person being praised for philanthropy in the 1780s. Mr J. Richards of Clapham, recently deceased in 1785, was described as 'a man of great philanthropy' for his work in adjusting insurance premiums as a means of saving lives in the Atlantic. Granville Sharp, the anti-slavery campaigner, was praised for his 'great philanthropy'.[35] Dr Lettsom, the Treasurer of the Royal Humane Society, acted with 'a philanthropy which does honour to human nature'. The Society paraded those it had rescued from drowning at its annual anniversary, a sight that was 'a treat for Britons and Philanthropists'.[36] Above all, Jonas Hanway, who died in September 1786, was 'that illustrious philanthropist'. His memorial in Westminster Abbey describes him as 'the FRIEND and FATHER of the POOR', a 'CITIZEN of the WORLD'. There should, it was suggested, be a statue to Hanway to accompany the one to Howard, 'his illustrious Coadjutor in the cause of humanity'.[37] For consistent praise not only for his philanthropy, however, but also for being a 'philanthropist', John Howard, the prison reformer, stood preeminent.

The appeal for money for the statue met with success beyond expectation. In September 1787 a general meeting of subscribers heard that 609 people had subscribed a total just short of £1,500.[38] Four aristocrats, the Duke of Portland, the Duke of Rutland, the Earl of Carlisle and the Marquis of Carmarthen, headed the list, each giving ten guineas as did others such as Lettsom and Warner. The four aristocrats were all participants in high politics, Portland a past and future prime minister, Carmarthen, who became Duke of Leeds in 1789, secretary of state for foreign affairs. There were other notable subscribers: the prime minister, William Pitt, gave five guineas as did William Wilberforce and Josiah Wedgwood. Sir Joshua Reynolds gave two guineas, the anti-slave trade campaigner Granville Sharp one guinea. These were notable contributors. Howard's name and fame were endorsed at the highest level, and with that went recognition that philanthropy was a national virtue. Of over two hundred subscribers listed in the *The Times*, only thirteen were women (three of these Lettsoms).[39] Overall, it was thought, the sums given would provide a surplus that could go into a 'Howardian Fund for Prison Charities and Reforms'.[40]

Both Warner and Lettsom recognised that there might be a problem in erecting a statue. Howard was abroad on a hazardous quest, reaching as far as Constantinople, to find the cause of and cure for the plague. After a sea journey under attack by privateers, he subjected himself to quarantine in the lazaretto in Venice for the requisite forty days, thinking that it might have lessons for other countries. But it was not the possibility that Howard might die abroad that worried the backers of a statue, rather that Howard might return to England before the statue was completed. If he did, Anglus recognised, 'Mr. Howard's humble sense of his own merits would most certainly prevent it'. Lettsom was more robust in his assessment of this risk. 'The present moment', he argued, 'during his absence in Turkey, is the most proper to accomplish such a design. With goodness of heart he unites exemplary humility; and a perfection of mind rarely equalled is veiled by a modesty that shuns praise and adulation; but the public applause which is due to great and virtuous actions cannot be ungrateful to the god-like breast of Howard'. In effect, Howard would accept a *fait accompli*. And there was more at stake than recognition of Howard's virtues. 'Public approbation of private and public virtues', wrote Lettsom, 'whilst it acknowledges a debt due to intrinsic merit, reflects the highest honour on the community; for to reward virtue is a pleasing proof of its prevalence'.[41] Raising money for a statue was recognition not only of Howard's virtues but also, and perhaps equally importantly, of those of the subscribers. As 'A Subscriber' put it, 'I never remember an occasion which so much inspired me with a sensation of doing honour to myself'.[42]

It is difficult to enter into the minds of people who proposed to take advantage of someone's absence from the country in order to carry out a project, supposedly to honour that person, even though they knew that person would prevent it if he had been present. J. P. Andrews, who claimed to be a relative of Howard's, found that many people wondered whether Howard would actually want such a memorial, and suggested that any money raised might go towards relieving the distress of prisoners.[43] This was a theme taken up in a series of letters by 'A Philanthropist' writing from Pall Mall in the *Morning Chronicle*. Addressing the Duke of Portland whose name headed the list of subscribers, and claiming that 'I speak the sentiments of Howard's great soul', he argued that the establishment on a firm basis of funds for prison charities (he wanted there to be an annual 'free-will gift' on a Sunday every August) and the implementation of prison reforms were a crucial preliminary to a statue. Attacking the 'credulity' evident in England, he argued that 'In the case of a subscription for the erection of a statue to Mr. Howard, there is such a spectacle exhibited in this present moment, as future generations will hardly give credit to, and which none but Englishmen would be capable of countenancing'.[44] Junius Junior, in support, asked of Howard, 'Surely ... we do not mean to gratify his *vanity*, instead of seconding his *philanthropy*?' He imagined Howard riding into London on 'the Howardian way' only 'to see my attempt applauded, but my ends unexecuted! Fame, I travelled not for you!'[45]

Howard's probable unwillingness to consent to a statue was compounded by the fact that there was no likeness of him that a sculptor could work from. Howard always resolutely refused to allow his portrait to be painted. 'There is no picture', he wrote, 'there is no Bust and I shall never sit for any'.[46] He had adopted a method of putting off those who might try to sneak a view of him. Standing outside a print shop one day he noticed that someone was trying to draw him; he immediately pretended to find the print he was looking at uproariously funny and contorted his face in laughter in such a way that no likeness could be taken.[47] John Sanders (1750–1825), a portrait painter, and John Hickey (1751–95) and John Flaxman (1755–1826), both best-known as sculptors, 'in a most liberal and disinterested manner' offered to furnish the committee with a likeness of Howard if instructed by any of Howard's friends who might be 'intimately acquainted with his features'.[48]

The ideal location and design of the monument was much debated. No one doubted that it should be in London. There was considerable support for the proposal in the provinces, but that such signal virtue should be honoured in the capital was taken for granted. Some suggested an obelisk or column, but a statue was always favoured – people, it was felt, could relate to it better than to anything abstract and would be more likely to be inspired to try to emulate the philanthropist. There was support for an indoors site, either Westminster Abbey, but it was thought to be too crowded with memorials, or St Paul's Cathedral.[49] Alongside this, there were many suggestions for an out of doors site, including various locations in the City and Shooter's Hill, but the one that attracted most attention was to place the statue within a crescent to be built in St George's Fields. As James Martin put it, it was 'one of the most frequented spots that could be found. It is the *most* common Entrance for all Foreigners to our Capital'.[50]

In the event all these plans had to be put on hold. Howard's friends had written to tell him what was afoot. Howard replied to Richard Price in October 1786, stating in the most emphatic tones the distress the proposal was causing him and urging that a stop be put to it.[51] Writing from the Venice lazaretto to Charles Dilly, Howard described how 'it mortifies, humbles, and distresses me; persons far over-rate my performance; and even what is in our best? – a miserable alloy of folly and sin; many things plead for me against such a measure; a private man, a Dissenter, peculiarities – diet, etc, dislike to shew and parade'.[52] Price on 3 November copied to Lettsom part of the letter he had received and asked him to take steps to bring a halt to the statue proposal; if not, Price would advertise Howard's objections in the newspapers. Lettsom had no alternative but to accede to the request put to him.[53] Alderman Boydell, who ran an engraving and print selling business and was to be Lord Mayor in 1790–91, chaired a general meeting of subscribers on 22 November 1786 where John Nichols moved resolutions to halt the statue proposal while hoping that Howard may still 'consent that a grateful community may, by erecting a statue to him, do itself the honour of shewing that it is not unworthy of such a member'. Once again, the statue was intended to honour the subscribers as much as Howard. Meanwhile, it was agreed, the Howardian Fund would remain open for subscriptions.[54]

Howard tried to put an end to any hope that he might change his mind. His only comfort was that his friends had had nothing to do with the proposal. Of Lettsom, Howard wrote that 'I have never passed one hour' in his company. The committee set up to forward the proposal for a statue was made up of people 'not one of whom I know'.[55] In a letter from Vienna on 15 December to the promoters of the plan he wrote how the execution of the plan 'will be a punishment to me', and that it was 'my particular and earnest request, that so distinguished a mark of me may *for ever* be laid aside'.[56] But to little effect. A committee of twenty-five people resolved in January that the erection of a statue 'be, for the present, laid aside'.[57] So much for Howard's wish that the proposal be laid aside 'for ever'. In the *Gentleman's Magazine* S. P. [Samuel Pratt] urged that 'To Mr. Howard's extreme delicacy, I trust that you will not yield' and hoped that 'Mr. Howard will at last respect that decision which he is unable to controul'.[58] Howard then addressed the subscribers directly, repeating his wish that 'the execution of your design may be laid aside for ever', and pouring the coldest of waters on the proposed Howardian Fund. He could not permit it in future to go by that name and he would 'have no concern in the disposal of the money subscribed; my situation and various pursuits render it impossible for me to pay any attention to such a general plan, which can only be carried into due effect in particular districts, by a constant attention and a constant residence'.[59]

In early March the committee tried to put some gloss on the difficult situation it found itself in. It resolved:

> That Mr Howard's refusing to let the subscribers do an honour to themselves, in erecting a statue to him, was an event to be apprehended, as, in the very first hint of this business which was given to the Publick, it was foretold that, if it could not be executed before his return (which was impossible, for want of a likeness), Mr. Howard would certainly prevent it; but still there can be no cause to regret the having made an endeavour, which even in its failure has proved a striking memorial of his merit, by convincing the world that his modesty, like his other virtues, exceeds the common scale of human excellence.[60]

In the bluntest of terms, the committee was acknowledging that, in supporting the proposal for a statue, the subscribers were honouring themselves, and were impeded only by Howard's exceptional modesty (or what we may suppose they more likely thought of as his stubbornness).

The committee also arranged for a meeting of subscribers on 12 March 1787 to decide what to do with the money raised. Subscribers could ask for the return of their donations. Of the 609 subscribers, 126 asked for their donations to be returned to them. These included a donation from Glasgow that was to be put to building a 'Public Infirmary' in the city.[61] The first call on the remainder was to be to 'strike a medal in honour of the great Philanthropist'. A statue, Lettsom reflected later, would have been seen only by Londoners, a medal would be more widely diffused. King George III and any other ruler in Europe who had helped Howard would receive a gold one, and there would be copies in silver for those who had subscribed five guineas or more and in bronze for those whose subscriptions were less.[62] Progress on implementing this scheme was slow, a sub-committee of seven including Sir Joshua Reynolds and Lettsom, Warner and Nichols was not set up until September, and no medal seems to have been struck in the more than two years from then until Howard's death in January 1790. As Nichols's son remembered, 'The medal was not proceeded with'.[63] Lettsom himself hoped that the remainder of the fund 'will never be annihilated; but, by accumulation, augment the channels of beneficence'. A society might be formed that would 'reward the philanthropy of virtue by the mitigation of calamity'. In fact all that was done to mitigate calamity was a donation of £200 in August 1788 for the relief of prisoners in London from what was still called, despite Howard's objections, 'the Howardian Fund'.[64]

Howard had wanted the idea of a statue to be buried 'for ever', but the subscribers thought that his death in Kherson in Ukraine in January

1790 relieved them from any longer holding back. In March 1790 it was agreed that the original idea of a statue should be revived, the sculptor to be John Bacon. Bacon had an established reputation with, to his credit, a bust of George III and the national monument to the Earl of Chatham in Westminster Abbey. He was envied by contemporaries for his ability to win prestigious commissions and criticised by some for his tendency towards sentimentality rather than neo-classical austerity. A large committee with thirty-one members was set up in May to oversee the siting and design of the statue. Rev. John Pridden, one of the committee, suggested St Paul's Cathedral as the site; it was, as those who were now termed 'the Howardian subscribers' agreed, 'peculiarly adapted to the greatness of his character and the dignity and gratitude of the British Empire'.[65] Prolonged negotiations ensued with the Dean and Chapter and the Trustees of the Fabrick (the archbishop of Canterbury, the bishop of London and the Lord Mayor), no one certain who had the responsibility of decision. In the event in March 1791 the Dean and Chapter gave permission.[66] St Paul's until then had no statues in the body of the cathedral. Sir Horace Walpole had hoped that the Earl of Chatham on his death in 1778 might be accorded a statue 'that there might be some decoration in that nudity', but it was not to be. Visitors complained about the 'void, barren space'.[67] The agreement to allow the statue of Howard was a significant break with tradition. Aware of this and of what was at stake for the future of St Paul's as a national and international building (the second in Europe and the first in Britain, according to the Marquis of Lansdowne), the Dean and Chapter insisted that 'no monument should be erected without the design being first approved by a Committee of the Royal Academicians'. They also agreed that Howard's statue should be matched with one of Samuel Johnson.[68]

On 19 May 1791 a high-powered delegation from the Royal Academy, headed by Sir Joshua Reynolds, and including Sir William Chambers, Benjamin West and Joseph Nollekins, met in St Paul's with members of the committee overseeing the Howard statue, and sites for the two statues were agreed: the south-east recess of the dome for Howard, the north-east for Johnson. The Howard committee then agreed that the monument to Howard should be 7' 8" high on a 7' pedestal and should show Howard bending down to relieve a prisoner. Bacon's model for this 'was unanimously approved of' in June; moreover it was agreed that the statue of Howard should be unveiled at least a month before that of Johnson.[69]

The Royal Academicians, however, were less than happy with the design. They regretted that what they thought had been agreed, a single figure of both Howard and Johnson, had been ignored. Bacon argued that he could not properly delineate Howard's character without a secondary figure, but Benjamin West and the Royal Academy committee considered this as 'of no weight'.[70] Sarah Burnage has argued that behind this lay a clash of styles, classical simplicity against the injection of emotion sought by Bacon and, more than this, a deep concern within the Royal Academy about the dangers of radicalism at a time when events in France were particularly threatening.[71] It would appear, however, that neither the Dean and Chapter nor the Howard committee disputed the Royal Academy's right to express its opinion. Moreover the Howard committee accepted the Royal Academy opinion and its agreement to Bacon's original model was 'rescinded'.[72] Howard in Bacon's sculpture stands upright, clad in a Greek tunic, a large key in his right hand, a sheaf of papers in his left. In a bas-relief Howard stoops to raise up a prisoner, an assistant brings food and water, and a gaoler unlocks a door to release those unjustly imprisoned.[73]

More money had to be raised. The Society for Giving Effect to His Majesty's Proclamation against Vice and Immorality, popularly known as the Vice Society, gave fifty guineas in 'appreciation of the design to do honour to the memory of that most respectable and respected character'.[74] John Bacon himself gave £50.[75] An even larger gift of £100, supplementing an earlier donation of £200, came from Samuel Whitbread. Whitbread, like everyone else who knew Howard well, had held back from donating while Howard was alive, his scruples now at an end. He became a member of the committee set up in May 1790 and a year later was chair of it.[76] He and his son, also Samuel, were thereafter important figures in the statue project. The son, insisting that his anonymity be preserved, composed the lines in memory of Howard that adorn the statue – and donated 30 guineas. Nichols's son recalled in 1850 that once there was agreement for a statue in St Paul's, the two Whitbreads 'took a lively interest in the erection of the monument'.[77]

The statue was opened to the public on 23 February 1796, nearly ten years after the proposal was first mooted. The mood of the nation, now at war, had changed dramatically in that decade. Howard was no longer at the centre of attention and no newspaper seems to have reported the opening. It was, however, an important moment in the history of St Paul's. It was some achievement to have got permission for the statue, not least, as the Marquis of Lansdowne pointed out, that the Dean and Chapter had to agree to a Dissenter being the first to be so honoured.[78] Once the monument to Howard had been agreed, the floodgates protecting St Paul's were opened, though perhaps not as might have been anticipated by many of the subscribers to the Howard statue. Between 1794 and 1823 thirty-two monuments were erected in the Cathedral, not to harbingers of peace but to military and naval leaders.[79] St Paul's hosted ways of remembering and enshrining in the country's history the Revolutionary and Napoleonic Wars.

Howard as philanthropist

Between 1780 and 1792 there were numerous publications and prints praising Howard. The process of placing Howard on a pedestal had been growing through the 1780s. Howard was imagined as descending into loathsome, disease-ridden dungeons to rescue individual and deserving prisoners. Edmund Burke, in dispute in 1780 with the electors of Bristol, took the occasion to lavish praise on Howard, describing how he visited all Europe

> to dive into the depths of dungeons; to plunge into the infection of hospitals; to survey the mansions of sorrow and pain; to take the gage and dimensions of misery, depression, and contempt; to remember the forgotten, to attend to the neglected, to visit the forsaken, and to compare and collate the distresses of all men in all countries. His plan is original; and it is as full of genius as it is of humanity. It was a voyage of discovery; a circumnavigation of charity.[80]

From the alliteration at the beginning to the comparison with the dangers of voyages of discovery at the end, Burke's words capture the magnitude of Howard's 'circumnavigation of charity'. They were frequently reprinted, the 'circumnavigation of charity' sometimes changed to 'a circumnavigation of philanthropy', or 'the voyage of discovery' becoming one of 'philanthropy'.[81]

In the same year, 1780, William Hayley published his 'Ode inscribed to John Howard'. Hayley pictured the miseries and gloom of dungeons, suddenly lightened by 'sacred beams':

> Oppression drops his iron rod!
> And all the bright'ning dungeon seems
> To speak the presence of a God.
> Philanthropy's descending ray
> Diffuses unexpected day!
> Loveliest of angels! – at her side
> Her favourite votary stands; – her English pride,
> Thro Horror's mansions led by this celestial guide.
> Hail! Generous HOWARD!

Philanthropy was an angel, diffusing light, Howard himself led 'by this celestial guide'. He was the 'New star of philanthropic zeal', 'a Patriot of the World'.[82]

Painters depicted Howard coming to the rescue of prisoners. In Francis Wheatley's 'John Howard offering relief to prisoners' (1787) an old man, probably a debtor, ill and supported by his family, lies on a rotten pallet. Howard's servants bring a mattress and a basket of bread. A boy is kneeling at Howard's feet.[83] 'The triumph of benevolence' (1788), probably by James Gillray, shows Howard visiting a soldier in chains supported by his family, a daughter on her knees beseeching help from Howard. In both paintings a little light filters in through a high-up grating, naturally falling on Howard's head and face: it is an aura.[84] In April 1790 *The Times* advertised a plate of Howard 'Visiting and relieving the miseries of a prison' which also held out 'to the world the acknowledged best likeness of its amiable Philanthropic Hero that can now ever be obtained'.[85]

George Romney could be said to be obsessed with Howard. A friend of William Hayley, he had provided a vignette for Hayley's *Ode to Howard* in 1780. Howard and the gaoler attend to a prisoner who is chained to the wall of a dungeon that in this instance was 'clean, lofty and well-lit'.[86] After Howard's death, over four years Romney 'made a huge number of studies for a proposed painting of Howard, under the eye of a satanic gaoler, visiting a dungeon full of sick and dying prisoners'. The final picture was never completed. In the drawings half naked and distorted bodies lie in disturbing profusion, Howard and Satan competing for their allegiance, Satan sometimes seeming to be winning.[87]

Aside from the depiction of Howard saving prisoners two pronounced and often linked themes dominated the writings about Howard. Howard was to be remembered for what he brought both to humanity across the globe and to Britain in particular. The 'tribute of praise and admiration from all religions, all nations … has made *an Era in the history of mankind*'.[88] He was a 'Patriot of the World' (a phrase much repeated); he was 'that illustrious Cosmopolite, Mr Howard'. 'Each nation felt and owned the blest effects of his universal philanthropy.'[89] Erasmus Darwin in *The Lives of the Plants*, first published in 1789, set out this worldwide role for philanthropy as exemplified by Howard.

> And now, benevolence! Thy rays divine
> Dart round the globe from Zembla to the Line;
> O'er each dark prison plays the cheering light,
> Like northern lustres o'er the vault of night.
> From realm to realm with cross or crescent crown'd,
> Where'er mankind or misery are found.
> O'er burning sands, deep waves, or wilds of snow,
> Thy HOWARD, journeying, seeks the house of woe.

As with Burke's eulogy in 1780, where 'charity' became 'philanthropy', so in Darwin's verses the 'benevolence' of the first line often became changed to 'philanthropy'.[90] Howard, as 'the Philanthropist of the World', was 'the friend of humankind'.[91]

Alongside his near divine status lay his 'humanity', another word much invoked. He 'had no profession but that of Humanity'.[92] It was for his work 'in the Cause of Humanity' that Trinity College Dublin in 1782 conferred on him an Honorary Degree of Doctor of Laws. John Aikin wrote to him before he set off on his final journey that 'the eyes and good wishes of all the friends of humanity in Europe will be upon you'.[93] He would be remembered 'as the best and dearest FRIEND TO THE RIGHTS OF HUMANITY', his life at length falling 'a sacrifice to his universal exertions in the cause of humanity'.[94] '[N]othing human', as Anglus had put it, 'is alien from him'.[95]

Philanthropy meant a love of humankind, and Howard was the ideal exemplar of it, his achievements 'hail'd by all the grateful earth'.[96] Howard was

> A mortal whose soul's with philanthropy bless'd,
> Who visits all climes, to relieve the distress'd:
> To Jew, Turk, or Christian, he is not confin'd,
> He has but one object – the Good of Mankind![97]

Such humanity reflected particular glory on the country that had produced Howard. 'The PHILANTHROPIC HOWARD', it was said, 'has extended the fame of BRITISH VIRTUE all over the globe'. 'Wherever his deeds are rehearsed', it was said, 'there the name of Britain is venerated'.[98] In *The Triumph of Benevolence; occasioned by the National Design of Erecting a Monument to John Howard, Esq*, S. J. Pratt lavished praise on Howard for his boundless philanthropy and rejoiced that a statue was going to be erected, 'Not to Grandeur, Pride, or Gold, nor War' as in other nations, but to endorse Howard's values as British or English:

> Well may the *Spirit of the Isle* arise,
>   With loud accord its best good man to grace;
> Well may the statue point to yonder skies,
>   And call on Cherubim to guard the place.[99]

It was, wrote another poet, unprecedented for a country to define itself as philanthropic. On the contrary, from the ancient Romans to the present, statues had been erected to honour conquerors and rulers:

> To British hearts a nobler praise be due,
> Than arms, or skill, or conquest can pursue ...
> Blest man, to thee shall future ages bend,
> And foreign nations hail thee for their friend![100]

From the erection of a statue 'more honour arises to *Britain* than to Mr. Howard. Never since the beginning of time was a public tribute paid to universal benevolence'.[101] Anglus in his opening letter in the *Gentleman's Magazine* reminded readers how France, the country that purported to be the most civilised in Europe, had refused Howard permission to enter the Bastille and sought to arrest him as he travelled in disguise through the country.[102] Britain, by contrast, could take pride in its commitment to humanity. Worldwide acclaim reflected glory on Britain.

From 1786 onwards Howard was 'John Howard, the Philanthropist'. When he passed through Newcastle in August 1787, pausing to visit the gaol and infirmary and 'bestow many handsome encomiums', he was 'that celebrated philanthropist ... this great ornament of human nature'.[103] John Aikin's biography published in 1792, *A View of the Character and Public Services of the late John Howard, Esq., LL.D, F.R.S* became *A View of the Character and*

Philanthropic Labors of the late John Howard, Esq., LL.D, F.R.S. when it crossed the Atlantic and was published in Philadelphia and Boston in 1794. Even Aikin, so critical of the '*extravagance* of philanthropy' in 1786, described Howard as 'this great philanthropist' in his biography.[104] 'Howard the Philanthropist' was the heading for a *Times* article in 1818 on his abstemious habits.[105] John Baldwin Brown's major biography of 1818 was entitled *Memoirs of the Public and Private Life of John Howard, the Philanthropist*, not, as it might have been, 'John Howard, the prison reformer'. As Brown put it, Howard was 'emphatically and deservedly styled *The Philanthropist*'.[106] For John Field, editing Howard's correspondence in the 1850s, Howard was 'known in every civilised nation as the Philanthropist'.[107] Book titles highlighted Howard as philanthropist: *The Life of John Howard, Esq. the Philanthropist* (1825) was in a series on 'Eminent Philanthropists'. Thomas Taylor in 1836 advertised his *Memoirs of John Howard, the Christian Philanthropist*. 'John Howard the Philanthropist' headed long extracts in *The Times* in 1849 from a book by Hepworth Dixon.[108]

Howard's philanthropy was the benchmark against which the philanthropy of others was measured. In 1823 at the Court of Common Council in London, Mr Favell proposed that a vacant pedestal in the room in which they met 'could not be better filled than by placing on it the bust of a philanthropist who, if inferior to any, was only inferior to the immortal Howard'. His candidate was Granville Sharp. When the matter came to a vote, S. Dixon objected: 'If philanthropy was the merit of Mr Granville Sharpe [*sic*] (and he did not seek to depreciate his merit) why not vote a bust to the memory of one who was a much greater philanthropist, the celebrated Mr Howard.'[109]

In 1856 Rev. W. Arnot delivered a lecture on 'Christian Philanthropy' to the Manchester Young Men's Christian Association. He told how 'The good exemplar of the philanthropist in the popular mind is of course John Howard' – he was 'the Homer of this sublime enacted epic' – and went on to describe how the

> undefined shadow of John Howard lying in the memory of the people … serves the whole nation as the *beau ideal* of a philanthropist. Other men appear from time to time with some of the peculiarities and some of the human kindness understood to belong to the original, and they are accounted the philanthropists of the day – lesser Howards in their smaller sphere. They stop the slave trade, emancipate the negroes, gather ragged urchins from the streets into the school and the kitchen, tend wounded soldiers in the rear of the battle-field, pay the widow's rent, and clothe her children.[110]

Conclusion

John Howard might be described as 'the reluctant philanthropist'. He never claimed or wanted the title. With a lifelong conviction of his own sinfulness he tried to carry out what he thought God asked of him. While that certainly involved giving relief to individual and deserving prisoners, his much larger aim was to reform the prison system in its entirety. Yet, both in St Paul's and in paintings he is always depicted as tending to the miseries of individual prisoners. Howard's much-proclaimed 'philanthropy' lay in putting his life constantly at risk, gaol fever a deadly presence in many prisons; he was seen as relieving those chained up in what were normally described as 'dungeons'. Viewed in this way, Howard was 'god-like'.[111]

Howard's achievements were also testimony to the present as against the past, to, in short, the Enlightenment. As Anglus put it, this was an 'age, when so much more light than heretofore, and, one would hope, consequent goodness, are diffused'.[112]

V. P., writing from Shrewsbury, perhaps best captured the self-congratulation that pervaded the commentary:

> If the actions of the eminently brave, or the talents of the eminently skillful, have in all ages been thought to deserve such publick tributes of applause, how much more are they due to that exquisite humanity, which is forever employed in alleviating the anguish of the most wretched of our fellow-creatures! The sublimest of all pleasures, I conceive, arises from the practice of such virtues; and the next to it, is the pleasure of praising and rewarding them. The first we may be allowed to envy Mr. Howard, the last is in our own power; and I will not doubt but the generosity of Britons will feel some delightful sensations round the heart whilst they contribute towards a purpose so honourable to themselves, to their country, and to the cause of virtue.[113]

Howard, who would never have admitted to 'the sublimest of all pleasures' in practising virtue, was placed, literally, on a pedestal. The subscribers could happily enjoy 'delightful sensations round the heart' for their generosity in erecting a testimony to philanthropy in its widest sense, to Britain, to 'the cause of virtue' – and to themselves.

If Howard was the model of a philanthropist, his life was not a guide to how philanthropy itself would develop. A large part of the reason for this, explored in Chapter 6, lay in the reaction against universalism prompted by the French Revolution. The values that Howard had come to personify in the 1780s were often ridiculed by 1796 when his statue was unveiled. But, more than this, Howard was a loner. He had a network of friends and helpers but on his journeys he was on his own except for a servant. He influenced policy but he instituted no organisation. Philanthropy in the nineteenth century was often taken to refer to the huge array of voluntary organisations, many of them founded in the period, philanthropists to be the people who ran them. Howard knew nothing of such a world.

In one respect, however, Howard's life pointed to the future. He was undoubtedly generous with his funds. Baldwin Brown claimed, without providing evidence, that he spent £30,000 in his philanthropic work.[114] He had apparently inherited £20,000 when his sister died in 1777 and probably devoted this sum to philanthropic work.[115] £30,000 was a colossal sum, equivalent in value in 2016 to over £4 million. Howard may well have impoverished himself through his philanthropy. In 1785 he nearly sold his house in Cardington, rescue coming from Samuel Whitbread, on whose funds Howard drew in the remainder of his travelling.[116] Despite this, financial generosity was not why Howard was remembered as a philanthropist.

Howard did, however, leave two major legacies. First, it was almost universally acknowledged in the century ahead that no philanthropist measured up to Howard. And, second, philanthropy was and remained closely associated with prisons and crime.

Notes

1 T.West, *The Curious Mr Howard: Legendary Prison Reformer* (Hook: Waterside Press, 2011) is the best recent biography. Other important sources for Howard are J. Aikin, *A View of the Character and Public Services of the late John Howard, Esq., LL.D, F.R.S* (London, 1792), and J. Baldwin Brown, *Memoirs of the Public and Private Life of John Howard, the Philanthropist* (London: Rest Fenner, 1818).

2 West, *Curious Mr Howard*, pp. 122–3.

3 Brown, *Memoirs of Howard*, pp. 684–5.

4 West, *Curious Mr Howard*, pp. 149–52; P. Lucas, 'John Howard and Asperger's Syndrome: Psychopathology and philanthropy', *History of Psychiatry*, 12 (2001), 73–101.

5 Quoted in West, *Curious Mr Howard*, p. 121.

6 Quoted in ibid., p. 152.

7 Ibid., pp. 53, 307, 312.

8 W. B. Peach (ed.), *The Correspondence of Richard Price*, 3 vols (Cardiff: University of Wales Press, 1994), Vol. III, p. 70.

9 See Howard's letters to Price in Peach, *Correspondence of Price*, Vol. III, esp. pp. 9, 138, 169, 326.

10 Bodleian Library, MS Eng. Misc, c. 332, fo. 68.

11 Ibid., MS Eng. Misc. c. 332, fos. 61, 72–3.

12 L. Aikin, *Memoir of John Aikin MD*, 2 vols (London: Baldwin, Cradock and Joy, 1823), Vol. I, pp. 41–2, 63.

13 Quoted in R. Morgan, 'Divine philanthropy: John Howard reconsidered', *History*, 62 (1977), 391.

14 R. Evans, *The Fabrication of Virtue: English Prison Architecture, 1750–1840* (Cambridge: Cambridge University Press, 1982), p. 94.

15 M. De Lacy, *Prison Reform in Lancashire, 1700–1850* (Manchester: Chetham Society, 1986), pp. 80, 91, 243; M. Ignatieff, *A Just Measure of Pain: The Penitentiary in the Industrial Revolution, 1750–1850* (London: Macmillan, 1978), pp. 84–5.

16 Evans, *Fabrication of Virtue*, p. 116; De Lacy, *Prison Reform*, p. 188.

17 Morgan, 'Divine philanthropy', 395; for a higher estimate of the proportion of debtors, see Ignatieff, *Just Measure of Pain*, p. 28.
18 J. M. Beattie, *Crime and the Courts in England, 1660–1800* (Oxford: Clarendon Press, 1986), pp. 540–3, 546, 562–3.
19 Ibid., pp. 549–52, 557, 569–71.
20 J. Innes, 'Parliament and the shaping of eighteenth-century English social policy', in J. Innes, *Inferior Politics: Social Problems and Social Policies in Eighteenth-Century Britain* (Oxford: Oxford University Press, 2009), p. 43.
21 J. Innes, 'Power and happiness: Empirical social enquiry in Britain, from "political arithmetic" to "moral statistics"', in Innes, *Inferior Politics*, pp. 162–3.
22 Quoted in Evans, *Fabrication of Virtue*, p. 68.
23 Quoted in ibid., p. 71.
24 J. Howard, *The State of the Prisons* (London: Everyman, 1929), p. 43.
25 Ibid., pp. 38–9.
26 E. A. L. Moir, 'Sir George Onesiphorus Paul', in H. P. R. Finberg (ed.), *Gloucestershire Studies* (Leicester: Leicester University Press, 1957), pp. 199, 206.
27 West, *Curious Mr Howard*, pp. 257–61, 275–6.
28 Ibid., pp. 239–40, 282–3.
29 *Gentleman's Magazine*, 56 (May 1786), 359–61.
30 Ibid., 56 (June 1786), 447–8.
31 J. C. Lettsom, *Hints Designed to Promote Beneficence, Temperance and Medical Science*, 3 vols (London: Nichols, Son, and Bentley, 1816), Vol. II, pp. 143, 155; for Warner, see *ODNB*.
32 Aikin, *Character and Public Services of John Howard*, p. 89.
33 *Gentleman's Magazine*, 56 (July 1786), 535; *ODNB*.
34 *Gentleman's Magazine*, 56 (Aug. 1786), 627–30.
35 *The Times*, 12 Dec. 1785; 5 Mar. 1788.
36 Ibid., 26 Apr. 1786; C. D. Williams, '"The luxury of doing good": Benevolence, sensibility and the Royal Humane Society', in R. Porter and M. M. Roberts (eds), *Pleasure in the Eighteenth Century* (Basingstoke: Macmillan Press, 1996), pp. 93–102.
37 *The Times*, 18 Sept. 1786.
38 British Library, Add MS 26055, fos. 43–4.
39 *The Times*, 14 Aug. 1786 and 18 Sept. 1786.
40 Ibid., 18 Sept. 1786.
41 *Gentleman's Magazine*, 56 (May and June 1786), 359–61, 447–8.
42 Ibid., 56 (July 1786), 536.
43 Ibid., 56 (Aug. 1786), 628–9.
44 *Morning Chronicle*, 1 Sept. 1786.
45 Ibid.
46 Peach, *Correspondence of Richard Price*, p. 70.
47 Brown, *Memoirs of Howard*, pp. 136–9.
48 Lettsom, *Hints*, p. 163.
49 *Gentleman's Magazine*, 56 (Aug. 1786), 628–32.
50 Add MS 26055, fos. 19–20.

51 Lettsom, *Hints*, p. 186.
52 Ibid., p. 188.
53 Ibid., pp. 182–5.
54 Ibid., pp. 189–91.
55 J. Field, *Correspondence of John Howard, the Philanthropist* (London: Longman, Brown, Green, Longmans, 1855), pp. 123–4.
56 Lettsom, *Hints*, p. 192.
57 Ibid., pp. 193–4.
58 Ibid., p. 195; Add MS 26055, fos. 33, 38.
59 Lettsom, *Hints*, pp. 196–7.
60 Ibid., p. 198.
61 Ibid., p. 146.
62 Ibid., pp. 148–9, 204.
63 Ibid., p. 207; *Gentleman's Magazine*, 33 (1850), 180.
64 Lettsom, *Hints*, pp. 205, 209.
65 Add MS 26055, fos. 3, 53; Lettsom, *Hints*, pp. 210–14.
66 Add MS 26055, fos. 3, 53.
67 R. Bowdler and A. Saunders, 'The post-Reformation monuments', in D. Keene, A. Burns and A. Saint (eds), *St Paul's: The Cathedral Church of London* (New Haven and London: Yale University Press, 2004), p. 272; H. Hoock, 'The British military pantheon in St Paul's Cathedral: The state, cultural patriotism, and the politics of national monuments', in R. Wrigley and M. Craske (eds), *Pantheons: Transformations of a Monumental Idea* (Aldershot: Ashgate, 2004), p. 81.
68 Add MS 26055, fos. 4, 62; Marquis of Lansdowne in Lettsom, *Hints*, pp. 217–18.
69 Add MS 26055, fos. 62–7.
70 Ibid., f. 75.
71 S. Burnage, '"A mere massy monument": The contested monument to John Howard (1786–96) at St Paul's Cathedral, London', *Journal of the Church Monuments Society*, XXV (2010), 148–62.
72 Add MS 26055, f. 75.
73 Bowdler and Saunders, 'Post-Reformation monuments', p. 274.
74 Add MS 26055, f. 65.
75 Lettsom, *Hints*, p. 222.
76 Add MS 26055, fos. 50, 54, 62.
77 *Gentleman's Magazine*, 33 (Feb. 1850), 181.
78 Lettsom, *Hints*, p. 220.
79 Hoock, 'The British military pantheon', p. 83.
80 *The Writings and Speeches of Edmund Burke*, Vol. III, ed. W. M. Elofson and John A. Woods (Oxford: Clarendon Press, 1996), p. 638.
81 *The Life of John Howard, Esquire, LL.D and F. R. S* (Newcastle upon Tyne: W. Thompson, 1790), p. 50; *The Life of the Late John Howard, Esq, with a Review of his Travels* (London: Printed by the author, 1790), p. 10.
82 W. Hayley, *Ode Inscribed to John Howard* (1780).
83 Evans, *Fabrication of Virtue*, pp. 92–3.

84 West, *Curious Mr Howard*, pp. 334–5; the Gillray is reproduced opposite p. 193.
85 *The Times*, 22 Apr. 1790.
86 A. Crookshank, 'The drawings of George Romney', *Burlington Magazine*, 99 (Feb. 1957), 47; many of the drawings are held in the Fitzwilliam Museum, Cambridge; see P. Joffé, *Drawings by George Romney: From the Fitzwilliam Museum, Cambridge* (Cambridge: Cambridge University Press, 1977).
87 A. Kidson, Introduction to *Heroic Drawings inspired by Shakespeare, Milton and Howard*, Exhibition at Abbott and Holder Ltd, Feb.–Mar. 2016.
88 *The Life of John Howard, Esquire*, p. 10.
89 *Anecdotes of the Life and Character of John Howard, Esq. F.R.S. Written by a Gentleman whose acquaintance with that celebrated philanthropist gave him the most favourable opportunity of learning particulars not generally known* (London: Hookham, Sewell & Mrs Harlow, 1790), pp. 2, 4; *Public Advertiser*, 11 Mar. 1790.
90 E. Darwin, *The Botanic Garden: The Love of the Plants* (London: Scolar Press, 1973), pp. 80–1. For the change from 'benevolence' to 'philanthropy', see Brown, *Memoirs of Howard*, p. 471.
91 Brown, *Memoirs of Howard*, p. xi.
92 [W. Hayley], *The Eulogies of Howard: A Vision* (London: G. G. J. and J. Robinson, 1791), p. 9.
93 Bodleian Library, MS Eng. Misc. c. 332, fos. 3, 48–9.
94 *Life of the Late John Howard*, p. 75; *Anecdotes of the Life and Character of John Howard*, p. 4.
95 *Gentleman's Magazine*, 56 (May 1786), 359.
96 Ibid., 56 (Oct. 1786), 824.
97 Ibid., 56 (Sept. 1786), 793.
98 *English Chronicle and Universal Evening Post*, 2 Mar. 1790; *The Life of John Howard, Esq. The Philanthropist* (Edinburgh: Archibald Allardice & Co., 1825), p. 3.
99 S. J. Pratt, *The Triumph of Benevolence; occasioned by the National Design of Erecting a Monument to John Howard, Esq.* (London: J. Nicholls, 1786).
100 *Gentleman's Magazine*, 56 (Oct. 1786), 890.
101 Ibid., 56 (Aug. 1786), 629.
102 Ibid., 56 (May 1786), 360–1.
103 *The Times*, 28 Aug. 1787.
104 Aikin, *Life of Howard*, p. 208.
105 *The Times*, 12 Nov. 1818; see also 13 Sept. 1819; 20 May 1841.
106 Brown, *Memoirs of John Howard*, p. 2.
107 Field, *Correspondence of Howard*, p. 1.
108 *The Times*, 22 Nov. 1836; 11 July 1849.
109 Ibid., 26 Sept. 1823; 23 Jan. 1824.
110 W. Arnot, *Christian Philanthropy* (Manchester: YMCA, 1856), pp. 4–5, 20–2.
111 See, e.g., Lettsom, *Hints*, pp. 157, 163; *Gentleman's Magazine*, 56 (Oct. 1786), 890.

112 *Gentleman's Magazine*, 56 (May 1786), 360.
113 *The Times*, 18 Sept. 1786.
114 Brown, *Memoirs of Howard*, pp. 576, 643.
115 Field, *Correspondence of Howard*, pp. 88–9.
116 Ibid., pp. 108, 115, 128, 134–5, 148, 154, 157.

5

Howard's legacy:
Philanthropy and crime

Howard's preeminence as a philanthropist meant that after his death in 1790 philanthropy's reputation was heavily dependent on success in the reform of prisons. It was perfectly plausible for George Eliot in *Middlemarch*, set in the early 1830s, to have Mr Brooke say of Rev. Casaubon that 'he doesn't care much about the philanthropic side of things; punishments, and that kind of thing'.[1] Through no fault of Howard, prison reform proved much more difficult and contentious than was at first imagined. Philanthropists were accused both of being too harsh in wanting solitude for prisoners and for being too soft in making prisons too comfortable. Howard's name, however, continued to carry weight as is testified by the foundation of the Howard Association in 1866, the forerunner of today's Howard League for Penal Reform.

Philanthropy's links with crime and reform were further sealed through a development that started in Howard's lifetime, the Philanthropic Society.

Robert Young and the Philanthropic Society

In 1788 Robert Young initiated the moves that would result in the establishment of the Philanthropic Society. Young had long been resident in France, and was perhaps influenced by the foundation of the Société Philanthropique in Paris in 1780. Settling in London in 1786, 'in a great degree, a stranger in the metropolis, and unpractised in the business of a public life', Young ruminated on his plan which he saw as 'a science, and a science entirely new'. In mid-1788 he opened a subscription among friends for funds 'to prosecute that design, the embryo of which had been so long in forming'.[2] The Philanthropic Society was instituted in September 1788 'for the Prevention of Crimes, and for a Reform among the Poor; By training up to Virtue and Industry Vagrant Children, and such who are in the Paths of Vice and Infamy; To save them from Ruin, and prevent their becoming injurious to Society'.[3]

Young is a tantalising figure. He gave philanthropy in Britain its first institutional base. Yet in 1790 he was in disgrace, accused of misappropriating
funds, and relieved of any role in the society he had founded. He embarked
on prolonged campaigns against those who he claimed had usurped the
Philanthropic Society. On Young's account, he, his wife and daughter were
seriously ill in the winter and spring of 1790. He admits that the accounts
were neglected – they seemed to him the least important aspect of his work,
and, in any case, 'The irregularities in my books were such as were injurious
to myself alone – neglect of charging payments made'.[4] By the end of June
1790, however, he was 'the late Treasurer'.[5]

Young did not take his dismissal lightly. He wrote and campaigned
against 'the usurpers' for another six years. The Philanthropic Society in
June 1793 was still willing to acknowledge that to Young's 'assiduity the original Institution of the Philanthropic Society is greatly indebted', but in 1794
instituted legal proceedings against him. Young, who served time in the Fleet
prison for debt, eventually found his way back to France.[6]

The Philanthropic Society would not have existed but for Young, and he
regarded it as very much his personal project. It is worth trying to unpick
his ideas and plans. The task is not made easier by the fact that his untitled
account of his thoughts and actions, held in the British Library, and dating
probably to 1792, is cut short at page 38, the remaining pages having been
removed. But from what remains something of the scope of his ambition
emerges. As a young man, he writes, before he was twenty, 'I contemplated
with deep regret, the miseries of the poor', and planned a remedy that would
'extend over the nation'. His design 'extended to the whole body of the poor,
and was aimed to accomplish an actual change in their favor'. When he
started the meetings in 1788 that led to the formation of the Philanthropic
Society he found that 'Whenever ... I had hinted at the design, I always found
it reprobated as the most visionary conception of an enthusiastic mind'. He
therefore held back. At the weekly meetings of the Committee held at his
house Young informed members 'of what was done and doing, but not always
of what I intended to do'.[7]

Early publications of the Philanthropic Society, doubtless written by
Young, hint at his ambitions. The young criminals or children of criminals
were to be housed in an 'Asylum not a Prison'; there would be no surrounding
wall.[8] Reform was the word he often used to describe his new society, 'the
Philanthropic Reform' becoming his preferred title. 'The Philanthropic
Reform', he wrote, 'was by me intended as the instrument of accomplishing
various important objects of moral, social and civil good', but after the
usurpers took over 'the institution passed into the hands of persons to whom
its very plan was not so much as known ... They have suppressed my Theory
of MORAL REFORM: they have extinguished its practice. A brick wall,
flogging, and dungeons, philanthropic dungeons! are their sole instruments
of reform'.[9] Before the usurpation the Society aimed at reforms that would
'lead to the reduction of every species of public burthen, which vice and

misery induce, poor rates, hospitals and prisons; and to the restoration of peace, good order and personal security'. Money invested would meet with a return from the profits of work undertaken. In Young's view, charity when 'divested of any view of return' was a perpetual 'current from the purses of the rich to the miseries of the poor' where it 'stagnated' and threatened to be 'destructive of the main pillars of civil society'.[10]

The eighteenth century was awash with progenitors of proposals that would transform society and in many ways Young can be seen as one of them – not least in the failure to carry through the proposal.[11] It was difficult, as Thomas Coram had found with the Foundling Hospital, to adjust from the period of planning for an institution to actually running it, not least because the person who saw himself and was seen by others as the founder lost ownership. Young, like Coram, had spent much time knocking on the doors of the wellborn and wealthy in order to assemble the requisite president, vice-presidents and committee members. He had been, on the face of it, remarkably successful. The Duke of Leeds, Secretary of State for Foreign Affairs 1783–91, a man who fancied himself in 1792 as prime minister, was President. The eight Vice-Presidents included an earl and two viscounts. On the twenty-three-man Committee sat J. C. Lettsom, the Quaker doctor well known in charitable circles, Jeremiah Bentham, father of Jeremy, Samuel Whitbread and a sprinkling of City figures. It looked thoroughly respectable. Given the impetus for reform of the criminal justice system, a plan to keep the young out of it altogether must have seemed eminently worthy. And once it had shed Young, the Philanthropic Society settled down as an institution housing young criminals and working for their reformation.

Young himself, however, clearly had a larger vision. His financial peccadilloes can perhaps be seen as the sins of a man who was under huge pressure both on the domestic front and in establishing the institution, and who both needed money and felt he had earned it. They do not take away from the interest of what he dreamed about. He was very much part of an Enlightenment belief that reform measures could turn lives around, could reintegrate outcasts into what he called 'civil society'. He was fertile in trying to launch scheme after scheme. In 1790 he published 'Proposals for Raising a Capital, for erecting and stocking a settlement for the employment and reform of discharged convicts, criminals, and others' for the *British Settlement for the Reformation of the Criminal Poor, Adults and Children*. £15,000 was needed to establish the Settlement 'in a centrical Situation of the Kingdom on some waste or cheap land'. Earl Grosvenor was President, his son, Viscount Belgrave, one of the vice-presidents. In the same year he promoted a Social Union Formed for the Improvement of Civil Society, 'an association composed of various parts, organized into a grand machinery of active powers, having virtue for its spring, reason for its guide, and happiness for its end'. There were to be committees for 'the redress of injuries, the Constitution, the Laws, the Police, Public Justice, Medicine, Charities, Political honour, Education, Parochial Affairs, Literature, Culture and Science, Elocution, New discoveries and

Foreign correspondence', the whole founded upon 'the Science of Society'.[12] This perhaps brings us closest to Young's vision: virtue and reason were the powers that would secure happiness. The Enlightenment project could hardly be more succinctly expressed. And what inspired the whole, what made it imaginable, was philanthropy, the love of humankind.

In early 1792 he was promoting his 'Undertaking for the Reform of the Poor, of which a principal branch is the Asylum of Industry' in eleven houses in Walworth. His clients were 'Youth discharged from gaols, female prostitutes, seamen and soldiers in want, vagrants, and in general, all who are willing to labour but who cannot procure employment'.[13] Young is next heard of in 1795 as head of the British Settlement at Tilgate Forest in Sussex 'for the self-support and reform of the criminal and destitute poor', perhaps the realisation of his 1790 plan for a British Settlement. He claimed that 'the usurpers of the Philanthropic Society' were attempting to destroy the Tilgate project, sending down a spy, William Houlton by name.[14]

Work, remunerative and profitable, was a key component of the reform regime. The Philanthropic Society intended 'to unite the spirit of charity with the principle of trade by erecting a Temple to Philanthropy on the foundations of Virtuous Industry'.[15] The 1791 Report, published after Young's dismissal, but much of it still bearing his mark, announced that 'The great object of this Society is to unite the purposes of charity with those of industry and police' – it was a 'plan of PREVENTIVE POLICE'. The word police signified the forces that contributed to good order. Conventionally enough, it was acknowledged that 'No nation has been more distinguished than Great Britain for its various and excellent charities', but, in a sting at the end, 'they have not always united wisdom and benevolence'. They had focused too much on the deserving. The Philanthropic Society, by contrast, was going to penetrate 'the haunts of vice, profligacy, and beggary', and select from them 'such objects as appear most likely to become obnoxious to the laws, or prejudicial to the community'. Four visitors were to 'allure' boys 'from their evil habits and connections by peculiar advantages and peculiarly good treatment'. The treatment would indeed be humane: Young was contemptuous of the way in which the Philanthropic Society after his departure had turned his asylum into a 'sort of mill for grinding children good'. But a crucial part of this good treatment was that the boys were to work; few charities, the Report claimed, 'have accustomed children to employment and useful labour', a statement dubious in its accuracy as many charities had indeed tried to do that, but indicative of the role of work and industry in the plans for reformation.[16]

Young's ambitions for a transformation of the condition of the poor were boundless. It is not entirely clear why he should have focused on young criminals or those likely to become criminals. His strategy seems to have been one of prevention: stop these children becoming criminals and the effects would be felt throughout society in the years ahead. Whatever the reasons, it meant that philanthropy in its origins in Britain was inextricably bound up with crime, its causes and its cures. It meant also that philanthropy's reforming instincts were institution-based: prisons or places designed to prevent crime (which all too often, as Young noted, could become scarcely distinguishable from prisons).

Prison reform and the criticism of philanthropy

By the 1790s imprisonment had become the accepted punishment for property crimes, the vast majority of all crimes.[17] Howard had been an important influence in this development, and it followed that philanthropy was bound up with the process of prison reform. The philanthropists aimed to reduce imprisonment for debt and the extent of capital punishment, and to transform the prison experience into one that would reform as well as punish the convicted. As Sir George Onesiphorus Paul put it in his 1783 address, 'CONFINEMENT TO PUNISH should also be CONFINEMENT TO REFORM'.[18] *The Times* in 1785 set out the agenda for reform: 'Solitary imprisonment, with a perpetuity of hard labour, or otherwise their being obliged to work at some operation of general utility, are the principal modes that might be devised to accomplish so salutary a plan, and which would be pregnant with the spirit of philanthropy and justice.'[19]

Philanthropists were not alone in their concern with prison reform. The utilitarians, Jeremy Bentham most prominent among them, were important co-workers. At one level the philanthropists' differences with the utilitarians were profound, the philanthropists aiming to bring prisoners to a sense of their own sinfulness (in common with the sinfulness of all humanity), the utilitarians confident that reason alone would facilitate reform. But as to remedy for the current chaos, there was considerable agreement: institutional reform was critical. Howard and Bentham were personally in close accord. Bentham described Howard in a letter to a French correspondent as 'c'est un homme selon notre coeur – c'est le Las-Casas des prisonniers', and to his father wrote of 'my good friend Mr *Howard*'.[20]

Ever since Michel Foucault explored the movement from punishment of the body to invasion of the soul of the offender it has been impossible to depict prison reform as straightforwardly progressive or, for many people, progressive at all.[21] As Archdeacon Paley put it in 1786, 'Of the *reforming punishments* which have not yet been tried, none promises so much as that of solitary imprisonment, or the confinement of prisoners in separate compartments. This improvement augments the terrors of the punishment'.[22] An 'improvement' that augments 'the terrors of the punishment' was on the face of it difficult to reconcile with philanthropy, with a love of humankind.

Philanthropists' leadership role in the politics of criminal justice reform had two contradictory outcomes. On the one hand they could claim credit, and be accorded credit, for what through the nineteenth century was seen as a highly necessary reform of eighteenth-century practices in penal punishment. Invocation of Howard's name was enough to make this point. On the other hand they could not escape censorship for what went wrong. And things did go wrong.

Separating out different types of prisoner and imposing solitude was difficult, if not impossible, to implement. An Act of 1784 (24 Geo. III.c.54) set out eleven different groups to be kept separated. In 1818 a report claimed that this was being done in only twenty-three prisons. Most prisons simply did not have enough space or rooms to implement the Act.[23] Imposing solitude, even at night, failed for a simple reason, the rise in the number of prisoners, starting in the later eighteenth century and continuing to the mid-nineteenth century. It was apparent across all types of prisoner, debtors as much as felons, misdemeanants and petty offenders. The number of debtors committed to Lancaster Castle, for example, rose from 162 in 1798 to 526 in 1818. Total committals to Salford New Bailey, covering all except debtors, rose from 685 in 1801 to 4,034 in 1827.[24] The outcome was that prisons became seriously overcrowded. The ideal of solitude could not be implemented.

The new regime, insofar as it was implemented, met with strong opposition from prisoners and from those who could voice their concerns. Gilbert Wakefield, who had been a lecturer at Hackney Dissenting Academy and in 1799 was sentenced to two years in Dorchester penitentiary for seditious utterance, though he himself escaped solitary confinement, had sufficient contact with prisoners to make him wonder that 'men can endure solitary confinement without distraction, melancholy and despair'.[25] Members of the radical London Corresponding Society were imprisoned in Coldbath Fields House of Correction. The Society's *Moral and Political Magazine* had castigated solitary confinement before the men were imprisoned. Once there, they petitioned outside supporters, leading in 1800 to a House of Commons debate on solitary confinement in which a Foxite Whig acknowledged that 'the late Mr Howard was certainly one of the worthiest men who had ever existed', but went on that 'if he had been one of the worst, he could not have suggested a punishment of a more cruel and mischievous description'.[26] This was less than fair to Howard who had reservations about solitude, but there was no denying that amongst radicals philanthropists had become associated with the hardship of solitude. It did not help that defence of the prison was led by William Wilberforce who described the prison as a monument to the benevolence of John Howard. When Sir Francis Burdett took up the prisoners' cause and won an election, the *Morning Chronicle* described his victory as a 'spontaneous and honest expression of indignation against the system of solitary confinement'.[27] Coleridge had given his view of it, in the person of the Devil, in 1799:

As he went through Cold Bath Fields, he saw
A solitary cell;
And the Devil was pleased, for it gave him a hint
For improving his prisons in Hell.[28]

The philanthropists, inspired by the vision that they could reform criminals by a system of prison discipline, felt bitterly disillusioned. In 1808 Sir George Onesiphorus Paul, famous for his prison work in Gloucestershire, complained that he had 'been obliged to defend himself from charges of an unfeeling cruelty regarding those very acts in the performance of which he had religiously felt himself executing the duties of a Christian and the policy of an enlightened philanthropist'.[29] A year later he told a correspondent that, 'by birth and education a Whig (albeit of the old school)', and claiming still to be so, he had become profoundly disillusioned with the record and behaviour of the Whigs and had spent 'the subsequent twenty-five years of my life ... in the school of a political philanthropy which best accorded with my idea of civil government'.[30] It was a shrewd recognition that the reform of prisons was profoundly political.

A new period of activity commenced in the latter years of the Napoleonic Wars, sparked off by the Holford Committee of 1810 before which Paul and Jeremy Bentham outlined their respective schemes. By the 1810s and 1820s many of the prisons built in the Howard era seemed deficient, not least because they were overcrowded, creating conditions in which reform was unlikely. The most prominent landmark of the new prison building was Millbank in London, opened in 1816 and designed to house one thousand inmates. In the same year a group of London Quakers founded the Society for the Improvement of Prison Discipline (SIPD). It rapidly became the authoritative voice on prison design and construction, pressing hard for measures that would prevent communication between prisoners, and seeking reform at national level.[31]

William Allen, a London Quaker, played a key role in initiating and maintaining discussion. In the second volume of *The Philanthropist*, published in 1812, Allen devoted four articles to 'Remarks on the life of John Howard, and on the police of prisons'. Lauding Howard's 'Pilgrimage of Philanthropy', proclaiming that Howard's *The State of the Prisons* 'may be regarded as constituting an aera in the history of humanity', Allen could not disguise his disappointment that so little had resulted from it: 'Manifold and heinous were the abuses ... which Howard brought to light. How feeble and thin are the instances of their eradication.'[32] 'We call ourselves a humane nation', wrote Allen, but 'For our own part, we freely confess, we never hear the praises of English humanity sounding in our ears, but the image of the numerous wretches who are wasting away under the slow torture of famine in our prisons arises in all its horrid deformities into our imagination'.[33] This led Allen to a pessimistic assessment of the progress of philanthropy:

It is unhappily ... not easy to rouse mankind (and our self-loving countrymen among the rest) to a very lively sense of the sufferings of others ...
It requires *public spirit*, a mind accustomed to look beyond the individual
to the *species*; a mind which has cultivated within itself a love for its *kind*; –
it requires a mind of *this* sort (of which we have as yet learned the art of

breeding very few) to have a quick sensibility to the concealed and silent sufferings of the tenants of our dungeons.[34]

If for a time accusations of cruelty could be thrown at philanthropists, a more damaging and lasting line of attack was that they were soft on crime. This criticism came to the fore at the end of the Napoleonic Wars, gathering steam in the crime wave that followed the wars. In 1815 a London alderman was complaining that the reformers would not stop until every prisoner had a 'Turkey carpet' in his cell. The SIPD, forced onto the defensive, declared in its *Rules* (1820) how determined it was that 'everything which borders on sensual gratification or unnecessary comfort should be entirely prohibited'. Magistrates across the country turned away from the idea that prisoners could be reformed. In the words of a Staffordshire JP 'nothing but the terror of human suffering can avail to prevent crime', so the experience of imprisonment should be 'as lonely and as inconvenient and irksome as the human mind can bear'. In tune with the new ethos, the treadwheel, first publicised by the SIPD in 1818, had spread to twenty-six counties by 1824. Ten years later silence was added to separation as a way of tightening up discipline and order in prison, leading to bitter debates between those who relied on separation alone and those who wanted total isolation for prisoners. Reflecting on these trends, Elizabeth Fry, famous for her work with female prisoners in Newgate prison, warned in 1835 that 'In some respects, I think there is more cruelty in our Gaols than I have ever before seen'.[35]

Advocates of the new harsh discipline were in no doubt that philanthropy and philanthropists were to blame for making prison become for offenders 'a sure and comfortable asylum, whenever their better fortunes forsake them'.[36] Philanthropists' reputation for being soft on crime is illustrated in an incidental comment by Thomas Fowell Buxton in a 1821 debate in the House of Commons on the Forgery Punishment Mitigation Bill where he cites evidence in support of mitigation from the Solicitor of the Excise whom 'nobody would accuse ... of being an enthusiast, or, what might be deemed worse by some persons, a philanthropist'. A month earlier *The Times* had referred to 'the principles of our modern philanthropists, who constantly uphold the necessity of mitigating punishments'.[37] *The Times* itself in 1846 had little time for 'the maudlin philanthropists of these charitable times' who wanted to allow pleas of temporary insanity in murder cases. Later in the same year, with reference to prison reform, it commented that 'The treatment recommended for prisoners is in perfect uniformity with sickly sentimentality which is prevalent among a certain very numerous class of talking philanthropists.' Discussing juvenile crime, *The Times* lambasted those who 'talk a vast deal of speech-and-pamphlet philanthropy about what the nation ought to do with the myriads whom they have already disgraced, contaminated, and ruined beyond redress'.[38] In similar vein a Mr Alcock in 1849, commenting on a report for a proposed new prison at Holloway, reflected that 'The more he looked back upon our forefathers the more he condemned the morbid philanthropy which interfered at the present day to prevent the punishment of crime'.[39]

In his Latter Day Pamphlet on 'Model prisons', published in 1850, Thomas Carlyle put the case against philanthropy with characteristic invective. There was, he asserted, a 'philanthropic movement', the 'indiscriminate contributions of philanthropy' to 'remedying social injustices' disastrous in their outcome: 'Philanthropy, emancipation, and pity for human calamity is very beautiful; but the deep oblivion of the Law of Right and Wrong; this "indiscriminate mashing-up of Right and Wrong into a patent treacle" of the Philanthropic movement, is by no means beautiful; this, on the contrary, is altogether ugly and alarming.'[40] The leaders of philanthropy were castigated as 'Solemn human Shams, Phantasm Captains, and Supreme Quacks'. Carlyle had nothing but contempt for 'this sugary disastrous jargon of philanthropy, the reign of love, new era of universal brotherhood', for 'philanthropic twaddle'. The typical philanthropy platform speaker was a 'little spouting wretch .... envious, cowardly, vain, splenetic hungry soul'. The pity expressed for criminals was 'cowardly effeminacy; maudlin laxity of heart'.[41]

Philanthropy and the state

The inspectorate of prisons, set up in 1835, and its gradual increase in powers in effect rendered the SIPD, the creation of the philanthropists, redundant. The management of prisons was henceforth in the hands of government. The philanthropic input to the development of prisons, however, was so marked that even after the central state began to take control of prisons philanthropy was seen as influential in policy-making and practice – and normally in criticism. A letter to *The Times* in 1853 by Edward Meryon, MD neatly sums up the prevailing views of critics of the philanthropic input to prison life. The present system, he maintained, was 'a delusion, which has been nurtured and maintained by a plausible pretension to reform and a philanthropic intention to restore the criminal to society in the shape of a regenerate and virtuous man'. There was, he felt, 'a pseudo-philanthropy' at work. At the same time he agreed with *The Times* itself that 'under the pretext of reformation, the prison philanthropist, by his paternal régime, subjects the object of his solicitude to a vast amount of mental torture'.[42] In short, it was a delusion to hope for reform of prisoners, and it was wrong in pursuit of this to subject the prisoner to the 'mental torture' involved in such practices as total solitude. This perspective became an orthodoxy in the later 1850s and early 1860s, a period marked by growing alarm about crime, particularly garroting, allied to criticism of the reformatory prison and other aspects of the criminal justice system. The ticket of leave arrangements that let prisoners out on what would now be called parole unsupervised were under vocal scrutiny.[43]

For *The Times* philanthropy had become something carried out by state officials. In 1858, claiming that life was too comfortable for prisoners, it focused on 'the annual reports of our professional philanthropists – the Inspectors of Prisons'. In county gaols, it asserted, 'every expedient for the reformation of criminals which experimental philanthropy could devise has been brought into play, with more or less success'. On the same theme in 1862, critical of the indulgence of criminals, it lamented that 'The philanthropists ... had got the control of penal administration'.[44] But in fact there was criticism of philanthropy from within the system. Herbert Voules, a prison inspector, speaking before a House of Lords select committee, condemned the 'ultra-philanthropy' that led offenders to see themselves as 'aggrieved parties'. W. L. Clay, son of the most famous prison chaplain John Clay, was equally critical of 'the hyper Christian philanthropy which, obliterating the eternal difference between right and wrong, regards the criminal as merely suffering from a moral disease'.[45] When in 1863 the Lord Chief Justice, Alexander Cockburn, declared that 'the reformation of the offender is in the highest degree speculative and uncertain and its permanence in the face of renewed temptation exceedingly precarious',[46] *The Times* commented that it did not think it had been previously known 'how far the philanthropists had been allowed to go in their pious frauds' – the adjective 'pious' linking philanthropists to evangelical Christianity.[47]

By the end of the 1860s the tone was beginning to change. The philanthropists, it seemed, were losing influence. In 1869 the passage of the Treatment of Habitual Criminals Act prompted the comment from *The Times* that 'The general reaction from the philanthropic fancies which were fashionable a few years ago would, perhaps, have ensured public support to even a stronger measure; but it was necessary to avoid the risk of once more enlisting sympathy on the side of felons'. The philanthropists were still a force to be reckoned with, but a less potent one. *The Times* admitted that opposition to the Act was 'likely to proceed ... from philanthropists, who fancy it will obstruct the reformation of criminals', and the *Pall Mall Gazette* knew that in arguing for the execution of criminal lunatics 'we shall have all the philanthropists down upon us'; but times were changing.[48]

The Howard Association

It was perhaps in part a response both to the criticisms of philanthropy and to the sense that it was losing influence that lay behind the formation of the Howard Association in 1866. The immediate spur was the report of the Royal Commission on Capital Punishment of 1864–66. The Royal Commission had been the outcome of lobbying by the Quaker-dominated Capital Punishment Abolition Society. Its report rejected the call for abolition but was opposed to public executions. Sensing that calls for abolition were unlikely to meet with much response for the immediate future, the Quakers turned to lobbying more widely for penal reform. The Stoke Newington Meeting of the Friends was the Howard Association's hub and probably the provider of funds. Its first secretary, William Tallack, was a Quaker.[49] Stoke Newington was an area of London with which Howard had been closely associated and it was doubtless Howard's largely unsullied national fame and reputation deep into the nineteenth century that prompted the adoption of his name for an association bent on reform of penal practice. The Association's aims reflected what were for the time understood as progressive views:

> a much greater resort to industry of a reformatory and useful tendency than is at present enforced in prisons; the disuse of prolonged cellular isolation and of degrading punishments such as the shot-drill, crank and treadmill; the exercise of more preventive effort in the treatment of the large class of minor offenders; the permission to poor persons to pay by instalments the fines imposed for petty misdemeanours; and the promotion of adult reformatories, or otherwise, and of establishments by the state, for the temporary industrial occupation (under proper restrictions) of discharged prisoners.[50]

The Howard Association had close links with the Social Science Association, and, after its formation in 1869, with the Charity Organisation Society (COS). It was resolutely moderate in tone, taking care in electing members to the committee 'to avoid men of extreme or impractical views'.[51] William Tallack remained secretary until his retirement in 1901 and to a large extent he was the Howard Association, a prolific author of pamphlets and proposals. At the outset he frequently sparred with the Chairman of the new Prison Commission, Sir Edward du Cane, but from the 1880s onwards the two were more often close to one another in thinking and policy.[52] The Howard Association's position as the public voice of penal reform began to be accepted. In 1879 there was no hint of criticism in the news report that 'Among modern philanthropic institutions there are none more characteristic than those which have been established for the aid of prisoners on their discharge' and the Howard Association, and its Secretary received respectful reporting and comment – in 1879 there was acknowledgement of 'highly estimable philanthropists like the authorities of the Howard Association'.[53] Differences of course remained. In 1880 the Howard Association was seen as 'mounting sentry in the camp of philanthropists against the evil devices of the Prisons Commissioners', but *The Times* was sympathetic to much of what it was suggesting. Again with reference to the Howard Association it was accepted that 'there are frequently wide differences of opinion between rigid disciplinarians and even sensible philanthropists', but the tone of comment was respectful – and Tallack's book on *Penological and Preventive Principles* received an even-handed review.[54]

The Times's editorial on the centenary of Howard's death in 1890 captures the new tone of comment on philanthropy in relation to crime:

He is loosely spoken of as a philanthropist who went from prison to prison and from hospital to hospital of Europe ministering to the wants of prisoners and sick persons. Howard was without doubt a good and char- itable man. But the errand upon which he traversed Europe over and over again was not an errand of mercy in that sense. He had a far deeper con- ception of the philanthropist's function than to be a scatterer of doles. Nor was he one of those 'Friends of Humanity' whose friendship to their fellow creatures consisted in evolving grand theories out of a so-called 'natural law'. Howard really did for imprisonment what Beccaria and Bentham did for criminal legislation – placed it upon a humane and logical basis. To his credit, he applied to philanthropy, almost for the first time, a patient pro- cess of research and inductive reasoning.

Now, concluded *The Times*, prisons are run well on uncontroversial lines. 'Rightly are we proud that the philanthropist whose unwearying efforts impelled civilized nations to civilize their prisons was a countryman of ours.'[55]

The Times in these comments was setting out a role for what philanthropists should and should not do. Scattering doles or loudly proclaiming friendship to humanity were, by implication, faults that so-called philanthropists had too often committed. The effective philanthropist was a patient researcher, a reasoner, applying him or herself to the solution of problems that straddled the boundaries between the social, the political and the economic. Over the course of a century philanthropists, in relation to crime, had first been lauded to the skies, then subjected for decades to the accusation that they cared only for the mitigation of punishment, then finally restored to a position where they had an acknowledged role to play in the criminal justice system.

For the Howard Association a degree of acceptance by both the prison authorities and the press carried with it the danger that it would be thought to be too close to established thinking. The Humanitarian League, founded in 1891, asked in 1896 'Where is the Howard Association?' and claimed that it 'is no longer a progressive, but a reactionary institution'.[56] The Penal Reform League, linked to the suffragette movement, and formed in 1907, was more cooperative and the two organisations merged after the First World War in 1921 as the Howard League for Penal Reform. Neither of the two organisations, however, could claim to be strong in either membership or money.[57]

Conclusion

In 1868 John Stuart Mill, opposing a proposal in Parliament to abolish cap- ital punishment, said that

It is always a matter of regret to me to find myself, on a public question, opposed to those who are called – sometimes in the way of honour, and sometimes in what is intended for ridicule – the philanthropists. (A laugh.) Of all persons who take part in public affairs, they are those for whom, on the whole, I feel the greatest amount of respect; for their characteristic is, that they devote their time, their labour, and much of their money to objects purely public, with a less admixture of either personal or class self-ishness, than any other class of politicians whatever. On almost all the great questions, scarcely any politicians are so steadily and almost uniformly to be found on the side of right ... It is through their efforts that our crim-inal laws ... have so greatly relaxed their most revolting and most impolitic ferocity ... This vast gain, not only to humanity, but to the ends of penal justice, we owe to the philanthropists.

Mill favoured the retention of capital punishment out of what he described as 'humanity to the criminal', for whom the alternative to quick death was years of incarceration.[58] He knew that on this issue he was standing aside from those with whom he would normally be in agreement. His speech is full of interest. The philanthropists are a 'class of politicians', distinguishable from others. He paid similar respect to them, as we shall see in Chapter 6, in his criticisms of Carlyle on slavery. They addressed themselves to 'the great questions' and were nearly always in the right. The improvements in penal justice 'we owe to the philanthropists'. He was aware, however, that there were those who ridiculed them.

For a century after his death in 1790 Howard held an unparalleled pos-ition in public esteem. He had successors who carried on where he left off and inspected prisons throughout the country, the most prominent of them James Neild. The Howard Association was testimony to the potency of his name. Yet most of what philanthropists did in relation to prison reform differed in one crucial respect from what Howard had done – they formed organisations whereas Howard, while always networking, was essentially a loner. Philanthropic reform after Howard became the work of pressure groups and committees – what critics called 'professional philanthropy'. The Philanthropic Society was the first of a long line of such organisations. It kept itself in the public eye with 564 mentions in *The Times* between 1788 and 1899. This type of philanthropy rarely escaped criticism, partly because its practitioners could not hope to live up to the standards set by the Howards and Frys of former years, and partly because they could never hope to please everyone. The Howard Association, as we have seen, was either too distant from government or too close to it. Any organisation that set out to change policy engaged in politics, and politics rarely escaped criticism. On crime – and not only on crime – philanthropy became political.

For Mill the philanthropists could hold their heads high for what they had done for prisons and penal reform. Mill spoke to a large constituency, but all the progressive causes he endorsed drew forth opposition.[59] From that oppositional stance it was tempting to focus criticism as much on philan-thropy as on policy.

Notes

1 G. Eliot, *Middlemarch* (1871; Oxford: Oxford University Press, 1997), p. 49.
2 British Library Tracts, T 84 Philanthropic Society, pp. 1–6.
3 Eighteenth-Century Short Title Collection, Tract in John Rylands Library, Manchester.
4 British Library Tract 84, pp. 17, 20.
5 *Address to the Public from the Philanthropic Society* (1791), pp. 30–2.
6 M. Whitten, *Nipping Crime in the Bud: How the Philanthropic Quest was put into Law* (Hook: Waterside Press, 2011), pp. 30–3, 98–110 gives a good account of these developments. For further details, see Clifford Papers, DDCC/144/13 in East Riding of Yorks Archives and Records Service.
7 British Library Tract 84, pp. 1–2, 10, 16.
8 Quoted in Whitten, *Nipping Crime in the Bud*, p. 24.
9 *Mr. Robert Young's Address to the General Body of Subscribers of the Philanthropic Society, and to the Nation, on the unparalleled Abuses, and Atrocious Delinquency of the Usurpers of the Philanthropic Reform, since its usurpation, in the year 1790; and on the ultimate means of their redress* (Covent Garden: Office of the British Settlement, 22 Mar. 1796), pp. 2, 4.
10 Quoted in Whitten, *Nipping Crime in the Bud*, p. 27.
11 S. Lloyd, *Charity and Poverty in England, c. 1680–1820: Wild and Visionary Schemes* (Manchester: Manchester University Press, 2009).
12 Whitten, *Nipping Crime in the Bud*, pp. 32–3.
13 Ibid., p. 32.
14 *Address to the General Body of Subscribers*, p. 6; Whitten, *Nipping Crime in the Bud*, p. 106.
15 Whitten, *Nipping Crime in the Bud*, p. 27.
16 *Address to the Public from the Philanthropic Society*, pp. 4–6, 9; Whitten, *Nipping Crime in the Bud*, p. 106.
17 J. M. Beattie, *Crime and the Courts in England, 1660–1800* (Oxford: Clarendon Press, 1986), p. 601.
18 E. A. L. Moir, 'Sir George Onesiphorus Paul', in H. P. R. Finberg (ed.), *Gloucestershire Studies* (Leicester: Leicester University Press, 1957), p. 209.
19 *The Times*, 20 Oct. 1785.
20 *Collected Works of Jeremy Bentham: Correspondence* (London: Athlone Press), vol. 2 (1968), pp. 105–8, 150, vol. 4 (1981), p. 43.
21 M. Foucault, *Discipline and Punish: The Birth of the Prison* (New York: Vintage Books, 1979).
22 Quoted in R. Evans, *The Fabrication of Virtue: English Prison Architecture, 1750–1840* (Cambridge: Cambridge University Press, 1982), p. 74.
23 R. Morgan, 'Divine philanthropy: John Howard reconsidered', *History*, 62 (1977), 407.
24 M. De Lacy, *Prison Reform in Lancashire, 1700–1850* (Manchester: Chetham Society, 1986), pp. 59–64.
25 M. Ignatieff, *A Just Measure of Pain: The Penitentiary in the Industrial Revolution, 1750–1850* (London: Macmillan, 1978), pp. 125–6.

26 Ibid., pp. 128–30.

27 Ibid., pp. 132, 135–9.

28 Quoted in Evans, *Fabrication of Virtue*, p. 192.

29 Quoted in Ignatieff, *Just Measure of Pain*, p. 142.

30 Quoted in Moir, 'Sir George Onesiphorus Paul', p. 201; Ignatieff, *Just Measure of Pain*, p. 120, transcribes 'a political philanthropy' as 'apolitical philanthropy', but Moir's reading seems correct.

31 R. McGowen, 'The well-ordered prison: England, 1780–1865', in N. Morris and D. J. Rothman (eds), *The Oxford History of the Prison: The Practice of Punishment in Western Society* (Oxford: Oxford University Press, 1998), pp. 85–8.

32 *The Philanthropist*, 2 (1812), 22, 142, 5.

33 Ibid., 250.

34 Ibid., 360.

35 Ignatieff, *Just Measure of Pain*, pp. 166–79.

36 Ibid., p. 175.

37 *The Times*, 24 May 1821; 25 Apr. 1821.

38 Ibid., 11 July 1849.

39 Ibid., 17 Feb. 1846; 27 Oct. 1846; 9 Jan. 1849.

40 T. Carlyle, 'Model prisons', in *Latter Day Pamphlets* (London: Chapman and Hall, 1899), pp. 49–51.

41 Ibid., pp. 61, 66, 68, 70, 83.

42 *The Times*, 22 Oct. 1853.

43 W. J. Forsythe, *The Reform of Prisoners 1830–1900* (London: Croom Helm, 1987), pp. 150–1.

44 *The Times*, 24 July 1858; 5 Jan. 1859; 30 Dec. 1862.

45 Quotes in Forsythe, *Reform of Prisoners*, pp. 155–6, 143.

46 Quoted in Ignatieff, *Just Measure of Pain*, p. 204.

47 *The Times*, 21 July 1863.

48 Ibid., 11 Aug. 1869; 25 Aug. 1869; 7 Sept. 1869.

49 M. J. D. Roberts, *Making English Morals: Voluntary Association and Moral Reform in England, 1787–1886* (Cambridge: Cambridge University Press, 2004), p. 207; G. Rose, *The Struggle for Penal Reform: The Howard League and its Predecessors* (London: Stevens & Sons, 1961), p. 19.

50 Rose, *Struggle for Penal Reform*, p. 17.

51 Ibid., pp. 17–19; Roberts, *Making English Morals*, pp. 208–9, quoting William Tallack.

52 Rose, *Struggle for Penal Reform*, pp. 41–2, 44, 46–9.

53 *The Times*, 15 Aug. 1879; 8 Dec. 1879.

54 Ibid., 24 Sept. 1880; 27 Sept. 1889.

55 Ibid., 20 Jan. 1890.

56 Rose, *Struggle for Penal Reform*, pp. 56–65, quoting p. 65.

57 Ibid., p. 91.

58 J. S. Mill, *Collected Works*, Vol. XXVIII (London: Routledge, 1988), pp. 266–7.

59 S. Collini, 'Their master's voice: John Stuart Mill as a public moralist', in S. Collini, *Public Moralists: Political Thought and Intellectual Life in Britain 1850–1930* (Oxford: Clarendon Press, 1991), pp. 121–69.

6

Universal philanthropy versus patriotism: The impact of the French Revolution, 1789–1815

John Howard's death in 1790, and the celebrations of his life and achievements that flowed immediately from the press, seemed likely to herald a golden age for philanthropy. The foundation of the Philanthropic Society in September 1788 was an early sign that philanthropy was poised to play an increasing role and to enjoy greater prominence. The outbreak of the French Revolution was welcomed by those of a philanthropic disposition. Howard himself rejoiced in the fall of the Bastille from which he had been barred.

By 1793, however, the world had changed. Britain was at war with France. Philanthropy in the aftermath of Howard's death proclaimed a love of all humankind. But for the ensuing twenty-five years, except for a brief break with the treaty of Amiens in 1802–03, war captured public attention. Philanthropy was in tension if not in conflict with patriotism. Philanthropists could be depicted as unpatriotic. 'Universal benevolence' or 'universal philanthropy' seemed unrealistic, naive and potentially dangerous to the interests of the nation.

Prison reform, the field in which through Howard philanthropy had come to prominence as a political movement, encountered severe criticism. As Chapter 5 has shown, progress was slow, results discouraging. Philanthropy lost its sheen. But there were also opportunities: numerous individuals and organisations laid claim to philanthropy. They included political radicals, self-help benefit societies, a journal, the *Philanthropist*, that was an organ for moderate reformers, and a poet who claimed that the coalition Ministry of All the Talents in 1806 embodied philanthropy. Philanthropy, in a way, was up for grabs.

If the prospects for philanthropy were in many respects dimmed and difficult there was one field where it emerged eventually triumphant. No one could dispute that philanthropy played a major role in the build-up to the abolition of the British slave trade in 1807. In this respect, universalism won out over a narrow concern with national interests. It was accompanied, moreover, by a significant shift in the social meaning of philanthropy. Philanthropy for most of the second half of the eighteenth century can be seen as the product of the Enlightenment and of the Romantic Movement. In the anti-slavery movement it became closely associated with evangelical Christianity, a social location that remained with it through the nineteenth century.

Radicals, philanthropy and the French Revolution

The French Revolution politicised philanthropy. Philanthropy – a love of humankind – could not easily recognise boundaries, whether geographical, national, religious, cultural or racial: it was universal. The French Revolution initially boosted such hopes but when it turned towards Jacobin terror it challenged them. The battle lines were clearly drawn. 'Nearly every supporter of the Revolution spoke in favor of universal benevolence' claims Evan Radcliffe.[1] Reflecting on the French Revolution the Unitarian minister Joseph Towers remembered in 1797 how 'Many of the inhabitants of England, from motives of genuine philanthropy, rejoiced at this event; they rejoiced, that a great nation had shaken off its fetters, and asserted the rights of human nature'. In opposition were those whom Towers called 'the mean, the selfish, and the sordid, men incapable of any noble or generous sentiments'.[2]

William Wordsworth exemplified the emerging rupture in British politics. He had first visited France in 1790, arriving just in time to witness and delight in the celebrations of the first anniversary of the fall of the Bastille. He then spent a year in France, a supporter of the Girondins, returning to England in late 1792. He was horrified at the outbreak of war, and equally horrified at the rise of Robespierre. In May 1794 he replied to a letter from William Mathews, a friend from Cambridge days. Mathews had suggested that they might collaborate in establishing 'a monthly miscellany from which some emolument might be drawn'.[3] Wordsworth was keen but thought it essential that they should be in agreement on politics. He set out his stall: 'You know perhaps already that I am of that odious class of men called democrats, and of that class I shall for ever continue.'[4] Delighted with Mathews's reply ('I read the explicit avowal of your political sentiments with great pleasure'), Wordsworth expanded on his own political convictions: he disapproved of 'monarchical and aristocratical governments, however modified'. He was 'not amongst the admirers of the British constitution'. Averse to revolution, though fearful that the British government's policies might bring it about, he called, as must every 'enlightened friend of mankind', for a commitment to 'political justice'. He then suggested a title for the new journal: '*The Philanthropist, a monthly Miscellany*'.[5]

'*The Philanthropist*' as planned by Wordsworth, Mathews and a third collaborator never saw the light of day. By early November 1794 the project had been abandoned. Wordsworth was in the Lake District, and his absence from London was fatal to progress. Mathews was taking up a post as a parliamentary reporter.[6] That may be the end of the story of Wordsworth and *'The Philanthropist'*. There is, however, another intriguing probability. In February 1795 Wordsworth came to London, keen to make his mark and some money in the world of journalism. On 27 February he attended a tea party at William Frend's lodgings. Six of his Cambridge contemporaries were there together with four others of an older generation: William Godwin, Thomas Holcroft, George Dyer and William Frend. Godwin's *Enquiry Concerning Political Justice* had been published two years previously and had created a considerable stir. Wordsworth was familiar with it and admiring of it. Holcroft was a prolific writer who had been one of those arrested on a charge of treason in 1794. Dyer was a Unitarian and reformer. His *The Complaints of the Poor People of England* came out in a second edition in 1793, *A Dissertation on the Theory and Practice of Benevolence* in 1795. Frend, a convert from Anglicanism to Unitarianism, had been banished from the University of Cambridge in 1794 for his *Peace and Union Recommended to the Associated Bodies of Republicans and Anti-Republicans*. In short, Wordsworth was at the centre of London radicalism.

Less than three weeks after the meeting an eight-page weekly, *The Philanthropist: Or Philosophical Essays on Politics, Government, Morals and Manners*, issued its first number. Published by Daniel Eaton, it ran for forty-two issues from 16 March 1795 up to 25 January 1796. Eaton, self-proclaimed 'printer and bookseller to the supreme majesty of the people', had escaped conviction after cases brought against him for publishing *The Rights of Man* in 1793 and for seditious libel in 1794. On the closure of the *Philanthropist* he fled to the United States. Was there a connection between the abortive Wordsworth/Mathews project and the new journal? It seems probable.[7]

The participants in the meeting at Frend's house were committed to benevolence or philanthropy that was universal. William Frend in his 1793 account of the proceedings taken against him by the University of Cambridge, wrote that 'if we neglect the principle of universal benevolence, our faith is vain, our religion is an empty parade of useless and insignificant sounds ... every christian is bound to entertain sentiments of universal benevolence, to love his fellow creatures of every sect, colour or description'.[8]

George Dyer's participation in the new journal is as uncertain as Wordsworth's, but seems likely. He was contemptuous of existing public charities: 'The philanthropy that attends public charities', he wrote in 1793, 'is frequently selfishness in disguise. He is the greatest philanthropist who enables the poor man to help himself'.[9] Returning to the theme in 1795, he wrote

It may be laid down as a safe position, that in proportion as a country abounds in poor, the state of society is bad ... There would be less occasion to erect so many temples to Charity, if we erected more to Justice. To remove the defects and excesses of governments; to give a just direction to the laws; and to preserve the course of industry from being obstructed, would be attended with more advantages to the poor, than the erecting of a thousand hospitals; and, on this ground, every philanthropist should be a reformer.[10]

This programme was profoundly political, aiming at reform of the practices and scope of government, changes to the statute book and removal of impediments to free trade. It would be more philanthropic to do this, urged Dyer, than to erect 'a thousand hospitals', hospitals shorthand for the most up to date forms of what Dyer described as public charity. In the *Philanthropist* (No. 37) someone, perhaps Dyer, or almost certainly someone who had read Dyer, described how 'A nation is not to relieve distresses of the poor by acts of charity; it ought to prevent their existence by acts of justice'.[11] Discussion of rights and duties in early modern European thinking drew a distinction between perfect rights and duties that were the domain of justice and enforceable in law and imperfect rights and duties where charity came into play. Dyer and others in the 1790s, in particular William Godwin, challenged this distinction, arguing that the domain of justice should be extended to include what had previously been thought of as charity.[12]

Justice, political justice, was William Godwin's theme. 'If justice have any meaning', he wrote, 'it is just that I should contribute every thing in my power to the benefit of the whole'.[13] This was, implicitly, a strong call that a good life would be a life dedicated to improving the lot of humankind. Such a goal should be achieved peacefully, by reason and persuasion – though it would amount to a revolution. 'The revolutions of states, which a philanthropist would desire to witness', he wrote, 'or in which he would willingly co-operate, consist principally in a change of sentiments and dispositions in the members of those states. The true instruments for changing the opinions of men are argument and persuasion'.[14] To advocate 'revolutions', even peaceful ones, in the febrile atmosphere in England in 1793, was to risk being counted as a Jacobin. To imagine that 'philanthropists' might 'willingly co-operate' in them was to place philanthropy in the same category.

In 1793, however, Godwin condemned some manifestations of philanthropy, claiming that 'Philanthropy, as contradistinguished to justice, is rather an unreflecting feeling, than a rational principle'.[15] Anyone who had read about philanthropy in the periodicals of the 1770s and 1780s knew that it was inextricably associated with emotions and feelings. This seems to have been the kind of philanthropy that Godwin had in mind in his critique. In the second edition (1796), composed in 1795, the year when the *Philanthropist* was launched, he rewrote this passage, giving an entirely favourable view of philanthropy. In advocating sincerity, he now saw it as 'intimately connected with the general dissemination of innocence, energy, intellectual improvement and philanthropy'. It was 'practised from a consciousness of its utility, and from sentiments of philanthropy'.[16] By 1795 philanthropy was being claimed by radicals in the circles in which Godwin was a leading participant.

Initially critical of philanthropy, Godwin began to speak up for it. In 1801, far from contradistinguishing justice and philanthropy, Godwin saw them as acting in harmony: to act justly a human 'must elevate philanthropy into a passion'.[17] Looking back in 1824 on the writing of *Political Justice*, he declared that 'No man perhaps has at any time been animated with a more earnest spirit of philanthropy, than I was in the composition of that work'.[18] Writing of 'Self-Love and Benevolence' in 1831 he argued that 'He who for ever thinks, that his "charity must begin at home", is in great danger of becoming an indifferent citizen, and of withering those feelings of philanthropy, which in all sound estimation constitute the crowning glory of man'.[19] Reversing what had been and remained a widely held view, that love of those close to us would spread wider and wider until it encompassed all humankind, Godwin argued that all too often such love looked in on itself and never spread.

In the mid-1790s the young Samuel Taylor Coleridge set himself up in opposition to Godwin and promoted a different view of philanthropy. From 1796 to 1799 'The idea of a critical treatise on Godwin's *Political Justice* increasingly occupied his mind'.[20] He was deeply influenced by David Hartley's *Observations on Man* (1749). Hartley argued against those who thought that a moral sense was innate, it came rather from the association of ideas. Love of those close to us could through association rise up to love of mankind. Coleridge set this out in a letter to Robert Southey in 1794:

> The ardour of private Attachments makes Philanthropy a necessary *habit* of the Soul. I love my *Friend* such as *he* is, all mankind are or *might be*! The deduction is evident -. Philanthropy (and indeed every other Virtue) is a thing of *Concretion* – Some home-born Feeling is the *center* of the Ball, that, rolling on thro' Life collects and assimilates every congenial Affection.[21]

Coleridge elaborated on this in 1795 in his *Conciones ad Populum* where the opposition to Godwin's ideas was explicit: 'Let us beware of that proud Philosophy, which affects to inculcate Philanthropy while it denounces every home-born feeling, by which it is produced and nurtured.' He went on to argue in one of his 1795 lectures in Bristol, that 'the Love of our Friends, parents and neighbours lead[s] us to the love of our Country to the love of all Mankind. The intensity of private attachment encourages, not prevents, universal philanthropy'. Coleridge was here, consciously or otherwise, picking up on Alexander Pope's well-known lines in his *An Essay on Man* (1733–34) where he compares the movement from self-love to love of all to the ripple effect of a pebble dropped in a lake:

> Friend, parent, neighbour, first it will embrace,
> His country next, and next all human race.
> Wide and more wide, th' overflowings of the mind
> Take every creature in, of every kind.[22]

Love of country both preceded and perhaps took precedence over love of humankind. 'Jesus', wrote Coleridge, 'was the friend of the whole human Race, yet he disguised not the national feelings, when he foresaw the particular distresses of his Countrymen'. In a later version of this passage 'his natural feelings' replaced 'the national feelings', yet the effect was similar: it was 'natural' to have 'national' feelings.[23]

Coleridge and Godwin differed profoundly in their approaches to philanthropy and to religion. Against Godwin's atheism Coleridge, a Unitarian from his time in Cambridge, saw philanthropy and religion as inextricably linked. He described Jesus in his 1795 'Lecture on the Slave-Trade' as 'the inspired Philanthropist of Galilee'. Later, having abandoned Unitarianism, he changed this to 'the redeeming Theanthropist'.[24] Either way, philanthropy and religion were inseparable. Important as these differences were, they should not obscure what Godwin and Coleridge had in common: both were politically radical. Coleridge's lectures in Bristol in 1795 attacked the war and the government – and the slave trade – with quite as much fervour as any of the London radicals.

However they interpreted philanthropy, radicals were laying claim to it and stressing that it was political. They promoted their views in a journal entitled the *Philanthropist*. John Thelwall, one of those on trial for treason in 1794, wrote in 1795 that 'The real lover of mankind must ... labour to redress their wrongs by purifying the fountains of political dispensation. What are these impure and polluted fountains? Parliamentary Corruption! – the system of Cabinet intrigue! – the system of Rotten Boroughs!'.[25] A 'lover of mankind' of this stripe lived dangerously. To be known as a reformer or radical in the years after 1792 was to be at risk of arrest and, if found guilty, of imprisonment, banishment to Botany Bay or execution. A network of spies covered the country. Wordsworth's name was on the spies' lists, and he and Coleridge in 1797 were under observation on the suspicion, unfounded, that they were laying the ground in the West Country for a French invasion. After 1795 most radicals abandoned active politics, driven out of it by restrictive laws and constant surveillance of their movements and correspondence. By adopting the language of philanthropy, by publishing the *Philanthropist*, radicals were ensuring that philanthropy would come to be seen by supporters of the government as extremist, Jacobin, foreign and deeply unpatriotic.

Universal philanthropy under attack

Universal philanthropy came under particularly severe criticism. People continued to invoke the sense of it, sometimes avoiding the words. Thus the Society of Friends of the Constitution, sympathising with Dr Priestley on the destruction of his property in Birmingham, was confident of 'the development of that philanthropic patriotism which regards all men as *in solido* associated in the common interest of general felicity'.[26] It would soon become difficult for such people to make their claim for patriotism. For some 'universal philanthropy' was uncontroversial. A letter in the *Gentleman's Magazine* in 1793 proposing a 'Plan for Assisting the Industrious Poor' hoped that his ideas would 'coincide with the sentiments of those persons, who, like the Divine Founder of Christianity, are actuated by universal philanthropy'.[27] Priscilla Wakeful in 1797, quoting Terence, the second century BCE Latin playwright's 'Homo sum: humani nihil a me alienum puto', went on to translate it as 'I am a man, and concerned about the affairs of all mankind. How valuable a character! This is the foundation of universal philanthropy. This is what constitutes a citizen of the world'.[28] The *Methodist Magazine* in 1798, discussing 'zeal', distinguished bad and good zeal. 'True Christian Zeal', it affirmed, 'is a generous philanthropy and benevolence, which, like the light of the Sun, diffuses itself to every object and longs to be the instrument of good, if possible, to the whole race of mankind'. The same periodical carried a long article on the Stranger's Friend Society, ending with the claim that 'Sectarian prejudices of every kind we sacrifice (in this work) at the shrine of universal philanthropy'.[29]

Others, sympathetic to universal philanthropy, faced up to the difficulties inherent in it. John Aikin's *Monthly Magazine* in 1796 asked 'Is Private Affection inconsistent with Universal Benevolence?' Quoting Pope's lines, the article asked whether this meant that 'private affections' might 'be lost in general philanthropy?' 'In order to be a philanthropist, must I cease to be a father, a friend, a patriot?' The answer of course was no. 'Universal benevolence' was indeed 'a divine principle, never to be abandoned' but, as Coleridge had argued, it was built on and out of private affections: 'No man is born a philanthropist'. It was a little tame after this to conclude that for most people, their horizon rarely raised above their locality, 'the general principle of universal benevolence' was of no relevance in their lives, though 'where it can be applied *with certainty*, it ought to be followed without reserve'.[30]

Opponents of the Revolution had no time for such quibbles. Even charity was under suspicion; in *Pigott's Political Dictionary* of 1795, it was defined as 'enormous contributions for French rebels: an utter neglect of our own poor'.[31] More influential was Edmund Burke's depiction of universal benevolence as a threat to the order of society and to family life. Burke wrote of 'the homicide philanthropy of France' where families tore each other apart: a love of humankind extinguished love for those nearest to you.[32] Furthermore, universal benevolence was incompatible with love of country. Burke, claimed William Hazlitt, set 'the two noblest impulses of our nature, the love of country and the love of kind … in hostile array … armed with inextinguishable fury against each other'. Demonstrating the truth of this astute observation, in 1798 the *Anti-Jacobin* painted a portrait of

> Philanthropy … beneath whose baneful sway
> Each patriot passion sinks, and dies away.[33]

To describe Tom Paine as a 'philanthropist', as the *Anti-Jacobin* did in dog-gerel verse, was not intended as a compliment; on the contrary it suggested someone whose love of people in other countries (America and France) cast serious doubts on his loyalty to his own country.[34] In a parody of Robert Southey, the paper mocked a 'Friend of Humanity', who, finding that a poor knife-grinder apparently had no grievances against the established order, kicked him and exited in 'a transport of universal philanthropy'.[35] When it was claimed in 1798 that French prisoners in England were being mistreated, the *Anti-Jacobin* deplored 'this instance of *Jacobin Philanthropy*'. It noted that the letter making the claim was 'signed *Philanthropos*, a Signature which the *Jacobin* cant has rendered justly suspicious to every honest man'. Bad living conditions in Switzerland, the *Anti-Jacobin* claimed, were not in any way alleviated by 'the *Charity* of the Pupils and Practitioners of the *Rights of Man*, of the Preachers of Universal Humanity, of general Philanthropy, of Liberty and Equality'. Philanthropy was here linked with all that Burke had found so disturbing about the French Revolution. As the paper put it in reflecting on the 'Manners and Character of the Age', there had been a deplorable spread of 'those principles, which, under the Imposing names of Philosophy, Philanthropy and Freedom, attack the very foundations of Society, by inspiring a contempt for all authority, human and divine'.[36] For the *Anti-Jacobin* philanthropy was 'Jacobin': it was akin to dangerous radicalism.

More moderately, in Hannah More's novel, *A History of Mr Fantom, the New-Fashioned Philosopher* (1794), Mr Fantom is a man of 'wide-stretched benevolence' who, rather like Mrs Jellyby in *Bleak House*, preferred to think of 'Poles and South Americans' rather than of a local parish apprentice who has been wronged.[37] Samuel Parr, who had once been a friend of William Godwin, elaborated on this in a Spital Sermon in 1800. 'The new doctrine of universal philanthropy', he contended, 'has found its way to our own country', from France. '[T]he philanthropic system', he admitted, had 'an engaging form', but 'by a thousand secret spells, it wins over to its purposes our vanity and our credulity, and from the service in which our affections are usually engaged, it would decoy them away … When any dazzling phantoms of universal philan-thropy have seized our attention, the objects that formerly engaged it shrink and fade'.[38] More's Mr Fantom and Parr's 'dazzling phantoms' suggest some-thing like a common agenda for anti-revolutionary writers to depict philan-thropy as fantastical, unreal, unconnected to everyday life.

The experience of the French Revolution left philanthropy tainted with the suspicion that in their attachment to 'universal benevolence' and 'uni-versal philanthropy' philanthropists were not only indifferent to sufferings close at home but also posed a danger to that attachment to family and to 'little platoons' that Burke had set out as the foundation blocks of an ordered and safe society.

The Philanthropist: Or Repository for Hints and Suggestions Calculated to Promote the Comfort and Happiness of Man, a quarterly magazine published from 1811 to 1819 and then subsequently from 1829 to 1830 and 1835 to 1842, attempted to restore confidence and belief in universal philanthropy. At one level it can be placed alongside the reports of the Society for Bettering the Condition and Increasing the Comforts of the Poor that had been set up in 1796 under the editorship of Thomas Bernard, aiming to 'make the enquiry into all that concerns the POOR, and the promotion of their happiness, a SCIENCE'.[39] Its seven volumes accumulated accounts of schemes to this end. The first five dated from 1797 to 1805, there was then a gap until 1811 and another until 1817. It seems possible that the Society for Bettering the Condition of the Poor was losing momentum (Bernard's health was in decline) and that the *Philanthropist* was a replacement and continuation. It too gave accounts of soup kitchens, savings banks, schemes for clothing the poor and so on, but its remit was wider and its tone broader.

William Allen, the *Philanthropist*'s founder and editor, was a successful Quaker businessman who had established his reputation in the charitable world from 1797 with the Spitalfields Soup Charity.[40] Allen was also from 1808 the first secretary of the Society for the Diffusion of Knowledge Respecting the Punishment of Death and the Improvement of Prison Discipline, and then of its successor, the London Society for the Improvement of Prison Discipline. He established and maintained extensive links with reformers in Britain, America and Europe. Allen spoke the language of the Enlightenment. There were constant appeals to 'friends of humanity'. Since the 'Creator's purpose is the happiness of his creatures', so also as we humans 'approach more nearly to the standard of perfection, we shall be more fully imbued with love to our species'.[41] Allen, however, was uneasily aware that the tide of opinion was running against him. Promoting an appeal on behalf of Poland in 1814 he drew attention to it in order 'to endeavour to insinuate into the minds even of a few, some considerations of justice and philanthropy'. Public interest, he noted, was greater the narrower the object of concern, and went on: 'It is to counteract this miserable tendency, that is one of the main objects of *The Philanthropist*; to enlarge the benevolent feelings of mankind; to make their narrow sympathies gradually expand; to give them habits of attending to masses.' How to achieve this was a problem: 'We own that it is through the people, that we have any hope of rendering princes and ministers philanthropists. Mere exhortations to humanity, addressed in opposition to immediate and powerful interests, have, with exceptions wonderfully small, proved always unsuccessful.' It was only through better education that 'this enlargement of mind, this more exalted virtue, this more productive and useful philanthropy, is to be produced'. But the education on offer was itself woefully inadequate.[42]

Allen was taken to task by one correspondent for using too strong language in condemnation of some current practices. His reply was robust and indicative of the platform that philanthropy had by this time adopted:

> Every thing which concerns man as a member of a community is *political*
> ... It is impossible for the principal topics of The Philanthropist *not* to be

political. The police of prisons is political, the provision for the poor is political, the system of education is political, the abolition of the slave-trade is political, the doctrine of peace is political; almost every thing, in short, is political, upon which it can be of any use for the philanthropist to write.[43]

Allen and others like him were attempting in what they wrote to mould the public mind on matters political. It was a hard task, 'even in our own country, the most enlightened as yet upon the surface of the globe'. The public must be 'awakened ... until the proper degree of feeling, and the proper mode of thinking, are planted, and rooted in their bosoms'.[44] To achieve this in time of war only added to the difficulty. Rather, it seemed, in the words of the Unitarian Robert Aspland in 1809, that philanthropy had been 'driven from the abodes of men by the din of war'.[45]

The range of philanthropy

In the 1790s and beyond 'philanthropy' and its derivatives were floating free of any fixed meaning, contested, without any certain destination. If the French Revolution challenged philanthropy on the issue of universality, it also opened up space for anyone to make claims for it.

The association of philanthropy with radicalism was not lost. Radicals began to use the word, and to link it with their 'patriotism'. Huddersfield radicals in 1793 urged the London Corresponding Society to 'send us the word of enlightenment and philanthropy' for although 'Huddersfield abounds in true patriots ... we are beset by masses of ignorant aristocracy'. 'True patriots' in this articulation were those committed to a democratic reform of the British constitution, to the Enlightenment and to universal philanthropy.[46] When the land reformer Thomas Spence died in 1814 his disciples set themselves up as the 'Society of Spencean Philanthropists', and were involved in the Spa Field riots and the Cato Street conspiracy. In 1818 the first attempt to form a General Union of all trades was known as the 'Philanthropic Hercules'. Philanthropy continued to be invoked by radicals. In 1831 Oldham radicals urged organisation in favour of Henry Hunt: 'Let us enter on this pleasing task in the fine spirit of energetic philanthropy.'[47]

Freemasons' lodges, benefit and friendly societies, growing apace in the late eighteenth century, sometimes described themselves as 'Philanthropic' in their titles. 'Rural Philanthropic Lodge No. 291' was set up in Burnham-on-Sea in Somerset in 1793. In Leeds 'The Philanthropic Lodge, No. 304' 'was named and established in 1794'. Skipton also had a lodge.[48] Stockton upon Tees in 1796 boasted a Lodge of Philanthropy; we know because of the publication of the oration delivered on the removal of Lodge No. 19 to new premises.[49] In 1806 'the Philanthropic Society', held at the Blind Beggar, near Mile-end Turnpike, gave £6 5s 0d to the Patriotic Fund to relieve relatives of soldiers and sailors. It was still doing good work as the Mile End Philanthropic Society in 1814.[50] The Philanthropic Society of House Carpenters and Joiners in Newcastle in 1812 was a mutual aid society, dedicated 'upon all just occasions to assist and support each other'.[51] Blackburn in 1839 was home to a Philanthropic Burial Society, with over 130,000 members by 1872.[52] In these examples and others, philanthropy seems close to ideas of mutualism rather than to giving by the rich. When William Beveridge wrote about *Voluntary Action* in the 1940s he distinguished between philanthropy and mutual societies, yet in the history of such societies there was a tradition of seeing themselves as philanthropic. Not only did they support members in times of difficulty, they also contributed to communities hit by mining accidents and by the 'cotton famine' in Lancashire in the 1860s. Moreover, in their rituals, their feasts, their rules and conventions, their place in their local communities, there was much that was akin to charitable organisations.[53]

Radicals were not alone in laying claim to philanthropy. The author of *The Reign of Philanthropy; or the Auspices of the New Ministry: A Poem* (1806) claimed that

> true philanthropy is distinguished by an extensive union of public and private virtue, which diffuses itself through society, the state, and the world. It is always efficient, and its effects are every where manifest – but in nothing more than a generous policy, both foreign and domestic, in the government of a great empire.

Philanthropy was here promoted as a force that would inform government. The 'new ministry' of the title was a coalition, the so-called 'Ministry of All the Talents'. The author saw its formation as 'unprecedented in the British annals', and foreshadowing 'THE REIGN OF PHILANTHROPY'. What he called 'the legitimate philanthropy' of many of the members of the new ministry afforded 'the happiest prospect to mankind'.[54] The author's hopes came to nothing, the Ministry lasting only one year.

The Anniversary Festival of the Royal Humane Society was an annual occasion for the celebration of the philanthropy that it embodied and for wider reflection. The highlight of the event was the procession round the dining hall of those whose lives had been saved in the course of the year. In 1793, 'Philanthropist', in a letter in the *Gentleman's Magazine*, described the procession as a 'sight ... at once so noble and sublime as to fill the minds of the spectators with an ineffable mixture of joy and surprize'. It prompted 'Philanthropist' to break into verse:

> Philanthropy a HOWARD once could boast,
>   Nor was a HANWAY backward in her cause;
> But, since these guardians of our lives were lost,
>   Humanity still boasts a COGAN and a HAWES.
> To foreign climes their precepts wide extend;
>   To *Afric* and *Americ's* distant shore
> Humanity her onward course doth bend,

Mankind to save, till dying is no more.[55]

Cogan and Hawes were the leading figures in the society. Later in the 1790s the Anniversary Festival was said to be '"the feast of Reason" realized', the organisers' 'philanthropy ... a blessing to the indigent, a consolation to the afflicted, and guardians to the lives of the people'.[56]

John Stoyle, a Royal Navy Lieutenant, was moved by the reports of the Royal Humane Society to write two 'Odes to philanthropy'. In the first he saw 'Divine Philanthropy' as an 'Emanation from above' that might spread to all:

> Still may thy power, Philanthropy, prevail,
>   Thy loveliness bring joy to every face;
> While lisping children breathe the artless tale,
>   And tell how they were saved from Death's embrace.

The 'lisping children' were those saved from death by drowning by the Society. In the second Ode Stoyle returned to the same theme:

> Thus, O Philanthropy, thy reign
>   Assume in every breast,
> Till nought of passions base remain,
>   To mar thy halcyon rest!
> Thus, Daughter of most happy skies, pervade
>   The Monarch and the Subject with thy love
> Till in each heart thy image be pourtay'd,
>   To fit the soul for happier scenes above;
> Where War or warlike hosts shall ne'er appear
>   To stain th' unsullied bliss of one eternal year.

Stoyle envisaged philanthropy spreading throughout the world to reach 'each savage tribe'.[57]

Evangelicals, slavery and philanthropy

One group who had a clear sense of where philanthropy should be heading were the evangelicals. Philanthropy's roots lay in a belief in the innate benevolence of human beings. Non-Calvinist evangelicals, convinced of the intrinsic sinfulness of humans, might believe that salvation was available for all but they were instinctively suspicious of any notion that only the wrong environment prevented humans from being good. Philanthropy, it might be thought, would have little appeal for them. Yet in the first half of the nineteenth century philanthropy came to be almost exclusively associated with evangelicalism. How did this happen?

It started with an engagement with benevolence and with a reiterated statement that benevolence without Christianity was hollow. Beilby Porteus, bishop of London, and sympathetic to the evangelicals, preached that unless charity 'be grounded on true evangelical principles, it may be very good pagan morality, but it is not Christian godliness'.[58] *The Love of Christ the Source of Genuine Philanthropy* on the death of John Thornton, a key figure in establishing Clapham in south London as a powerhouse of evangelicalism, rejoiced that 'Even our degenerate times may boast of a Howard, or a Thornton, who in different ways have caused astonished multitudes to applaud their disinterested, and generous philanthropy', but regretted that those multitudes 'have not understood that the love of Christ constrained them thus to act'.[59] For evangelicals true benevolence came not from some instinct of the human heart but from the gospel. For William Wilberforce

> Benevolence ... when not originating in religion, dispenses but from a scanty and precarious fund; and therefore, if it be liberal in the case of some objects, it is generally found to be contracted towards others. Men who, acting from worldly principles, make the greatest stir about general philanthropy or zealous patriotism, are often very deficient in their conduct in domestic life; and very neglectful of the opportunities, fully within their reach, of promoting the comfort of those with whom they are immediately connected. But true Christian benevolence is always occupied in producing happiness to the utmost of its powers.[60]

Thomas Rennell was more outspoken in 1795: 'we may *absolutely deny*, that the frame of man *naturally* conducts him to sentiments of benevolence'. In a sermon entitled 'Benevolence exclusively an Evangelical Virtue', he argued that 'the ONLY basis of charity is faith in Christ'.[61]

In this belief Rennell was aiming directly at those who argued the opposite case. It was put most clearly, and provocatively, by the Unitarian George Dyer who in 1795, the same year as Rennell preached his sermon, claimed that

> No system of theological opinions is, exclusively, essential to form the benevolent character. Infidels and professed Christians may be full of malevolence; Infidels or Christians may possess the milk of philanthropy. The social affections are dictated by nature, and confirmed by habit; and dwell in the heart of that man, who is least corrupted by base passions, whatever his religion be.[62]

Dyer upheld Enlightenment beliefs. 'With respect to man', he wrote, 'that happiness is his ultimate good, the centre to which his warmest wishes move, is the universal opinion of mankind', a statement that might have been more likely to be widely accepted some years previously. Whereas in 'dark ages' of superstition, people had looked to saints or guardian angels for help, 'Benevolence … is the hope and guide of more enlightened periods … A good man is the well-wisher, and, to the utmost of his power, the bene-factor of his species'.[63] But Dyer's unsectarian 'benevolence' was becoming difficult to uphold.

From the 1790s evangelicalism was a growing force in Britain. It had powerful appeal amongst Dissenters. Within the Church of England high church and more conventional Christians saw it as a threat to the Establishment. Evangelicals, it was claimed, were an increasing proportion of the clergy. In politics critics detected an evangelical party, 'the Saints', most famous for their opposition to the slave trade, but also active on the domestic front, clamping down in any way they could on lack of Sunday observance, alehouses and traditional forms of leisure. Charitable organisations, both old and newly founded, boasted substantial numbers of aristocratic evangelicals on their letterheads as Patrons and Vice-Presidents.[64]

The evangelicals first became associated with philanthropy in their opposition to the slave trade. That they were motivated by philanthropy was an accusation thrown at them by their opponents. When Wilberforce in December 1790 moved for a committee to be established on the African slave trade, Col. Tarleton, MP for Liverpool, speaking 'from a duty he owed to his constituents … considered himself bound to oppose *this modern pro-duction of false and mistaken philanthropy*'. Tarleton returned to the theme in March 1791. Those in favour of abolition of the trade, he said, 'had been led on by a very mistaken idea of humanity, a sort of modern philanthropy, which had made them lose sight of many objects nearer their views, and more worthy of their humane and charitable feelings'.[65] In June 1791 Sir William Young, criticising Wilberforce in the House of Commons, 'would maintain that his philanthropy was mistaken, and his good-will towards mankind only specious'. In November 1791, Wilberforce again to the fore in speaking in the House of Commons on the subject, Lord Carhampton criticised his 'ill-judged philanthropy'. The *Northampton Mercury* in 1792 gave space to a letter from a Gentleman from Kingston, Jamaica, critical of Wilberforce's 'Quixotic Philanthropy'.[66] Philanthropy in this perspective was 'modern' (an adjective often used in criticism), 'mistaken', 'ill-judged', 'false' and 'quix-otic'. It was most manifest in these regards in connection with the slave trade. The opposition to the British slave trade was led by evangelicals, Wilberforce preeminent.

Attacks of this kind on philanthropy continued up to abolition of the slave trade in 1807. In 1804, for example, the *Morning Post* printed Bryan Edwards's attack on 'the pestilent doctrines of those hot-brained fanatics and detestable incendiaries, who, under the vile pretence of philanthropy and zeal for the interests of suffering humanity, preach up rebellion and murder to the contented and orderly Negroes in our own territories'.[67] In the same year a member of parliament stated his opposition to 'every proposition for granting … money for the support of visionary schemes of philanthropy'.

The Lord Chancellor, Baron Eldon, 'recommended it to those persons who pretended to be philanthropists, to make their philanthropy a little universal, and to consider not only the condition of the blacks, but of their countrymen, who might be ruined by the abolition of this trade'.[68]

British public opinion was mobilised to an unprecedented extent in opposition to the slave trade and later to slavery.[69] A formidable economic interest was under attack. In 1792 400,000 people signed a petition for abolition, around 13 per cent of the adult male population. There were widespread boycotts of slave-grown sugar, involving perhaps 300,000, many of them women.[70] If, as supporters of the slave trade and slavery maintained, philanthropy lay behind these expressions of opinion, then there could be no disguising the fact that philanthropy was attacking an established economic interest and that it was engaged in a fundamentally political cause.

Wider currents of opposition to philanthropy were circulating around opposition to the slave trade. In 1790 in the *Universal Magazine of Knowledge and Pleasure,* a writer in defence of the slave trade declared how 'I very much fear that a relaxation and effeminacy of manners, rather than genuine tenderness of heart, has been the cause of this violent paroxysm of philanthropy'. That philanthropy was 'effeminate' had, as we shall see, a long history ahead of it. In the same journal in 1791 it was perhaps the same author who, discerning a decline in Christianity, wrote how 'Even the prevalence of a liberal and warm philanthropy is secretly sapping the foundation of christian morals, because many of its champions allow themselves to live in the open violation of the severer duties of justice and sobriety, while they are contending for the gentler ones of charity and beneficence'.[71]

Anti-slave trade campaigners did proclaim their philanthropy. When Colonel Tarleton said that the defeat of an abolition motion in 1791 was a 'triumph', Charles James Fox replied that 'it is a *triumph* which patriotism and humanity are strangers to, and which every philanthropist considers as disgraceful to the nation – the triumph of self-interest over mercy!' The *Northampton Mercury* hoped that 'a principle of philanthropy may, at length, effect a purpose in which the interests of humanity are so very particularly concerned'. When money was being raised for the cause in 1792 the *Chester Chronicle* was delighted that 'The stream of philanthropy is flowing over every part of our island'. In March 1792 the *Lincoln, Rutland and Stamford Mercury* reported on a petition for abolition in Lincoln where the inhabitants were 'actuated by the same liberal Principle of Philanthropy that has distinguished so many of his Majesty's Subjects on this Occasion'.[72]

When abolition was achieved in 1807 the *Chester Chronicle* saw it as a key date in the nation's history:

It is with the most heartfelt satisfaction that we congratulate the public on the full accomplishment of this beneficial measure – a measure which will render sacred, to the lovers of mankind, not only the man [Wilberforce] with whom it first originated, but the philanthropic Administration which carried it into effect. The history of England tells us of the *long Parliament*, the *rump Parliament*, etc., but the present will be handed down to posterity as the JUST and HUMANE PARLIAMENT![73]

In similar vein, when the British public in 1814 pressed hard for the slave trade to be abolished across the world, the *Leeds Mercury* rejoiced that

> the British nation has risen up as one man against the continuance of the Slave Trade; that all distinctions of political party, of religious sects, and even of rank, have been forgotten, and that she has with the voice of her collective population proclaimed aloud 'let there be no Slave Trade'. The call will vibrate through Europe, it will reach the shores of Africa, and it will ultimately prevail, for it is the voice of God.[74]

This, needless to say, was less than entirely accurate. It was an attempt to forge a narrative of a nation that responded to 'the call of justice and the voice of humanity' and acted as God's agent on earth. It had no time for the caution of the *Morning Post* that urged that 'the real philanthropist' would not press France to abolish the trade, and even less for French newspaper reports that British philanthropy was a mask for self-interest.[75]

In the debates on the abolition of the slave trade philanthropy was invoked by both sides, condemned by the opponents of abolition, held up for admiration by its supporters. Wilberforce, 'that great Philanthropist', led the parliamentary campaign, and was the person most receiving praise and obloquy. He was a leading evangelical and that helped to place a focus on evangelicalism.

The fear provoked by the growth of evangelicalism was voiced from 1798 by the *Anti-Jacobin Review* and then by one of the most powerful writers of his age, William Cobbett. It was not only the opposition to the slave trade that aroused alarm. 'Fanatics', it was claimed, were subverting church, state and nation, in ways similar to Puritan initiatives in the seventeenth century. The difference was, as William Cobbett put it in the first issue of his *Political Register* in 1802, that

> Those of that day were destitute of many of the specious pretexts, and many of the other advantages, which their more fortunate successors enjoy. Legislative solicitude for bettering the conditions of Negro slaves had not then made an opening for the intrusion of their hypocritical compassion, nor had the philanthropic title of citizen of the world sanctioned indifference to country, and broken the more sacred bonds of allegiance.

Evangelical opposition to rural sports 'which string the nerves and strengthen the frame, which excite an emulation in deeds of hardihood and valour, and which imperceptibly instil honour, generosity, and a love of glory, into the mind of the clown' meant that 'the sect are incessantly laboring to eradicate, fibre by fibre, the last poor remains of English manners'.[76] Cobbett spoke for many in seeing evangelicals as fanatical and hypocritical, their actions destructive of traditional English virtues. And, most germane for us, these negative qualities were bound up with their claim to 'the philanthropic title of citizen of the world'.

Cobbett was fiercely critical of the anti-slave trade movement and of causes associated with it. The foundation and travails of Sierra Leone, 'the philanthropic colony', roused his contempt. When a petition was presented to the House of Commons for government money to aid the ailing settlement, Cobbett let fire: 'What! troubles, and battles, and bloodshed, in that new Utopia, where Philanthropy reigned in person, where the tears were to be wiped from all eyes, and the weals from all backs, where the *harmless* African was, at last, to find rest from his labours! The annals of Bedlam do not furnish a stronger instance of madness than the establishment of this colony.' Fearful of black immigration to England, Cobbett declared that 'It is time the nation should be roused from its philanthropic dream'. On Toussaint L'Ouverture, leader of the revolt in Haiti, he described how 'The Puritans and Philanthropists (who are very nearly related) prayed and sighed for the negro, the former regarding him as one of the elect (for the *blacker* the sinner the brighter the saint), and the latter as a "fellow man", a brother citizen of the world'.[77]

War with France also preoccupied Cobbett. He wanted the British to become 'a *military people*' without interference from 'canting philanthropic societies'. He was scornful of 'your bawlers for *peace and plenty on any terms*; your philanthropic haters of *all war*'. When peace terms with Napoleon were under discussion in 1802, Cobbett, deeply opposed to them, thought it 'a folly, worthy only of a whining hypocritical philanthropist, to declaim against the horrors of a war *ad internecionem* when the matter is not left to your choice'.[78]

The enemies of the evangelicals did not let up in their expression of concern. The Reverend Sydney Smith, for example, in 1808 and 1809 had four articles attacking the evangelicals published in the *Edinburgh Review*, fearing that 'fanaticism will increase rather than diminish'.[79] The *Anti-Jacobin* retained its hostility and in 1816 began to emphasise what Cobbett had referred to, the linkage between evangelicalism and philanthropy. In doing so it put into the public domain what was to remain deep into the nineteenth century a language that was used to criticise philanthropy and philanthropists. In July 1816 it called for steps to be taken against 'the fanatical exertions of those spurious philanthropists, who are laboring to *puritanize* ... the public mind, and, consequently, to destroy the best energies, and the best feelings, of Englishmen'. As with Cobbett, philanthropists, so-called, were seen as destructive of Englishness, their philanthropy 'spurious', a mask for something else that turned out to be professional and financial gain. James Stephen, active in the anti-slavery cause, had, it was claimed, completed his 'philanthropic harvest' by becoming Master in Chancery and law adviser to the Colonial Department. 'And Mr. Macaulay has driven a still more lucrative trade, by his traffic in philanthropy, which has, at once, filled his coffers, and introduced him to respectable society.' Others were climbing on the philanthropic bandwagon: 'So much for the disinterested efforts of these noisy philanthropists.' How had Zachary Macaulay done this? '[B]y the employment of smooth words, and oily professions, the whine and cant of the tabernacle'.[80] Spurious, noisy, smooth and oily, their discourse imbued with whine and cant, evangelical philanthropists were tarred with words and images that it proved difficult to shake off. And philanthropy itself was coming to be seen as inseparable from evangelicalism.

For the critics, the danger to church and state could not be exaggerated. These 'fanatics … from the immense profits which accrue from their trade of philanthropy, may be enabled to buy boroughs and so to acquire a preponderance in the senate, that may restore the times of the usurpation!' – and this time 'without the chance of a second restoration'.[81] Philanthropy was not some harmless exercise of benevolence, but a potent political danger, equivalent to the opposition that Charles I had faced in the seventeenth century.

Conclusion

In 1819 Abraham Rees, a leading Unitarian minister, in his thirty-nine volume *Cyclopaedia; or Universal Dictionary of Arts, Sciences and Literature*, defined charity as 'one of the three grand theological virtues; consisting in the love of God and our neighbour', and philanthropy as 'a general benevolence towards the species'.[82] In its contrast between the specifically Christian definition of charity and the more secular one of philanthropy, and in seeing philanthropy as benevolence or good feeling rather than action, it might have been written in the eighteenth century before John Howard had associated philanthropy with doing good. It is a definition that is testimony to a degree of continuity and constancy in the history of philanthropy.

In the war years, however, the changes that philanthropy underwent were the most striking feature. No one in 1789 could have predicted them. Philanthropy had roots in France and the outbreak of the Revolution could be seen as a harbinger of a spread of philanthropy across the world. But once Britain was at war with France, the Enlightenment belief in progress, reform, rationality and philanthropy came under severe pressure and quickly fragmented. Above all, a belief in universalism, at philanthropy's core, became difficult to uphold. True, there were before that, powerful critics, Adam Smith preeminent, of the philanthropists' dedication to universalism. But it was war with France that set up patriotism in opposition to philanthropy. What might have been predicted at the time of Howard's death in 1790, a spread widely through society of the philanthropy that he had come to embody, never happened. On the contrary, that kind of philanthropy was in retreat.

Looking back on that period we can now see that philanthropy was under attack from two directions. First, there was the attack on what came to be called Jacobin philanthropy; politically radical and uncompromising in opposition to the government and the war, it was an easy target for the virulent government-sponsored press. Second, there was the attack on the advocates of abolition of the slave trade, identified as primarily evangelicals. Wilberforce and the Saints did not proclaim their own philanthropy, though some of their supporters did, but they were lambasted for being philanthropic – naive at best, at worst spurious, self-interested and effeminate. After 1807 and more strongly after the 1814 campaign to urge the government to push for worldwide abolition of the trade at the peace negotiations, there was the beginning of the construction of a narrative that made abolition a propitious moment in the history of the nation, one in which Wilberforce and the 'Saints' were the heroes. Equally important, however, in forging links between philanthropy and evangelicalism were the attacks on them by the *Anti-Jacobin Review* and William Cobbett. Their line of attack continued unabated deep into the nineteenth century.

Notes

1 E. Radcliffe, 'Revolutionary writing, moral philosophy, and universal benevolence in the eighteenth century', *Journal of the History of Ideas*, 54 (1993), 229.

2 Quoted in G. M. Ditchfield, 'Rational philanthropy: Theory and practice in the emergence of British Unitarianism, c. 1750–1820', in C. Binfield, G. M. Ditchfield and D. L. Wykes (eds), *Protestant Dissent and Philanthropy in Britain, c. 1660-c. 1920* (Woodbridge: Boydell, 2019), pp. 81–2.

3 A. G. Hill (ed.), *Letters of William Wordsworth: A New Selection* (Oxford: Oxford University Press, 1984), p. 12.

4 Ibid., p. 12.

5 Ibid., pp. 14–16.

6 S. Gill, *William Wordsworth: A Life* (Oxford: Clarendon Press, 1989), p. 87.

7 K. R. Johnston, 'Philanthropy or treason? Wordsworth as "active partisan"', *Studies in Romanticism*, 25 (1986), 374; N. Roe, *Wordsworth and Coleridge: The Radical Years* (Oxford: Clarendon Press, 1988), pp. 276–9; M. T. Davis, '"That odious class of men called democrats": Daniel Isaac Eaton and the Romantics 1794–1795', *History*, 84 (1999), 89–91.

8 Quoted in Roe, *Wordsworth and Coleridge*, p. 112.

9 G. Dyer, *The Complaints of the Poor People of England*, 2nd edn (1793), p. 168.

10 G. Dyer, *A Dissertation on the Theory and Practice of Benevolence* (London: Kearsley, 1795), pp. 35–6.

11 Quoted in Johnston, 'Philanthropy or treason?', 401.

12 J. B. Schneewind, 'Philosophical ideas of charity: some historical reflections', in J. B. Schneewind (ed.), *Giving: Western Ideas of Philanthropy* (Bloomington and Indianapolis: Indiana University Press, 1996), pp. 54–75.

13 *Political and Philosophical Writings of William Godwin*, ed. M. Philp, 7 vols (London: William Pickering, 1993), Vol. III, p. 49.

14 Ibid., p. 115.

15 Ibid., p. 146.

16 Ibid., Vol. IV, pp. 161, 166.

17 Ibid., Vol. II, p. 184.

18 Quoted in Roe, *Wordsworth and Coleridge*, p. 159.

19 *Political and Philosophical Writings of William Godwin*, Vol. VI, p. 160.

20 L. Patton and P. Mann (eds), *The Collected Works of Samuel Taylor Coleridge: Lectures 1795 on Politics and Religion* (London: Routledge & Kegan Paul, 1971), p. xxxvii.

21 13 July 1794: E. L. Griggs (ed.), *Collected Letters of Samuel Taylor Coleridge*, Vol. I, 1785–1800 (Oxford: Clarendon Press, 1956), p. 86.

22 Patton and Mann, *Collected Works of Coleridge*, pp. 46, 163; *The Poems of Alexander Pope*, ed. J. Butt (London: Methuen, 1963), pp. 546–7 ('An Essay on Man', iv, lines 363–8).

23 Patton and Mann, *Collected Works of Coleridge*, pp. 163, 352–3.

24 Ibid., p. 248.

25 Quoted in Roe, *Wordsworth and Coleridge*, p. 174.

26 *London Magazine*, Sept. 1791.

27 *Gentleman's Magazine*, Nov. 1793.

28 *Universal Magazine*, Nov. 1797.

29 *Methodist Magazine*, May and Aug. 1798.

30 *Monthly Magazine*, May 1796.

31 Quoted in A. R. Humphreys, '"The friend of mankind" (1710–60): An aspect of eighteenth-century sensibility', *Review of English Studies*, 24 (1948), 216.

32 Quoted in Radcliffe, 'Revolutionary writing', 234.

33 Quoted in ibid., 235.

34 *Anti-Jacobin*, 11 Dec. 1797, p. 169.

35 Quoted in Radcliffe, 'Revolutionary writing', 235.

36 *Anti-Jacobin*, 5 Feb., 1798; 23 Apr., 1798; 2 July 1798.

37 Radcliffe, 'Revolutionary writing', 235.

38 S. Parr, *A Spital Sermon, preached at Christ Church, upon Easter Tuesday, April 15, 1800*, pp. 6, 11–12; Radcliffe, 'Revolutionary writing', 237–8. For Godwin's reply to Parr, see *Political and Philosophical Writings of William Godwin*, Vol. II, pp. 176–89.

39 J. Fowler, 'Scientific philanthropy and the Society for Bettering the Condition and Increasing the Comforts of the Poor, 1796–1824', in C. Rochester, G. C. Gosling, A. Penn and M. Zimmeck (eds), *The Roots of Voluntary Action: Historical Perspectives on Current Social Policy* (Brighton: Sussex Academic Press, 2011), pp. 171–81, quoting p. 172; see also M. J. D. Roberts, *Making English Morals: Voluntary Association and Moral Reform in England, 1787–1886* (Cambridge: Cambridge University Press, 2004), pp. 63–5, 75–6.

40 M. J. D. Roberts, 'Head versus heart? Voluntary associations and charity organizations in England, c. 1700–1850', in H. Cunningham and J. Innes (eds), *Charity, Philanthropy and Reform: From the 1690s to 1850* (Basingstoke: Macmillan, 1998), pp. 75–7.

41 *The Philanthropist*, I (1811), 'On the duty and pleasure of cultivating benevolent dispositions', pp. 2–5.

42 Ibid., IV (1814), pp. 136–8.

43 Ibid., III (1813), p. 87.

44 Ibid., VI (1816), pp. 1–3.

45 Quoted in Ditchfield, 'Rational philanthropy', p. 90; see also the Liverpool Unitarian, William Roscoe, writing in similar terms to Thomas Jefferson in K. Lloyd and C. Burgoyne, 'The evolution of a transatlantic debate on penal reform, 1780–1830', in Cunningham and Innes (eds), *Charity, Philanthropy and Reform*, p. 216.

46 H. Cunningham, 'The language of patriotism, 1750–1914', *History Workshop Journal*, 12 (1981), 12.

47 E. P. Thompson, *The Making of the English Working Class* (London: Gollancz, 1963), pp. 613, 775; *Manchester Guardian*, 12 Nov. 1831.

48 They are listed in *Access to Archives* under 'philanthropy'.

49 J. Brewster, *An Oration Delivered on the Removal of the Lodge of Philanthropy, No. 19, Stockton upon Tees* (1796).

50 *Morning Post*, 6 Jan. 1806; *Hampshire Chronicle*, 26 Dec. 1814.

51 R. Postgate, *The Builders' History* (London: National Federation of Building Trades Operatives, 1923), p. 19.

52 G. Finlayson, *Citizen, State and Social Welfare in Britain 1830–1990* (Oxford: Clarendon Press, 1994), p. 31. Ten friendly societies with 'philanthropic' in their title were listed in the 'Return of Friendly Societies certified or registered under the Friendly Societies Act 1850', *Parliamentary Papers* 1852, Paper No. 39.

53 W. Beveridge, *Voluntary Action: A Report on the Methods of Social Advance* (London: George Allen & Unwin, 1948), pp. 8–9; B. Harris and P. Bridgen, 'Introduction: The "mixed economy of welfare" and the historiography of welfare provision', pp. 4–5 and D. Weinbren, 'Supporting self-help: Charity, mutuality, and reciprocity in nineteenth-century Britain', pp. 67–88, in B. Harris and P. Bridgen (eds), *Charity and Mutual Aid in Europe and North America Since 1800* (London: Routledge, 2007).

54 *The Reign of Philanthropy; or the Auspices of the New Ministry: A Poem* (London: H. D. Symonds, 1806), pp. 3, 8.

55 *Gentleman's Magazine*, Apr. 1793, 324–5.

56 *The Times*, 22 Apr. 1799.

57 *Gentleman's Magazine*, Feb. 1807, 156; Aug. 1807, 755.

58 Quoted in D. T. Andrew, 'On reading charity sermons: Eighteenth-century Anglican solicitation and exhortation', *Journal of Ecclesiastical History*, 43 (1992), 585.

59 *The Love of Christ the Source of Genuine Philanthropy: A Discourse on the Death of John Thornton, Esq.* (London, 1791), p. 48.

60 W. Wilberforce, *A Practical View of the Prevailing Religious System of Professed Christians, in the Higher and Middle Classes in this Country, Contrasted with Real Christianity* (1797; Glasgow: William Collins, 1829), p. 383.
61 T. Rennell, *Benevolence Exclusively an Evangelical Virtue: A Sermon Preached before the Governors of Addenbroke's Hospital, 2 July 1795*, pp. 16, 23.
62 Dyer, *Benevolence*, p. 19.
63 Ibid., pp. 17, 5, 3.
64 F. K. Brown, *Fathers of the Victorians: The Age of Wilberforce* (Cambridge: Cambridge University Press, 1961), pp. 317–60.
65 *Town and Country Magazine*, Dec. 1790, 587; *Literary Magazine and British Review*, Mar. 1791, 231.
66 *Scots' Magazine*, June 1791; *The Bee*, 30. Nov. 1791, 133; *Northampton Mercury*, 21 Apr. 1792.
67 *Morning Post*, 31 May 1804.
68 *Morning Chronicle*, 10 July 1804; *Manchester Mercury*, 10 July 1804.
69 J. R. Oldfield, *Popular Politics and British Anti-Slavery: The Mobilisation of Public Opinion against the Slave Trade 1787–1807* (Manchester: Manchester University Press, 1995); S. Drescher, *Capitalism and Antislavery: British Mobilization in Comparative Perspective* (London: Macmillan, 1986).
70 Oldfield, *Popular Politics*, pp. 114, 140.
71 *Universal Magazine of Knowledge and Pleasure*, Dec. 1790, 276; Mar. 1791, 175.
72 *Leeds Intelligencer*, 3 May 1791; *Northampton Mercury*, 7 May 1791; *Chester Chronicle*, 3 Feb. 1792; *Lincoln, Rutland and Stamford Mercury*, 23 Mar. 1792.
73 *Chester Chronicle*, 3 Apr. 1807.
74 *Leeds Mercury*, 9 July 1814.
75 *Morning Post*, 25 Aug. 1814.
76 Brown, *Fathers of the Victorians*, pp. 156–83, quoting pp. 181–2.
77 *Cobbett's Weekly Political Register*, 5 June, 29 May, 12 June 1802.
78 Ibid., 9 July 1803; 27 Nov. 1802; 10 July 1802.
79 Brown, *Fathers of the Victorians*, 363–9, quoting p. 366.
80 Ibid., pp. 369–71.
81 Ibid., p. 371.
82 Quoted in G. M. Ditchfield, 'English Rational Dissent and philanthropy, c. 1760–c. 1810', in Cunningham and Innes (eds), *Charity, Philanthropy and Reform*, p. 195.

7

The Times and the telescope: Philanthropy, 1815–50

No one in the early nineteenth century could predict what future philanthropy might have, if indeed it had a future at all. A love of humankind could potentially be expressed in any number of ways. It might be secular or inspired by religion. Its politics might be radical or conservative. It might focus on neighbourhood or on the world. It might express itself in private life or through institutions. It might refer to the giving of money or simply to an attitude of benevolence towards fellow human beings. As it turned out 'philanthropy' was used in all these ways and others. There was a gender component to it, men and women being ascribed different roles, and male philanthropists being lambasted by critics for their effeminacy. Philanthropy came to be both praised as one of the glories of the nation and fiercely criticised as harmful to the national interest and demoralising to recipients of its largesse. To be called a philanthropist might bring down on you encomiums of praise or the most withering criticism, your motives, behaviour, even your body language held up to ridicule and scorn.

In this chapter I explore how these battles over the ownership and meaning of philanthropy were fought out over thirty-five years to the point where some of the potentialities of philanthropy were effectively closed off, but where philanthropy remained contentious. A leading player in these debates was *The Times*, fiercely critical of most philanthropy and philanthropists. One of the points it made was that philanthropists were too concerned with problems across the world to the neglect of those at home, what Charles Dickens was to call 'telescopic philanthropy'.

Philanthropy as a feeling

Samuel Johnson's eighteenth-century definition of philanthropy as 'Love of mankind. Good nature', a disposition to delight in the sight of human happiness, continued to have resonance through the first half of the nineteenth century. When peace came, temporarily, in 1814 there were many celebrations. *Wright's Leeds Intelligencer* reported how at the 'Public Rejoicings' at Skipton in Craven 2,000 of the poor were given dinner while 'the fashionable walked upon the terrace of the Castle, with hearts expanded by philanthropy, on this glorious occasion'.[1] Watching 'the happy multitude' of the poor dining, the well-to-do felt good about themselves. With an improvement in trade in September 1817 the *Manchester Exchange Herald* claimed that 'almost everyone exhibits that satisfaction which the philanthropist loves to be seated on the faces of his fellow-men'. 'Philanthropists and patriots', wrote the *Bath Chronicle* in October 1817, 'must receive pleasure in observing the laudable exertions to establish Savings Banks'.[2] The philanthropists' pleasure came from 'observing' what was being done, not by doing anything. The healthy, clean and 'apparently happy creatures' emerging from the St Giles's Poor House for a day at Christmas 1823 was 'a truly gratifying scene to the philanthropist'. The throngs of people visiting an art exhibition in Westminster Hall in 1844 was 'a sight that might do good to the heart of the philanthropist', just as the Isle of Thanet Horticultural Show in 1847 was 'to the philanthropist ... a most delightful spectacle'.[3] It was from scenes, sights and spectacles that a philanthropist derived pleasure. He or she was a spectator, an observer, the sights seen doing good to her or his heart.

Things read about but not seen could be equally gratifying. 'The progressive advances in cultivation of intellect, in virtue, and in happiness' of the people of Haiti in 1821 afforded 'pure and generous' 'grounds of satisfaction' to the philanthropist. In 1837 improved relationships between Great Britain and the United States accorded 'the most benevolent delight' to 'the philosopher and philanthropist'. For the Bishop of Winchester, reporting in 1847 on missions in Borneo, 'it must be a pleasing reflection to the philanthropist that so many of our fellow-creatures are thus gradually relieved from ignorance, barbarism, and self-destruction'. By contrast, the 'truly heart-rending' disclosures in the Children's Employment Commission of 1842 'must excite the most painful emotions in the mind of every true philanthropist'.[4] The philanthropist, it seems, was someone who delighted in scenes or reports of humans happy and improving, and was upset by reports of the opposite. Philanthropy was a cast of mind. It did not require you to do anything.

Philanthropy and national identity

More commonly, however, philanthropy was invoked in matters that affected the nation or the empire as a whole and as a valued element in the nation's identity. Philanthropists were frequently ranked alongside 'statesmen' as the people who might bring about a solution to deep-seated problems. 'The education of the poor is an essential object of the philanthropist and statesman', it was claimed at a meeting in support of Robert Owen's plans.[5] In the debates on the Poor Law in 1833 John Smith MP and William Allen urged 'the deep attention of the statesman and the philanthropist [to] what relates to the morals and comfortable subsistence of the great mass of the people in every country – the poor'. It was with education in mind that Edward Baines 'would lay it on the conscience of every Christian and philanthropist to aid in the moral reformation of the most degraded portions of society'. There was, wrote *The Times* in 1847, a new interest in the condition of the people, 'matters which affect the happiness of a nation too deeply to be neglected by the philanthropist, the lawyer, or the statesman'.[6]

It was not only the poor and degraded in Britain whose reformation was held up as the task of the philanthropist. Ireland was rarely out of mind. *The Times* in the 1840s thought that there was nothing with 'so many claims on the attention of the philanthropist and the legislator as the condition of the Irish peasantry'.[7] Infanticide in India, too, demanded attention. *The Times* had been confident in 1824 that 'All that the warmest philanthropist need require of [the British government] is to pursue the path on which it has already entered', but in 1833 J. Peggs thought more needed to be done: 'It behoves every philanthropist to seek the abolition of this unnatural and murderous custom.'[8] The issue of reform in Turkey, urged *The Times* in 1838, was 'well worthy of fixing the serious attention of the philanthropist, the economist, and the statesman'. And there was the persistent problem of the British West Indies; in 1840 *The Times* claimed that 'the present state of the British West India colonies is a subject that engages the attention of every British statesman and philanthropist'.[9] The 'wisdom of the statesman' and 'the humanity of the philanthropist' could work towards the same ends.

Politicians, however, were well aware that, strong though their feelings or declarations of philanthropy might be, they were wise to associate them with an even higher dedication to their country. Earl Fitzwilliam, at a public dinner held in his honour at Sheffield in 1823, stressed his local ties and commitments, for 'to carry that philanthropy to the scorched inhabitant of the sultry Equator, or the frozen Esquimaux under the Pole, was impracticable; because, however expansive were a man's intentions, they must always be controlled and limited by his means of practical benevolence'. Two days later in a speech at Plymouth George Canning, the Foreign Secretary, hoped that his 'heart beats as high for the general interest of humanity – I hope that I have as friendly a disposition towards other nations of the earth, as any one who vaunts his philanthropy most highly: but I am contented to confess, that in the conduct of political affairs, the grand object of my contemplation is the interest of England'.[10] In 1830 the rising young Whig politician Lord Morpeth, speaking as a potential representative for Yorkshire, declared that 'while as a patriot and a philanthropist, I cannot help expressing my general wishes for the triumphant and bloodless march of freedom in every corner of the globe', yet it was necessary to have more limited goals in mind, in his case the abolition of slavery.[11] These speeches, both Whig and Liberal Conservative, point to a widely held mode of discourse: pronounce your general sympathy for humanity across the globe, but declare such unboundaried philanthropy to be impractical – national and local interests must come first. You could be, or so Morpeth hoped, both 'a patriot and a philanthropist', but such a combination entailed choices, and the choice to be made involved a sacrifice of universal philanthropy. There was a 'moral geography', a boundary to philanthropy set by what could be deemed to be patriotic or, in Canning's words, 'in the interests of England'.[12] Philanthropy, *tout court*, was impractical. And practicality in Victorian Britain was highly valued.

The phrase 'universal philanthropy', battered by the experience of the French Revolution, dropped out of circulation, its use increasingly confined to radicals and those on the fringes of power and influence. Robert Owen, for example, was criticised by the *Morning Chronicle* for his utopian ideas and for hoping to inspire members of a community 'with sentiments of universal benevolence and philanthropy'.[13] People who had died and were remembered for their 'universal philanthropy' were all radical: Thomas Day, Charles James Fox and Major Cartwright, the latter's philanthropy extending to 'Spain, Italy, Naples, Greece, and the different states of South America', capped by his donation of his body for dissection to promote, in the words of his will, 'the good of mankind'.[14] Some continued to invoke the idea of 'universal philanthropy'. Collecting money in London in 1836 to relieve victims of a fire in New York, Dr Bowring MP declared that the aim 'was to show to the whole world the unbounded philanthropy by which the people of Great Britain were actuated towards not only the inhabitants of New York, but towards the whole family of mankind'. He put his case 'upon the principles of universal philanthropy'. In 1847 he was still hoping that 'what was called the spirit of nationality would be lost in a large philanthropy, embracing the whole world'.[15] But Bowring was a man without much influence.

Philanthropy, then, had to proclaim its patriotism. This, for many, did not mean confining it to the boundaries of Britain, it meant Britain being able to take pride in its global role. Philanthropy helped to forge the reputation and identity of the nation. A fund set up in 1815 to relieve sufferers from the war in Germany was, so it claimed, 'eminently distinguished among those unrivalled monuments of British philanthropy and beneficence, which will grace the descriptive page of future historians'.[16] In the year of revolution, 1830, welcoming events in France, the *Western Times* of Exeter, in a long leading article on 'Philanthropy', described how the paper had concentrated on foreign news in order to promote in its readers 'enlightened, philanthropic, and Christian views' rather than 'a contracted patriotism':

> Philanthropy, like charity, it is true, must begin at home; but it must not stop there; and when our own necessities are provided for, and our own liberties secured, then we must range abroad, and do what in us lies to provide for the political necessities of our fellow men, and guard and defend the liberties of other nations.

The editor was confident that 'No longer will the people of England be indifferent to the state of France, of Portugal, and of Greece. – No longer will they sanction the minister of a free people to put chains on an unwilling nation, or to support legitimacy, unless it be for the liberties of the nations'.[17]

Philanthropy here was being seen as a matter of foreign policy, a theme taken up in a series of letters by 'A Clergyman of the Diocese of Hereford' in 1837. Delighted with the general election results that returned the Whigs to power, he was confident that

> The reign ... of political and individual philanthropy will happily be extended. Oh, what a noble yet hitherto spurned character is the political philanthropist! A far prouder statue is Lord Brougham's, or Lord Melbourne's, when battling with the first of the realm for the independence, civilization, and education of mankind, far and near, than any position of the Duke of Wellington's on the field of Waterloo.[18]

In this vision, the future of mankind, 'far and near', was to be in the hands of 'the political philanthropist'.

The response to the French Revolution, in pitting philanthropy against patriotism, did much to tarnish its reputation, but it also reinforced the belief, originating in the mid-eighteenth century, that the benevolence, charity and philanthropy of the British stood preeminent among nations. This was the leading theme of William Seward Heald's *The Empire of Philanthropy; with a Portraiture of British Excellence as a National Example; a Dramatic Poem* (1822). Heald held up 'his benevolent and beloved Country as the great national example of Philanthropy to the world'. Philanthropy herself, one of the characters in the poem, declares that

> To the whole earth for empire I lay claim
> To make the spacious world a Heaven, I aim.

To this end it was '*Philanthropic Britain*' that led the way in spreading good around the world. Europe, Asia, Africa and America unite to sing:

> Britannia rose at Heaven's command,
>   With ardent flow of gen'rous fire –
> Warm is her heart, and kind her hand.
>   To bless mankind her high desire.
> Blessings she sends, with sails unfurl'd
>   Her Philanthropic range – the *World*.

There was only one big task left for Britain 'in this enlightened, philanthropic day', to free the slaves.

In France 'modern philanthropy condemned the benefactor of his country [Louis XVI] to a scaffold', whereas in England the Prince Regent had silk made up to help the Spitalfields weavers in their distress and 'no man need be ashamed to imitate a Prince in an act of useful philanthropy'.[19] In an appeal for the 'Distressed Poor in Northern Parts of their Metropolis' in 1817 the committee organising it was 'animated by their knowledge of that national philanthropy which has mitigated distress in every part of the wide world'. Greeks in Constantinople in 1822 appealed to fellow Greeks in London, 'the centre of philanthropy; you live amongst a people always famed for their generous feelings towards the unfortunate, for their dislike to tyranny, and their support of the oppressed'. When the Court of Common Council in London voted £500 for refugee Poles, 'acknowledging the obligations of a wide and extended philanthropy', it recalled similar donations to Greeks, Spaniards, Russians and Portuguese.[20]

People seeking to raise funds constantly tried to tap into what was seen as a national tradition. In 1825 the newly formed Society for the Prevention of Cruelty to Animals sought to draw on this and to extend its remit to animals:

> Our country is distinguished by the number and variety of its benevolent institutions. A tender care for our suffering brethren, of every colour and complexion, of every clime and country, of every age and condition of life, has been nurtured by many admirable institutions, all actuated by one common philanthropy, and all breathing the pure spirit of Christian charity and good will towards mankind.[21]

In the following year Alexis James Doxat, writing for support for Spitalfields weavers, described how 'under the banners of charity, we see men of the most opposite courses in the political world assemble continually and with alacrity, to explore every source of relief which British philanthropy can afford to humanity, not only in these realms, but in every part of the world where British influence can extend'.[22] Such philanthropy marked Britain out from all other countries – it was a source of national pride.

Philanthropy, evangelicals and political economy

It is easy to assume that philanthropy had an agenda that was broadly progressive and humanitarian. In fact, many philanthropists came under attack for their perceived lack of humanity. Political economy lay at the root of this. For many evangelical philanthropists the laws of political economy were seen as working in harmony with the laws of nature, both sets of laws under the oversight of God whose own interventions were in accordance with them. If God in his Providence inflicted plague or famine it was not random but as punishment for disobedience, for failure to keep to the laws. Nations as well as individuals could be punished. Wilberforce, for example, thought that Providence would bear down upon the nation if nothing was done about slavery, manifestly not free labour, 'in the way of natural consequence'; slavery offended the laws both of nature and of political economy.[23]

Philanthropy was by the 1820s closely linked to evangelicalism. Evangelicals were a dominant force in the proliferation in the late eighteenth and early nineteenth centuries of voluntary societies and institutions aimed at remedying all kinds of perceived ills.[24] Yet the term 'evangelical' was no more unchanging than 'philanthropy'. In the 1820s and 1830s evangelicalism was splitting and diversifying. The older generation, identified with what in retrospect in 1844 was termed 'the Clapham Sect', felt threatened by the criticisms flung at them by charismatic preachers, the most prominent of them Edward Irving. The pre-millenarianism that the latter preached, the belief that Christ would return to earth in the very near future, chimed in with the fashionable romanticism of the age and heralded an impatience with the established and methodical ways of the first generation of evangelicals. Whereas the first generation was inclined to believe in political economy, the pre-millenarians opposed it. At a different level, relations between evangelicals within the Church of England and those in Dissent grew more distant and hostile as Dissenters launched campaigns against the Church's privileged position. Dissent remained loyal to the older reforming tradition within evangelicalism. In the Church of England evangelicalism became associated with conservatism.[25]

The birth of philanthropy coincided with the birth and rise to prominence of political economy. Political economists preached market solutions to social problems. They were above all concerned that wages should be determined by the market. Earning a living through wages was fundamental both to a successful economy and to personal morality. In 1824 William Ellis, a young utilitarian, reflected on the impact that political economy had made:

> To convince the public, twenty or thirty years ago, of the goodness of a charity, it was sufficient to shew that the objects relieved were in a state of real distress ... But now, that the circumstances are more generally known, on which the condition of the labouring classes depends, all former reasonings on the subject of charity ... are invalidated ... The condition of the labouring classes with regard to the necessaries and comforts of life, is evidently determined by the rate of wages.[26]

Start giving to beggars or to the poor, it was said, and you began to create dependency. '[B]enevolence is useless or mischievous without knowledge', and the knowledge that was required was knowledge of political economy.

Existing charitable practices came under heavy fire. Nothing did more harm, it was said in 1815, than 'the misplaced benevolence of the charitable and humane', their 'injudicious benevolence' that so encouraged vagrancy and begging.[27] In the 1820s claims were being made for 'philanthropy' as the means by which political economy could set bounds to unlimited charity. Teaching the poor 'the knowledge of the laws which regulate wages', it was said, 'depends in a great measure upon the exertions of enlightened philanthropists'.[28]

In the 1840s John Stuart Mill reiterated these arguments. Writing to Henry S. Chapman in New Zealand in November 1844 he reflected on 'the state of the public mind': 'There is a prodigious current setting in every day more strongly, of superficial philanthropy. English benevolence can no longer be accused of confining itself to niggers and other distant folks; on the contrary everybody is all agog to do something for the poor.'[29] Mill set out his views in a long review article for the *Edinburgh Review* in April 1845, thinking it 'a most useful thing to enter a protest against the intolerable mass of pseudo-philanthropy now getting into vogue'.[30] Provocatively, Mill traced back what he called 'this philanthropic movement' to alleviate the condition of the labouring classes to the much-hated Robert Malthus who had argued that prudence on the part of those classes was the sole means by which conditions could be improved. But the means advocated by 'the present philanthropic movement', these 'new philanthropists', were very different from those of Malthus for they interfered with the iron laws of political economy whereby wage rates were at the mercy of supply and demand. Mill proposed a better education system and justice rather than kindness as the means by which conditions would improve. Justice would mean the repeal of the Corn Laws, the Game Laws and anything else that interfered with what he saw as the free course of human activity and fostered bad relations between the classes.[31]

Mill was a radical reformer but he was also a political economist and what he saw amongst these 'new philanthropists' was a willingness to ignore fundamental economic tenets. Far from philanthropy being at one with political economy, it seemed to be at odds with it. Moreover, with philanthropy expanding its repertoire to focus on the poor of England, there was a 'philanthropic movement' staffed by 'new philanthropists'. There were to be, as we shall see, quite a number of new philanthropies to come, but this was the only one identified by its critic rather than its proponents. But the question Mill raised continued to trouble future generations as well as his own: could philanthropy co-exist with capitalism? Or did it undermine it?

Mill was by no means alone in the mid-1840s in sensing that philanthropy was becoming a power in the land. Charles Greville, eminent diarist, wrote in 1844 that 'We are just now overrun with philanthropy, and God knows where it will stop, or whither it will lead us'. Greville was referring to the way in which legislation, such as factory reform, was being proposed or passed under the influence of philanthropy. When Lord Ashley's Ten Hours Bill came before Parliament, Greville reflected that 'a philanthropic agitator is more dangerous than a repealer, either of the Union [with Ireland] or the Corn Laws'.[32] It was extraordinary testament to the power that philanthropy was thought to possess for the Union and the Corn Laws lay at the heart of politics.

Mill was too sweeping in assuming that all philanthropists were ignoring the lessons of political economy. On the contrary, an adherence to political economy acted as a guide to many philanthropists in their attitudes to the Poor Laws and to factory reform. The strongest impact came from Thomas

Chalmers, Professor of Divinity at the University of Edinburgh. Deeply influenced by Malthus's fears about unrestrained population growth, he argued for the end to all Poor Laws. Without that, he wrote in 1832, 'every other device which philanthropy can suggest, or even an enlightened political economy can sanction, will turn out to be futile and abortive'. He was critical of much philanthropy for ignoring this. More positively, he saw a clear role for 'a Christian philanthropist' to teach the poor morality and especially the morality of restricting births in accordance with what he saw as the lessons of political economy.[33]

The 1834 Poor Law Amendment Act did not end the Poor Laws but it radically transformed them in ways that Chalmers could approve. Not surprisingly, it was broadly supported by philanthropists associated with the Clapham Sect. A majority of anti-slavery MPs either voted in favour of the New Poor Law or abstained.[34] Often generous themselves in relieving poverty, they also believed that any gifting should be voluntary and come from the heart as well as the head; above all it must not be legal as enshrined in the Poor Laws. Poverty for them was divinely ordained, setting a test for donors as to how much and to whom they should give. For Robert Montgomery 'The sublime cause of Philanthropy is greatly strengthened by the poor', the dependence of the poor the greatest of the 'benefits conferred by the poor upon the rich'.[35] Evangelicals of this kind agreed with the principles underlying the new law – less eligibility for those in receipt of relief, the workhouse test for the unemployed. The old Poor Law, they argued, subsiding wages, ran counter to the principles of political economy, encouraged the kind of growth of population that Malthus deplored and discouraged the poor from taking responsibility for their own welfare.

The New Poor Law, however, met with strong opposition. *The Times* shocked readers with the virulence of its disgust with the new workhouse test, but it was by no means alone in its stance.[36] Preaching on 'Christian Philanthropy' in a Spital Sermon in aid of London's hospitals in 1835, and with reference to the New Poor Law, James Anderson urged his congregation not to suffer 'the impulses of the heart to be deadened, and the sanctions of the Gospel to be weakened, by theories of utilitarian expediency; nor the doctrines of political economy to supersede the broad, unalterable principles of Christian Truth'.[37] The High Church *British Critic* in 1840 denounced political economy as 'this anti-Christian philanthropy; which most assiduously and disinterestedly forwards and invents all schemes of benefit and relief which throw the burden of the poverty of the poor upon themselves, and promote economy in giving'. 'H.O.' writing from Oxford in the same year thought that 'Christian philanthropy at the present time cannot take up a point more worthy of itself than the unchristian, cruel enactments' of the Poor Law, but as he was well aware many prominent in 'Christian philanthropy' were defenders of it. For *The Times* itself, 'The duty of providing for the poor has never been more overlooked than in our own age of boasted philanthropy'.[38]

Philanthropists were also under attack for their opposition to factory legislation. On this issue, as on others, evangelicals were divided. Those who accepted the laws of political economy as consonant with natural laws and with God's ordinances were instinctively opposed to any restrictions on the freedom that should determine the relations between employer and worker. Those, on the other hand, described by Boyd Hilton as 'the pentecostal, pre-millenarian, adventist, and revivalist elements' in evangelicalism provided much of the leadership of the factory reform agitation; both Michael Sadler and his successor as parliamentary leader for reform, Lord Ashley, were close to that wing of evangelicalism. Ashley frequently complained in the 1840s that he had little support from evangelical MPs, a reference to the Clapham Sect side of evangelicalism.[39] Such people were vulnerable to the accusation that they cared much more for black slaves in the West Indies than for 'little white slaves' in Britain's factories.

The Times **and 'telescopic philanthropy'**

In *Bleak House*, published in 1852, Charles Dickens gave the title 'Telescopic philanthropy' to his chapter introducing Mrs Jellyby. Dickens contrasted Mrs Jellyby's chaotic household and her neglect of her own children with her ambitions for growing coffee and spreading civilisation at Borrioboola-Gha on the left bank of the Niger. Esther Summerson, approaching and entering this household, was immediately drawn to one of Mrs Jellyby's children, his head stuck between railings, to another who had fallen down stairs and then to the eldest daughter who was required to take down dictation from her mother for letters to and about Africa. Amiable as Mrs Jellyby might be, Dickens left no doubt that her priorities were woefully wrong. And it was philanthropy that he was targeting. Mrs Jellyby's unctuous aide, Mr Quale, had the nerve to introduce himself as 'a philanthropist'.

Dickens here coined a new phrase for a phenomenon that had for long attracted the critics of philanthropy. Supporters of the slave trade and slavery, under criticism from philanthropists, counter-attacked by pointing to bad conditions in England that philanthropy seemed to ignore.

The Times was the most persistent and powerful critic of philanthropy. Under the editorship of John Barnes from 1819 until his death in 1841 *The Times* built up a reputation encapsulated in coming to be known as 'The Thunderer' after it had 'thundered out' an article in 1829 protesting against an attempt to conceal the truth about a suicide.[40]

There were three prongs to *The Times*'s critique of philanthropy. The first was that it was all talk. 'In these days of busy and garrulous philanthropy we hear of few Frys and still fewer Howards', Fry and Howard the exemplars of active philanthropy. Attacking Lord Dudley Stuart's philanthropy on behalf of the Poles, the paper claimed that 'post-prandial eloquence … often forms the sole donation of the talking philanthropist to the cause he advocates'.

'Talking' philanthropy was a cover for 'charlatanism' or 'the quackery existing in most pursuits [that] has grown to a fearful extent in that vaguest of all professions, the avowed object of which is the happiness of the whole human race, or the amelioration of the condition of certain classes of our fellow-creatures'.[41] 'The present', claimed *The Times* in 1846, 'is undoubtedly, as far as talking goes, the age of universal philanthropy. Humanity never had such hosts of friends'.[42]

The second prong of the critique dug deeper into the character of philanthropists; they were deficient in manliness. In 1832 Sir Charles Wetherell, set the tone; arguing in favour of capital punishment for forgery, he denounced the opposition of 'the pedantic and absurd, *soi-disant* philanthropists – the smelling-bottle and white handkerchief gentry of the present day'.[43] Proper men, was the subtext, did not use smelling bottles or white handkerchiefs. More open attack came in the 1840s. In 1846 there was a possibility, a danger thought *The Times*, that country gentlemen might enter into an unholy alliance with philanthropists over the issue of duties on the import of sugar. But

> nature never intended their manly forms and magnanimous minds, their open countenances and honest tongues for the trade of philanthropy. How in the world will they get up unction and tears in time? It takes a life to acquire the proper roll of the eye, and that particular nasal twang, without which the most cogent reasoning, the most heartrending appeals will not go down.

Even ten years of daily practice would not 'enable the Duke of Richmond or Mr Miles to come over one old woman. It is not in them'.[44] Philanthropists were not 'manly', the adjective implying magnanimity, openness and honesty. *The Times* attacked Buxton and others for engaging in 'mere platform parades in favour of savage tribes' rather than in the scandal of 'infant labour' in factories; they were, it said, 'self-perfuming coxcombs'.[45] When a Society for the Improvement of the Condition of the Labouring Classes was set up in London in 1845 *The Times* did 'not see the least prospect whatever of their emerging into a more masculine tone of operation than has usually characterized the encroachment of philanthropy into the province of commerce'.[46] In short, philanthropy was not properly gendered. It was not simply that women were involved in it, though that was bad enough: Jacob Omnium in 1845 mocked 'the spiritual tea parties of the hen philanthropists of Clapham'.[47] More important was that the men with their rolling eyes and nasal twangs, their body language marking them out from ordinary mortals, were deficient in manliness and masculinity. They were out of touch with the real world, the world of commerce, impractical and softhearted in their dealings with crime and other social problems.

Neglect of home problems in favour of distant ones formed the third and most persistent prong of *The Times*'s attack on philanthropy. The criticism nearly always emanated from the West Indies or was related to slavery and was first voiced by West Indian planters defending slavery in the 1780s.[48] It resurfaced in the 1810s and 1820s at precisely the time anti-slavery advocates were becoming more active in pressure and propaganda and began to be put more stridently and consistently from the early 1830s. Wilberforce was alert to the danger. Writing to Macaulay in 1817 when conditions in Britain were severe he advised not proceeding with a bill for the registration of slaves, for 'When Parliament meets, the whole nation, depend upon it, will be looking for relief from its own burthens, and it would betray an ignorance of all tact to talk to them in such circumstances of the sufferings of the slaves in the West Indies. We should specially guard against appearing to have a world of our own, and to have little sympathy with the sufferings of our countrymen'.[49] It was shrewd advice, but on its own not enough to guard against accusations that philanthropists did indeed live in a world of their own without sympathy for their fellow-countrymen.

Noting in 1823 that the law permitted a master to have his servant flogged, *The Times* thought it 'would not be amiss for our philanthropists to repeal degrading statutes like this, before they turn their entire attention to the West Indian slaves'. The paper gave publicity to a pamphlet by Lord Darnley that urged attention to the Irish poor and, as *The Times* summarised it, 'reprobating the fantastic and perverse philanthropy which leads men to undertake wild-goose chases over the most distant quarters of the earth – to Greece, the West Indies, the East Indies, Sierra Leone – on a search for remote misery or slavery, while they forget the supplications of wretched sufferers at their own doors'.[50]

Neglect of home problems was linked to an equal concern with the prominence and range of philanthropy and its disastrous consequences. In its correspondence columns, responding to 'Publius' who had criticised West Indian proprietors for blaming their ill-fortune on 'the interference of meddling philanthropists', 'A West Indian Proprietor' replied that 'the inconsistencies of our modern philanthropists are so numerous that they almost cease to excite surprise'.[51] A key phrase here was 'modern philanthropy', the adjective always conveying criticism. 'An Inhabitant of Demerara' took up the theme, attacking 'modern philanthropy, whose course is everywhere marked with misery, and often with disorder'. He went on to deplore the growing influence in the House of Commons of 'the party, formerly denominated "Saints", and now "Philanthropists"'.[52]

If in the House of Commons 'philanthropists' were growing in influence, in the country at large, claimed 'An Inhabitant of Demerara', things were even worse:

> their labours are discoverable in every village! Busily employed in plans which subdue the spirit, cripple the energies, and destroy the industry of the people; everywhere inviting humiliation and mendicity, but nowhere industry and independence. Here we find a society for some

new 'philanthropic' object or another – there, an hospital for the reception of the victims of increasing misery. In this place is founded a 'Home Missionary Society' – in that, conspicuously stands a 'Magdalen Asylum' to receive the unfortunate victims of growing vice! Until the land is covered with 'Philanthropic Societies', and establishments of every kind, instead of industrious and high spirited men! Instead of 'a bold peasantry, a country's pride'.[53]

In its tone and in its coverage this letter captures a message that the critics of philanthropy and philanthropists never tired of reiterating in the second quarter of the century, the climax coming in the late 1840s.

With the British slave trade abolished in 1807 and slavery itself in British possessions in 1833 the philanthropists had achieved their primary goals in their major field of endeavour. For a time the momentum was with them. Gladstone in 1849 recalled that 'In 1835 … philanthropy was at high-water-mark in this country; an aborigines committee was appointed; the Colonial-office was unable to check the excesses of philanthropic feeling … Of late years philanthropy had been at low-water mark, or rather at a discount'.[54]

With its achievements behind it, it was not surprising that the anti-slavery movement began to fragment. It was not for lack of issues to campaign on. Most immediate was concern that the 'apprenticeship' that was supposed to ease the transition from slave to free labour bore too close a resemblance to slavery. More long-term were the question of what to do about the slave trade carried on by other countries, whether to boycott slave-grown produce, whether sugar produced in the free labour British Caribbean should be protected in the British market, and how to help repair the damage done to Africa by slavery and the slave trade. Flashpoints flared over the exploration of the Niger supported by philanthropists, the use of the Royal Navy in attempts to suppress the Atlantic slave trade, and the question of whether slave-grown sugar should be discriminated against. Criticism, relatively muted up to 1833, felt fewer constraints thereafter.

In 1832 Thomas Fowell Buxton, perhaps the individual most targeted by the critics, was taken to task by a West Indian plantation owner, who contrasted treatment of the slaves with the long hours and Sunday work at Buxton's brewery, the slaves better treated than 'your labourers obtain though under the vertical rays of your philanthropy'. Gladstone administered a milder reproof in 1836 when Buxton proposed the setting up of a committee to inquire into the scheme whereby former slaves became apprentices: 'He could not but think that there was some little misdirected philanthropy here which might very well find objects of its sympathy nearer home' – Gladstone had earlier referred to children working twelve hours a day in factories.[55]

In 1840 the formation of the Society for the Extinction of the Slave Trade and for the Civilization of Africa, inaugurated with Prince Albert in the chair, and lauded at its outset as 'a great movement of Christian philanthropy', soon became the focus of attack.[56] When there was a meeting in

Norwich to support it, the Buxton and Gurney families prominent, 'flighty philanthropists' as *The Times* called them, Chartists were prominent in drawing attention to their neglect of problems at home. *The Times* highlighted another problem with the scheme: 'these self-styled philanthropists … deliberately propose to sacrifice thousands of their countrymen at the shrine of self-conceit, by enticing them to settle' in a climate where death rates for whites were notoriously high. Reviewing a pamphlet on schemes for the extinction of the slave trade, 'the misguided philanthropy of these crack-brained enthusiasts' such as Buxton was again to the fore.[57] Members of the Provisional Committee of the Society, noted a Correspondent, supported the New Poor Law: 'these boasting pretenders to philanthropy and patriotism … these friends of humanity towards the blacks stand forward as the unblushing advocates of the most grinding inhumanity towards the whites'. When reports of the failure of the Niger expedition came through, they should, hoped *The Times*, 'consign African philanthropy to everlasting ridicule and scorn'. The philanthropists, 'these charlatans', should be regarded with 'disgust and scorn … It is really sickening to think of them'.[58]

There was no escape for the Buxtons and Gurneys. When prison conditions in Norfolk and Suffolk were shown to be bad, what more, asked *The Times*, could you expect of 'your professing philanthropists … Their humanity is always in the horizon, and, like the horizon, it is always flying before them. What is more to be complained of, it is always lavished more generously on distant than on proximate objects. Its intenseness varies directly as the distance from home'.[59] George Eliot inserted a comment to the same effect in *Middlemarch*, set in the 1830s, reporting a newspaper's hostile reaction to Mr Brooke's candidacy for Parliament: 'we all know the wag's definition of a philanthropist: a man whose charity increases directly as the square of the distance'.[60] *The Times* did not let go of the topic: 'Was philanthropy', it asked, 'banished from our shores to the wilds of Australia, and the deserts of Africa, because she could literally find no sufficient object for her bounty in our own and the sister island?' '[T]hat peculiar section of ostentatious and meddling philanthropists who have become notorious under the title of the British and Foreign Anti-Slavery Society' were soon under attack, not least for seeing themselves as 'philanthropy impersonated'. Whether or not they did see themselves as impersonating philanthropy, *The Times*, highlighting the difficulties of the Niger expedition, distinguished between 'that humbug which prefers cheap philanthropy to costly and self-denying good deeds'.[61]

It was a commonplace to associate the Niger expedition and other philanthropic ventures with Exeter Hall, the meeting place in the Strand in London for evangelical societies. Opened in 1831, its largest hall seated 4,000. In his review of a book about the Niger expedition, published in 1848, Charles Dickens opened with the assertion that 'it might be laid as a very good general rule of social and political guidance, that whatever Exeter Hall champions, is the thing by no means to be done … The African Expedition … is in no respect an exception to the rule. Exeter Hall was hot in its behalf, and it failed'.[62] This reflected a deep antagonism on Dickens's behalf, and that of many other people, to the impact of evangelicalism on English social and political life.

On occasions, more moderately, *The Times* could see some good in 'philanthropy' if it was not restricted to those it saw as obsessed with slavery and the slave trade. 'We are a calculating age', it claimed in 1842, worried about the impending war in Afghanistan; 'men ask themselves now the meaning of words ... Philanthropy ... with all its cant, is not *all* hollow and unmeaning. There is a feeling, growing because true, that the statesman's care, though it begins, does not end, with his own country – that there is such a thing as national as well as individual selfishness'. But words in support of philanthropy were nearly always countered with criticisms of its practices and practitioners. 'Much has been said, and too much cannot, perhaps, be said, in favour of philanthropy. It is the circulating medium of humanity.' But 'philanthropy may exceed its price. It may be misplaced – it may be mistaken in its views – it may dilute into exaggerated sentimentality – it may be not only injudicious, but mischievous'.[63]

The true task of philanthropy lay at home. The *Leeds Times* in 1843 attacked those who 'go out fuming with liberalism and philanthropy, to an anti-slavery meeting, heedless, meanwhile of the beggar that lies starving at their very doorsteps'. It was the 'poor white slaves of our own country' who needed help and those sleeping out in parks, 'completely out of the reach of the fashionable philanthropy of this Christian and civilized country'.[64] There was, wrote *The Times*, 'an overstretched philanthropy towards the aborigines of New Zealand'. 'With many of the worthy people of Exeter-hall distance is essential to love', claimed *Punch*.[65] In 1846 *The Times* compared the regulations protecting 'coolies' in the West Indies with the condition of the Dorset peasantry, and urged 'the philanthropists of Exeter-hall' to turn their attention to Dorset where work was likely to be much more effective and outcomes measurable. As it was, philanthropy's concern for the West Indies was 'as unnatural and contemptible a perversion of feeling as to caress a china monster, or to weep over a pampered poodle'. The New Poor Law was a more lasting object of *The Times*'s concern, prompting the comment that 'Philanthropy has ... plenty of work at home, without seeking for distant objects of benevolence, while the pauper population of England is undergoing all the miseries of oppression and slavery ... Slavery exists at home under the New Poor Law in a form more oppressive towards its victims than has ever been experienced by the blacks in the English colonies'.[66]

The deployment of naval vessels in West Africa to stop the slave trade provoked sustained anger. It was, claimed a trustee of a West India property, 'an useless and Quixotic scheme of cosmopolite philanthropy'.[67] 'Cosmopolite' was a word in fashion in the 1840s, sometimes used with pride. In 1843 a delegate to the World Anti-Slavery Convention declared that 'We are not merely Britons, but cosmopolites. We go to the east and to the west, to the north and to the south, to seek for misery and to endeavour to relieve it'.[68] For *The Times* the patrols in West Africa were an instance of this 'cosmopolite philanthropy'; they were 'this cruel and barbarous philanthropy', a 'suicidal philanthropy', 'our facile philanthropy'. It cost half a million pounds a year, money much better spent on charitable work: 'It has become the mere crotchet of a minority, cherished with the more desperation as its folly has been more freely exposed'.[69] The *Manchester Times and Gazette* echoed these criticisms, writing of 'The Follies of Philanthropy' and 'Philanthropy at Fault'. Free trade, it argued, would end the slave trade, not 'promoting philanthropy by fire and sword'.[70]

In 1848 *The Times* asked, 'Were Clarkson and Wilberforce right or wrong in the steps they took in the cause of Negro Emancipation? Sentimentalism apart, are they to be numbered amidst the enlightened benefactors of humanity?' The answer was that they were not.[71] Globally the slave trade had increased, the British Caribbean islands had failed to flourish under a free labour regime. The abolition of the slave trade and of slavery came in time to be held up as the supreme achievement of British philanthropy, no one doubting that Clarkson and Wilberforce were right. But in the years immediately following their achievements they were subject to surprisingly vocal criticism.

Carlyle versus Mill

There is much evidence that by the end of the 1840s philanthropy had become associated not only with a particular group – for which the shorthand was Exeter Hall – but also with a sentimental view of human beings and social problems. Thomas Carlyle gave voice to these views in two articles in 1849 and 1850, the first on slavery, the second, discussed in Chapter 5, on prison reform. In 'Occasional discourse on the Negro question' (1849) Carlyle disguised himself as Dr Phelim McQuirk and purported to be speaking on behalf of 'the Universal Abolition-of-Pain Association, which is meant to be the consummate golden flower and summary of modern Philanthropisms all in one'. Addressing 'My Philanthropic Friends', he warned them that on the 'Negro Question' 'you will not in the least like' what he has to say. He contrasted 'Our beautiful Black darlings', eating pumpkins and living happily, with 'doleful Whites sitting here without potatoes to eat'. Carlyle then went on to mock the way reliance on 'supply' and 'demand' had led to a situation where whites could not get labour to work the sugar plantations. For Carlyle there was a human duty to work – that's what we were on this earth for – and whites had a right to enforce it, perhaps by some form of serfdom or even by a return to slavery. As it was, however, there had been in this and other matters an unholy marriage between 'Exeter Hall Philanthropy' and what he dubbed 'the *dismal science*', that is political economy. It will, he warns, 'give birth to progenies and prodigies; dark extensive moon-calves, unnameable abortions, wide-coiled monstrosities, such as the world has not seen hitherto!'[72]

The 'Occasional discourse on the Negro question', reprinted in 1853 as 'Occasional discourse on the nigger question', is an outspokenly racist tract, shocking both at the time and to the present. That, however, did not mean that its attacks on philanthropy did not resonate. 'Exeter Hall' is cited again and again, associating philanthropy both with the evangelicals and with talk not action, 'philanthropic stump-oratory'. But perhaps most interesting is the linkage Carlyle makes between philanthropy and political economy. It had been the assumption of those opposing slavery that the plantations would be worked by wage earners, supply meeting demand, but Carlyle claimed that that was not what had happened. We have seen how the links between philanthropy and political economy placed philanthropists in uncomfortable positions with regard to factory reform and the Poor Law. Carlyle took pleasure in rubbing salt into their wounds. And he did not tire of attacking philanthropy, denouncing in 1867 the 'rabid Nigger-Philanthropists' for their punitive action against Governor Eyre for the way in which he had suppressed the revolt in Jamaica in 1865.[73]

Not surprisingly there was a response from the philanthropy side. As Carlyle noted in his journal, 'Nigger article has roused the ire of all philanthropists to quite an unexpected pitch'.[74] It fell to John Stuart Mill who, as we have seen, had his reservations about philanthropy, to respond to Carlyle. According to Carlyle, Mill wrote, it appeared that the age 'is ill with a most pernicious disease, which infects all its proceedings, and of which the conduct of this country in regard to the Negroes is a prominent symptom – the Disease of Philanthropy'. Mill determined to 'set my anti-philanthropic opponent right on a matter of fact'. The opposition to slavery, he wrote, was not a mere

> affair of sentiment ... It triumphed because it was the cause of justice; and in the estimation of the great majority of its supporters, of religion. Its originators and leaders were persons of a stern sense of moral obligation, who, in the spirit of the religion of their time, seldom spoke much of benevolence and philanthropy, but often of duty, crime, and sin.

If Carlyle thought there was too much humanity in the present, Mill argued for its deficiency, 'deficiency even of philanthropy, and still more of other qualities wherewith to balance and direct what philanthropy it has'. There was much to be said, claimed Mill, for trying to diminish pain: 'It is precisely because we have succeeded in abolishing so much pain, because pain and its infliction are no longer as familiar as our daily bread, that we are so much more shocked by what remains of it than our ancestors were.' Philanthropy as the pursuit of justice was set against Carlyle's view of it as mere sentiment.[75]

Conclusion

There were two striking features of philanthropy in the period 1815–50. The first was that philanthropy was seen as embodying an outlook on the world that gave it a ranking equal with statesmanship. There were still those who thought of philanthropists, perhaps thought of themselves, as people who got pleasure from the happiness or improvement of others without requiring the necessity of doing anything. But much more important was the place that philanthropy established for itself as a force that had important things to contribute to the full range of social and political problems in Britain and around the world. The most important of these was slavery. Both campaigners against slavery and those who defended it recognised the role of philanthropy in bringing about change. Philanthropy had infiltrated to the heart of government, government and ministers acted philanthropically. Britain became an 'anti-slavery state', setting as a goal a delegalisation of slavery throughout the world.[76] A factor that both enabled this and fostered it was the widespread sense that Britain stood preeminent in the world for its philanthropy. Other nations, it should be said, were disinclined to buy into this view that the British had of themselves.

The second feature was the level of criticism that philanthropy attracted. This was in large part because philanthropy became closely associated with evangelicalism. The evangelicals were divided, both within the Church of England and in the relationship between the Church of England and Dissent, but critics were unlikely to attend to these divisions. 'Exeter Hall', the annual meeting place for evangelical societies, became the shorthand for what critics disliked: platform oratory, effeminate body language, talk without substance, neglect of home problems in favour of those far distant, and a sense of moral superiority over their fellow-citizens.

The high status of philanthropy alongside the virulent criticism of it attest that philanthropy, unlike charity and benevolence, had become thoroughly political. Radical versions of philanthropy of the kind put forward in the early days of the French Revolution were in this period rarely heard. At a different level there were interesting lines of allegiance. Tories, for the most part, disliked philanthropy. Some of them, influenced by Burke and the later writings of Coleridge, spoke up for a traditional localised paternalism built on the sanctity and authority of private property. As Arthur Helps put it in *The Claims of Labour* (1844), articulating the views of the paternalist, 'No sentimental philanthropy will do, nor even a warm and earnest philanthropy' for the need was for 'a sphere small enough for him to act'.[77] Philanthropy cast its net too wide. There were, however, eminent Tories who were unquestionably philanthropists: William Wilberforce, Michael Sadler, Lord Ashley, Richard Oastler and others involved in factory reform. On the other side Whigs were more favourably disposed towards the language of philanthropy, but for many of them political economy had a higher standing, and they supported the New Poor Law and were at best lukewarm on factory legislation.

At mid-century the status and future of philanthropy was poised. In 1849 *The Times* claimed that 'every gentleman of standing and pretension professes to be a philanthropist'.[78] This, with a degree of reluctance and the spice of hostility, recognised the important role that philanthropy was playing. But it was impossible for anyone not to be aware of the extent of criticism. Carlyle brought this to a head. Slavery emancipation and prison reform, his two targets, were the two key platforms of philanthropy. Philanthropy for Carlyle was a 'Movement'. It had its headquarters in Exeter Hall. Its leaders were mere talkers, not doers, shams and quacks, effeminate, maudlin and prurient. Where did all this false feeling originate? Carlyle traced it back to Howard, though Howard was the unintentional fountainhead. 'Howard', he wrote, 'is a beautiful Philanthropist, eulogised by Burke, and in most men's minds a sort of beatified individual'. That said, his reservations could be given play: 'I honour Howard very much; but it is on this side idolatry a long way.' 'Howard', he concluded, 'is to be regarded as the unlucky fountain of that tumultuous frothy ocean-tide of benevolent sentimentality, "abolition of punishment", all-absorbing "prison-discipline", and general morbid sympathy, instead of hearty hatred for scoundrels; which is threatening to drown human society as in deluges'.[79]

James Martineau, a prominent Unitarian, was much more sympathetic to philanthropy than Carlyle. Yet he too at mid-century had doubts about its role. They focused on the role of money in philanthropy. 'The *least* beneficent thing a man can do with his funds', he asserted, 'is to *give them*' and went on to ask,

> After all, do we not allow the *pecuniary* element of benevolence to engage too much of our attention? If more *personal labour and intercourse* were given by us, and maintained in a neighbourly way among the poor within immediate reach of our proper sphere, and occasions of kind deeds were seized, as they arose, throughout the range of our knowledge and acquaintance, without regard to the nominal distinction of rich or poor, the sorrows of the world would be more effectually lightened, than by the kind of systematic and semi-official and wholly officious philanthropy, which perverts the moral taste of the present day.[80]

Martineau here foreshadowed a distinction that was to become widely expressed in the late nineteenth and twentieth centuries between giving away money and personal service, these two forms of action seen sometimes as rival versions of philanthropy, sometimes as complementary. Martineau, criticising giving away money on political economy grounds as harmful to economic development as well as demoralising to the recipient, makes clear his preference for personal service, what for many would be called charity. His real distaste is for 'philanthropy' seen as an intrusive system, officially sanctioned and supported, powerful enough to pervert moral taste.

Possibly society could or should do without philanthropy altogether. It was a distraction from the real duty and purpose of life. Life, critics asserted, should be a struggle, a journey filled with self-discipline and duties. Arthur Clough at mid-century remarked that 'It is a good deal forgotten that we came into this world to do, not kindness to others, but our own duty, to live soberly, righteously, and godly, not benevolently, philanthropically, and tenderheartedly'.[81]

Carlyle, Martineau and Clough represented three different critiques of philanthropy, all with a future ahead of them. Carlyle was an outlier, on the extreme margin: no one could match his vitriol. But he had been preceded by *The Times* in the substance of much of what he wrote. Together they gave license to others to feel as they did – and sometimes to give voice to it. Martineau's criticism was more measured but in ways more challenging. If the giving of money was so dangerous, what did that say about not only indiscriminate almsgiving but about the huge institutional framework of charitable organisations and the fund-raising they engaged in? Clough denied the need for or desirability of philanthropy, imbued as it was with sentimentalism. In similar vein Fitzjames Stephen discerned a shift from a stern Puritanism to a 'kind of vapid philanthropic sentiment which calls itself undenominational; a creed of maudlin benevolence from which all the deeper and sterner elements of religious belief have been carefully purged away'.[82] Was philanthropy so contaminated with false feeling that it should be abandoned? Take these three critiques together, add to them the persistent worry about telescopic philanthropy, and the strength of the belief that too much philanthropy undermined adherence to political economy, and it's clear that philanthropy by mid-century carried baggage that it would be difficult to shed.

Chambers' Edinburgh Journal in an 1849 article headed 'Reaction against philanthropy', summed up the state of opinion at mid-century: 'Things are not at present looking well for philanthropy. The public is evidently turning against many of the schemes for lessening evil and promising good which have occupied attention for some years past.' 'The late philanthropic paroxysm', it wrote, 'was itself a reaction from a previous state of indifference'. There had been 'forty years of philanthropy' when punishment for crimes was softened and education spread, but things seemed worse rather than better. It called for an end to the 'system of impulsive philanthropy' and a renewed emphasis on the responsibility of individuals for their own welfare. The article was much debated, but the editors insisted in reply on the fact of 'the reaction against philanthropy'.[83]

Notes

1 *Wright's Leeds Intelligencer*, 4 July 1814.
2 *Manchester Exchange Herald*, in *The Times*, 4 Sept. 1817; *Bath Chronicle*, 16 Oct. 1817.
3 *The Times*, 26 Dec. 1823; 14 Aug. 1844; 10 Sept. 1847.

4 Ibid., 5 Oct. 1821; 3 Jan. 1837; 23 Nov. 1847; 6 May 1842.

5 Ibid., 28 June 1819.

6 Ibid., 15 Nov. 1833; 24 Apr. 1847; 22 Feb. 1847.

7 Ibid., 22 Apr. 1844.

8 Ibid., 25 Oct. 1824; 6 Aug. 1833.

9 Ibid., 20 Sept. 1838; 23 Sept. 1840.

10 Ibid., 1 Nov. 1823; 3 Nov. 1823.

11 Ibid., 7 Aug. 1830.

12 R. Huzzey, 'The moral geography of British anti-slavery responsibilities', *Transactions of the Royal Historical Society*, 22 (2012), 111–39.

13 *Morning Chronicle*, 21 Aug. 1817.

14 *The Times*, 5 Feb. 1818; 23 Aug. 1822; 3 June 1826.

15 Ibid., 14 Mar. 1836; 18 Sept. 1847.

16 Ibid., 8 Mar. 1815.

17 *Western Times*, 5 June 1830.

18 *Morning Chronicle*, 1 Sept. 1837.

19 *The Times*, 22 June 1814; 13 Sept. 1816.

20 Ibid., 5 Feb. 1817; 28 June 1822; 19 Dec. 1836.

21 Ibid., 11 Apr. 1825.

22 Ibid., 7 Feb. 1826.

23 B. Hilton, *The Age of Atonement: The Influence of Evangelicalism on Social and Economic Thought, 1795–1865* (Oxford: Clarendon Press, 1988), p. 210.

24 F. K. Brown, *Fathers of the Victorians: The Age of Wilberforce* (Cambridge: Cambridge University Press, 1961), pp. 353–60.

25 D. W. Bebbington, *Evangelicalism in Modern Britain* (London: Unwin Hyman, 1989), pp. 75–104.

26 *Poverty in the Victorian Age*, Vol. III, *Charity 1815–1870* (Farnborough: Gregg International Publishers, 1973), 'Charitable institutions', p. 99.

27 Ibid., 'Mendicity', pp. 121, 139.

28 Ibid., 'Charitable institutions', p. 113.

29 J. S. Mill, *Collected Works: The Earlier Letters of J. S. Mill, 1812–1848*, ed. F. E. Mineka (Toronto: University of Toronto Press, 1963), pp. 640–1.

30 Ibid., p. 655.

31 *Edinburgh Review*, Apr. 1845, esp. pp. 499–502, 506, 508.

32 *The Greville Memoirs: A Journal of the Reigns of King George IV, King William, and Queen Victoria*, ed. H. Reeve (Cambridge Books Online), Vol. V, p. 243.

33 T. Chalmers, *On Political Economy, in Connexion with the Moral State and Moral Prospects of Society* (Glasgow: William Collins, 1832), quoting pp. iii, 438, 423–4, 565; see also, pp. 48, 70–2, 173–4, 275, 319, 484.

34 D. Turley, *The Culture of English Antislavery, 1780–1860* (London: Routledge, 1991), pp. 147–8.

35 Hilton, *Age of Atonement*, pp. 100–8, quoting p. 103.

36 *The History of The Times*, 5 vols (London: The Times, 1935–52), Vol. I, pp. 293–8.

37 James S. M. Anderson, *Christian Philanthropy: A Spital Sermon* (London: J. G. and F. Rivington, 1835), pp. 15–16.

38 *The Times*, 9 July 1840; 17 Jan. 1840; 15 May 1843.

39 Hilton, *Age of Atonement*, pp. 212–13.
40 For the Tory and High Church attitudes of *The Times*'s leader writers, see D. Roberts, *Paternalism in Early Victorian England* (London: Croom Helm, 1979), pp. 194–6.
41 *The Times*, 11 July 1849; 19 May 1846.
42 Ibid., 27 Mar. 1846.
43 Ibid., 1 Aug. 1832.
44 Ibid., 22 July 1846.
45 Ibid., 3 May 1841.
46 Ibid., 27 June 1845.
47 Ibid., 23 July 1846.
48 C. L. Brown, *Moral Capital: Foundations of British Abolitionism* (Chapel Hill: University of North Carolina Press, 2006), pp. 370–1.
49 E. M. Howse, *Saints in Politics: The 'Clapham Sect' and the Growth of Freedom* (Toronto: University of Toronto Press, 1952), pp. 149–50.
50 *The Times*, 30 May 1829.
51 Ibid., 7 Oct. 1823; 10 Jan. 1824; 14 Jan. 1824.
52 Ibid., 10. Feb. 1824.
53 Ibid., 10 Feb. 1824.
54 Ibid., 27 June 1849.
55 Ibid., 31 Mar. 1832; 23 Mar. 1836.
56 Quoted from the *Morning Advertiser* in H. Temperley, *White Dreams, Black Africa: The Antislavery Expedition to the River Niger 1841–1842* (New Haven and London: Yale University Press, 1991), p. 3.
57 *The Times*, 21 Nov. 1840; 30 Nov. 1840; 4 Feb. 1841.
58 Ibid., 30 Mar. 1841; 9 Dec. 1841.
59 Ibid., 28 Jan. 1842.
60 G. Eliot, *Middlemarch* (1871; Oxford: Oxford University Press, 1997), p. 360.
61 *The Times*, 12 May 1842; 21 Oct. 1842; 22 Nov. 1842.
62 'The Niger Expedition', *The Examiner*, 19 Aug. 1848.
63 *The Times*, 29 Nov. 1842; 27 Feb. 1845.
64 *Leeds Times*, 4 Nov. 1843.
65 *The Times*, 15 Dec. 1843; *Punch* quoted in ibid., 17 May 1844.
66 Ibid., 25 July 1846; 30 Sept. 1846.
67 Ibid., 4 Dec. 1847.
68 Turley, *Culture of English Antislavery*, p. 205.
69 *The Times*, 27 Apr. 1849; 30 Apr. 1849; 27 Dec. 1849.
70 *Manchester Times and Gazette*, 1 Aug. 1846; 26 Feb. 1848.
71 *The Times*, 29 May 1848.
72 [T. Carlyle], 'Occasional discourse on the Negro question', *Fraser's Magazine*, 40 (Dec. 1849), 670–9.
73 Quoted in R. L. Tarr, 'The "Foreign Philanthropy Question" in "Bleak House": A Carlylean influence', *Studies in the Novel*, 3 (1971), 283.
74 Quoted in ibid., 281.
75 Mill, *Collected Works*, Vol. XXI, *Essays on Equality, Law, and Education* (Toronto: University of Toronto Press, 1984), pp. 87–95.

76 R. Huzzey, *Freedom Burning: Anti-Slavery and Empire in Victorian Britain* (Ithaca, NY: Cornell University Press, 2012); J. Oldfield, 'After emancipation: Slavery, freedom and the Victorian Empire', in M. Taylor (ed.), *The Victorian Empire and Britain's MaritimeWorld, 1837–1901: The Sea and Global History* (Basingstoke: Palgrave Macmillan, 2013), pp. 43–63.
77 Roberts, *Paternalism in EarlyVictorian England*, p. 34.
78 *The Times*, 11 July 1849.
79 T. Carlyle, 'Model prisons', in *Latter-Day Pamphlets* (London: Chapman and Hall, 1899), pp. 62–5.
80 J. Drummond and C. B. Upton, *The Life and Letters of James Martineau*, 2 vols (London: James Nisbet & Co., 1902),Vol. II, pp. 297–9.
81 Quoted in W. E. Houghton, *The Victorian Frame of Mind, 1830–1870* (New Haven and London: Yale University Press, 1957), p. 276.
82 Quoted in ibid., p. 275.
83 *Chambers' Edinburgh Journal*, 24 Feb. 1849; 31 Mar. 1849.

8

Mid-Victorian philanthropy, 1850–80

The mid-Victorian period was marked both by a running theme of praise for British generosity and by a continuity of the criticism of philanthropy that had marked the 1830s and 1840s. But the world was changing and a new phase in the history of philanthropy was opening. Its identification with evangelicalism became less pronounced, its relationship to capitalism more central. Political economy, the ideology of capitalism, continued to pose huge problems for philanthropists who tried to tackle poverty. On the other hand there were initiatives that suggested that philanthropy and capitalism might work in harmony, in the philanthropy plus 5 per cent that attempted to ease urban housing problems. Some tried to make philanthropy more 'professional', others deplored the growing signs of the emergence of the 'professional philanthropist'. The gender of philanthropy became explicitly an issue, some at war with what they saw as its 'effeminacy'. And novelists found scope in philanthropy for witty caricature laced with acerbic criticism. Outside the world of philanthropy its critics made more noise than its friends.

British generosity

In a leading article in January 1859 in the midst of a hard winter *The Times*, thankful for the donations that had 'flowed through our columns' to relieve distress, reflected that it showed 'the existence of a considerable mass of people who have a giving *habit*, who are in a state of mind prepared to give upon the proper claim being submitted'. It felt that, in contrast to previous generations, there was now

> A natural bent and attitude of mind in the direction of giving ... Society looks upon evil as something to be met and dealt with, and no longer stands passive in the matter. There is an active, inquiring, busy, penetrating,

intellectual spirit of benevolence which has come in, and which does not let people rest, but sets them to work.

True, 'a mechanical spirit' might 'creep into the agency and working of our benevolent schemes; every one who attends a committee meeting, or who puts his name to a packet of printed letters, is not a HOWARD'. Nevertheless, 'There is now a general understanding on the subject of the facts of human want and misery which come before us and are part of the law of our social system'.[1]

Less than a month later *The Times* extended the discussion to consider the growth of 'the philanthropic principle':

> It cannot fail to strike any one who goes over the history of the last half-century how strongly the philanthropic principle has come out as a practical public consideration – how, from being a beautiful idea, cherished in studies, it has become a political power, able to do things, to carry measures, to pull down and to build up, and make itself attended to ... it abolished the Slave Trade, and in this empire Slavery altogether; it had a great hand in repealing the Corn Laws, which might have stood to this day had they had only the financial ground to appeal to; but multitudes who did not understand a word about political economy took in the benevolent argument. This principle has obviously had a great deal to do with moulding our Indian policy of the last twenty years. On the European area it combined with classical element to erect the Kingdom of Greece. It is now an admitted member of the political circle, and one of the organizing and constructing forces of the day.

By the 'philanthropic principle', *The Times* continued, 'we do not mean exclusively an interest in negroes and savages, but any feeling for the interests and rights of society, or any portion of it'.[2] The potential scope of philanthropy had been set out earlier, in 1853: 'The African, the heathen, the old, the young, the sick, the maimed, the criminal, the ragged, and countless other forms of misery and deprivation have their respective patrons.'[3]

These articles set out a vision, rooted in the past, of the present and future in 'this philanthropic age'. The past stretched back little more than a half century. Howard marked the beginning, but he was like 'an Apostle of old' and 'modern philanthropy does not run such dangers'.[4] But there were substantial achievements, the abolition of the slave trade and slavery, the repeal of the Corn Laws, Indian policy and the establishment of the Kingdom of Greece. A narrative was being constructed and it was elaborated over the second half of the century. In 1879 when a monument to Thomas Clarkson was unveiled, *The Times* reflected that 'The efforts of the philanthropists whom Clarkson led have made the historical fact of British dealings in the [slave] traffic almost inconceivable'. No longer could be it said, as it was in 1848, that Clarkson and Wilberforce were not to be 'numbered amidst the enlightened benefactors of humanity'. In 1885 the Bishop of Colchester, proposing an Elizabeth Fry Memorial Church, described her as 'the mother of modern philanthropy'.[5] Howard the father, Fry the mother, both, as it happened, famous for their work in prisons. But philanthropy stretched beyond that, it was a political force both nationally and internationally, capable of defeating long-established economic forces (the slave trade, slavery and the Corn Laws), of 'moulding' imperial policy, of changing regimes. At a more local level in Britain, the emergence of 'the giving *habit*', together with 'a general understanding on the subject of the facts of human want and misery', suggested that poverty could at least be relieved if not abolished.

These mid-Victorian years were the highpoint of the reputation of philanthropy. It was not that there were no critics. Rather, what was important was the range of activity and of causes that could come under the aegis of philanthropy and the influence it was assumed to have at the highest level of politics. It was as if the governing classes had themselves taken on the mantle of philanthropy and would seek to do good across the globe. Philanthropy had a place in Britain's image of itself; it had political power.

Provincial newspapers often reflected on Britain's preeminence in philanthropy. Here are three examples. Writing in the *Derby Mercury* in 1855 a correspondent described how

> Among the distinctive features of our national character philanthropy stands prominent; in fact without its continued exercise our noble institutions, the pride and glory of Britain, would become useless, droop and die away. Our institutions for the orphan, the destitute, the widow, our infirmaries and hospitals, our unions for the maintenance of the poor and unfortunate, our asylums for the blind, the deaf and dumb, and our varied and multifarious plans which have for their special object the mitigation of human suffering, the elevation of our common humanity in a moral, religious, and social point of view, depend solely on the maintenance and development of philanthropy.

The writer was convinced that this philanthropy was 'emphatically peculiar to the present age in its more extensive and mighty operations ... in the world's wide domain'. The writer expatiated on the work of missionaries and concluded that 'in the cause of philanthropy we have set the world a noble example which they would do well to imitate'.[6]

The *Preston Guardian* in 1862 gave a long notice of Rev. J. Gutteridge's lecture on 'Philanthropy; or, are we not brothers?' For Gutteridge 'there was more humanity in this land than in any other land, and, as might have been expected, there was more philanthropy. The nations of Europe and the world had been held in wonder by the generosity of the people of this country'. There were more than six hundred philanthropic institutions in London alone. True, philanthropists needed to be careful and discriminating in their giving, but the generosity of the British was undeniable.[7]

The *Essex Standard* in 1877 carried a leading article on 'National phil-anthropy'. It praised 'the enormous machinery of Christian benevolence for the maintenance of Hospitals, and Orphanages, and Asylums ... the still vaster sums that are every year contributed for the promotion of Christianity in our own and foreign lands ... the still larger sums which are given in secret by Christian philanthropists'. It highlighted money given to relieve suffering in the Russo-Turkish War and in the Indian famine. All this was 'testimony to the noble spirit of philanthropy, which prevails in England as no where else on earth'. But there was a sting in the tail: 'the part borne in this work by the millionaires and large landed proprietors of the country is utterly disproportioned to the sacrifices of moderate capitalists and the middle classes. But so it always has been, and so it always will be: the burden of benevolence does not fall on those best able to bear it'.[8]

What shines through in reports of this kind is the assertion of the generosity of the British – that is to say the amount of money they gave. There were dissenting voices: Lord Shaftesbury speaking in 1864 at the anniversary meeting of the Systematic Beneficence Society, itself established by evangelicals in 1860, claimed that in the Irish famine, the Indian famine and the Crimean War 'The newspapers were loud in bepraising the munificence of the country ... but I confess I never saw any munificence'. Nevertheless, the existence of the Systematic Beneficence Society was itself a sign of the linkage between philanthropy and giving.[9] There is also in these reports a sense that key institutions of the nation were held together by a network and 'machinery of Christian benevolence'. It is notable that in the contribution from Derby the Poor Law counted as one of these institutions. Only in the *Essex Standard* was a class dimension explicit – that the middle class was the initiator and sustainer of these institutions.

There were many other positive notices of philanthropy in action. The Royal National Lifeboat Institute was the focus for an article on 'Philanthropy of the best sort'. The *Liverpool Mercury* was delighted with the 'Christian philanthropy' exemplified in Mrs Burt's work for the emigration of children to Canada.[10] *Good Words* in 1875, after commenting on the 'waste of money in the administration of our wealthier charities', praised the Peabody Trust under the title 'Philanthropy and common sense'. The *Sunderland Daily Echo* in 1879 commended the work of the Mayoress of Sunderland and Ladies' Local Relief Fund as 'Practical Philanthropy'.[11] The titles of many of these articles, however, could not help hinting that there was also philanthropy that was not 'practical', that was not 'Christian', nor consonant with 'Common Sense' and that was not 'of the Best Sort'. As we shall see, there were many only too willing to focus on philanthropy that failed to meet with approval.

Royalty took the lead in disseminating the view that Britain stood pre-eminent for its philanthropy – and by donation contributing to it. With a diminished political role, Victoria and Albert were fully alive to the important part that their philanthropy could play in reconciling classes and averting the danger of revolution. As Albert put it in a speech to the Society for Improving the Condition of the Labouring Classes 'the interests of classes too often contrasted are identical, and it is only ignorance which prevents their uniting for each other's advantage. To dispel that ignorance, to show that man can help man ... ought to be the aim of every philanthropic person'. To further this end Albert saw the purpose of royalty to be the 'headship of philanthropy, a guidance and encouragement of the manifold efforts which our age is making towards a higher and purer life'. He was tireless in visiting provincial cities and laying foundation stones accompanied by a speech. Institutions were fully aware of the value of the royal presence and of royal patronage to their reputation and their finances. Victoria in 1851 'contributed to more than 210 charities, including fifty schools, thirty-seven hospitals, twenty-one churches, and eighteen asylums'. 'Rules and Principles' were established in 1858 to guide donations and the use of the royal name. 'All the Queen's subjects', it was laid down, 'should consider it to be their privilege to apply to Her Majesty in distress and difficulty; and the poorest person ... has as much the privilege of a subject, as the richest'.[12]

In 1871 Gladstone as prime minister, the Queen, the Prince of Wales and palace officials discussed what role the Prince should play in public life. One suggestion was that philanthropy should be his main occupation. Gladstone, however, who had wanted the Prince to have a post as the Queen's representative in Ireland, considered that 'it is hardly possible for the Prince to make a worthy pursuit out of philanthropy; I do not mean one worthy in itself, but of adequate magnitude'. Philanthropy, he felt, would not give him 'a central aim and purpose'. It seems as if for Gladstone a preoccupation with philanthropy was not quite a becoming occupation for the heir to the throne. Yet philanthropy turned out to be what the Prince did. In the 1890s he was carrying out about forty-five philanthropic engagements every year; he had by then supported nearly 1,000 institutions or appeals, including seventy-five of the leading hospitals.[13]

The response to royal philanthropy was uniformly positive, whether in the size and demeanour of the crowds that assembled to watch the laying of a stone or the opening of an institution, or in the words fed back to royalty: the chairman of the Committee of the Sailors' Home in Liverpool congratulated Albert for 'associating your name with institutions formed for religious, scientific and philanthropic purposes, by these means securing the triumphs of peace and the blessings of Christianity'. Similarly, the contributor to the *Derby Mercury* in 1855 was delighted that 'Our noble Queen herself has given repeated proof of her philanthropy in her various and oft-repeated acts of beneficence to all classes and conditions'.[14]

Royalty flattered the public in turn, reinforcing the belief in Britain's exceptional philanthropy. Queen Victoria's children all inherited a belief that they should support charitable organisations. In 1879 Prince Leopold, perhaps the most active philanthropist of the royal children, speaking at a prize-giving at the Birkbeck Literary and Scientific Institution, declared that 'No nation, may I venture to say it, has produced a larger proportion of such philanthropists [as Birkbeck] than our own. No nation, I am sure I may assert, has been more eager to aid those philanthropists in life, or to honour them when they have passed away'.[15] A few months later the Prince of Wales, speaking at the Cabdrivers' Benevolent Association dinner, emphasised the royal family's keenness 'to uphold those great charities and philanthropic objects for which, I think I may say, our country is distinguished'.[16]

The May meetings of evangelical societies, their headquarters at Exeter Hall, excoriated by *The Times* in the 1830s and 1840s, came to be seen as a much-loved and valued moment in the calendar:

> They stand for just everything which the English nature loves best and approves most deliberately. Philanthropy and religious zeal at home and abroad, displayed alike to friends and enemies and strangers, undertaken at no light expense, and started and directed all through strictly voluntary agencies – all this is what the May Meetings represent in its most concrete shape, and assist very materially ... There is at the bottom a real desire to do good to others, with the added notion that the Anglo-Saxon race is the proper vehicle of good to everybody.[17]

The adjective most used to describe philanthropy that was approved of was 'practical', royalty to the fore. Prince Albert's philanthropic cottage building at Windsor was 'eminently practical'. The Royal Victoria Coffee-Hall had the support of 'the company of practical philanthropists'. The Gordon Boys' Home was praised in 1886 'as a scheme of practical philanthropy'.[18] More modestly, the opening of a room during the fair at Market Harborough for tea, coffee and songs was described by W. H. Gatty as 'a piece of practical philanthropy', doubtless designed to attract people from less salubrious entertainment. Practical philanthropy also had its part to play on the interface between public and private provision. A Voluntary (as opposed to a Board) School was described as 'a sort of centre for the practical philanthropy of its neighbours'.[19]

Philanthropy and political economy

'Earnest', 'thoughtful' and 'sober-minded' philanthropists joined ranks with those who were 'practical' on the positive side of the balance sheet but they were far outweighed by those who were subjected throughout the second half of the century, and with no signs of diminution, to the adjectives that had flourished in the criticism of philanthropy in the 1830s and 1840s. 'Morbid', 'puffing', 'pseudo', 'uninformed', 'inconsiderate', 'professional', 'ignorant', 'mistaken', 'well-meaning', 'spurious', 'so-called', 'false', 'mealy-mouthed', 'misplaced', 'pinchbeck', 'sham', 'blundering' and 'misapplied', these were the adjectives that philanthropy and philanthropists had thrown at them. At best philanthropy was 'well-meaning' or 'uninformed', but at worst it was driven by motives that were 'pseudo' (a common accusation), 'puffing', 'spurious' or 'sham', the pretence of philanthropy masking other ambitions, including profiteering.[20]

Ignoring the laws of political economy was for the critics the besetting sin of philanthropy. Too many institutions, thought *The Times* in 1850, 'disregard … the principles of political economy', philanthropy paying too little attention to 'the chasm which separates vice from virtue'.[21] In an 1853 article in the *Westminster Review*, tellingly entitled 'Charity, noxious and beneficent', W. R. Greg set out a role for philanthropy that distinguished it from charity:

> The profession of philanthropy, like every other, can be safely and serviceably practised only by those who have mastered its principles and graduated in its soundest schools. It is as dangerous to practise charity, as to practise physic without a diploma. He who would benefit mankind must first qualify himself for the task.

What that meant was '*ascertaining and enforcing those principles of social science* by which alone misery can be permanently removed or prevented, and distress, effectually and without mischief, relieved'. Once the principles of social science (i.e. political economy) were firmly established, 'our kindly impulses and deep consciousness of the debt we owe to others, will cast off the lazy shape of charity, and rise into the attitude and assume the garb of true philanthropy'.[22] For Greg there were 'two classes of philanthropists – the feelers and the thinkers', the latter those which he endorsed.[23]

Philanthropy, however, never entirely separated itself from 'the lazy shape of charity'. Greg himself in 1865, reviewing a new edition of J. S. Mill's *Principles of Political Economy*, claimed that

> There are none who have shown themselves more truly and earnestly desirous of promoting the welfare of the poor than those who have thoroughly mastered the principles of political economy. Their philanthropy may indeed take a different form from vulgar charity; but it is a difference not between hardness and benevolence, but between scientific and unscientific ways of being benevolent. It is not a moral, but an intellectual distinction. It is not political economy on the one side, and the Christian religion on the other; but it is knowledge on the one side, and ignorance on the other.[24]

Charity here was 'vulgar' and ignorant, philanthropy scientific and knowledgeable. But few held to this rigorous distinction, many using philanthropy and charity interchangeably. In 1859, for example, the factory inspector Mr Baker was confident that 'There is spring and energy enough, and the warmest sympathies and sufficient love of offspring among the working classes to provide for their bodily wants, if these are not rendered lukewarm by too much philanthropy'.[25] 'Philanthropy' here, surely what Greg would have denounced as 'vulgar charity', would demoralise the working classes. In 1865 Joseph Rowntree was withering in his assessment of much giving: 'Charity as ordinarily practised, the charity of endowment, the charity of emotion, the charity which takes the place of justice, creates much of the misery it relieves, but does not relieve all the misery it creates.'[26] Tackling the issue head on, Thomas Beggs in January 1869 lectured to the Social Science Association on 'Misdirected Philanthropy as an Economical Question'. He 'contended that £7,000,000 or more which was spent annually in London in charity went greatly to increase the distress it sought to relieve'. The 'machinery' of charitable organisations (a metaphor often used: Walter Bagehot in 1859 wrote that 'Philanthropy must submit to the machinery of philanthropy'), 'enabled the wealthy to do the duty of helping the poor by proxy, and without trouble to themselves'. The lecture was widely noted in the provincial press. The *Westminster Review* followed this up in April 1869 with 'The philanthropy of the age in its relation to social evils'. Citing Beggs with approval, the article claimed that 'the multitude of charities augments the amount of distress', and was scornful of 'a misguided and sanguine philanthropy'. 'Our restless philanthropy', it was claimed, threw a heavy burden on the taxpayer. It was time to pay attention to 'economic science' and 'political economy'. Indiscriminate almsgiving, asserted another writer in 1869, was 'a public nuisance, if not a grave moral offence'.[27] For *The Times* in the hard winter of 1878, too often 'the best intended machinery for the relief of poverty becomes a principal agent in fostering and promoting the evil it was intended to remedy'.[28]

In 1872 Walter Bagehot gloomily wondered 'whether the benevolence of mankind does most good or harm. Great good, no doubt, philanthropy does, but then it also does great evil. It augments so much vice, it multiplies so much suffering, it brings to life such great populations to suffer and to be vicious, that it is open to argument whether it be or be not an evil to the world'. The reason for the evil, Bagehot thought, arguing a social Darwinist case, was that philanthropists had 'inherited from their barbarous forefathers a wild passion for instant action'. If philanthropy was to do good, it must be the product of careful forethought and preparation, of adherence to the laws of political economy, not of a desire by otherwise excellent people to 'relieve their own feelings' in face of an 'evil'.[29]

Politicians absorbed the anxieties of political economists. Gladstone in 1875 feared that if W. E. Forster became Liberal party leader he might go for over-government and 'in … the propagandism of a vague philanthropy, he might go constantly astray' – astray, that is, from the principles of political economy. In 1877 G. J. Goschen, another Liberal, claimed that political economy had been 'dethroned' in parliament and 'Philanthropy has been allowed to take its place. Political economy was the bugbear of the working classes, and philanthropy, he was sorry to say, was their idol'. Two years later, he was arguing that extension of the franchise gave scope to 'Socialistic or ultra-philanthropic tendencies', and 'dwelt strongly on the growing predominance of philanthropy over political economy in our own Legislature since the Reform Act of 1867' though without, as *The Times* noted, being able to cite a single instance. From the Conservative side Salisbury complained about Gladstone's 'vague philanthropic phraseology'. Philanthropy had lost any claim to be better than the charity or benevolence from which it had tried to emancipate itself. It was no longer working in accordance with the laws of political economy. As Brian Harrison concluded, 'Philanthropy had become a pejorative term for some Mid-Victorians, a synonym almost for soft-headedness'.[30]

Reading warnings about the dangers of giving could reduce well-intentioned people to a state of paralysing uncertainty. Of John Ruskin, it was said that 'he never dares to give any thing in the streets without looking on all sides to see whether there is a political economist coming'.[31] But it was not only political economists he had to worry about, it was also Christians. When Brooke Lambert, a vicar in London's East End, preached before the University of Oxford in 1868, he lamented the money that had poured into the area from the West End indiscriminately. 'The marvel of Christ's life', he said, 'is His repression of His powers of beneficence'.[32] It was, if nothing else, a new take on the Gospel. Christians, like Christ, should repress their 'powers of beneficence'.

A powerful influence on thinking came from Edward Denison who in 1867 at the age of twenty-seven took up residence in Stepney. Denison's letters, published after his death in 1869, set out a template for the future. He was contemptuous of much charity. 'The gigantic subscription lists which are regarded as signs of our benevolence', he wrote, 'are monuments to our indifference'. J. R. Green, vicar of Stepney, knew Denison well, and commented on his 'resolute stand … against the indiscriminate almsgiving which has done so much to create and encourage pauperism in the East of London'. Supporting a firm application of the principles of the New Poor Law, Denison's work, wrote Green, was far distant from 'the fussy impertinence of the philanthropists who think themselves born "to expose" Boards of Guardians'. A friend of Green's, wondering what had been 'the greatest boon conferred on the poorer classes' in recent years, expatiated 'on the rival claims of schools, missions, shoe-black brigades, and a host of other philanthropic efforts for their assistance'. Green replied that 'the sixpenny photograph is doing more for the poor than all the philanthropists in the world'. Stuck over a labourer's fireplace, cheap portraits kept alive a sense of family, the boy in Canada, the girl out at service, the child who died young.[33]

The proponents of political economy did not have things entirely their own way. There were public figures, Cardinal Manning most famous, who refused to obey the economists' injunction never to give to beggars. Others engaged in charitable work sometimes raised their heads above the parapet to take on the political economists. In 1860 W. D. B. wrote to *The Times* saying that he found himself 'transformed from a peaceful philanthropist into a Red Republican of the most dangerous order'. Why? Because Lord Ebury had attacked the writer's scheme for a new relief society. Faced with distress, wrote W. D. B., 'Human nature says Yes; political economy and Lord Ebury say No. With which faction will the English public side?'[34] In 1879 Edward Clifford, writing in response to a claim by Sir Charles Trevelyan, arch political economist, the man who had denied aid to Ireland in the famine, that the Local Government Board and the COS were dealing well with problems, said that 'I try, as far as possible, to restrain my anger, but if I were a working man with a nearly naked wife and children, griped with hunger, I think I should hate certain philanthropists with a perfect hatred'. Clifford helped to provide 'dry bread and weak cocoa' in an Assembly Hall. 'And, thanks to English public opinion, we have money to feed them for some little time at least.'[35] A decade later, in the aftermath of the dock strike, it was felt that public sympathy had won out over political economy. 'It is common', reported a correspondent of *The Times*, 'to hear congratulation upon the disappearance of the heartless laws of political economy, and their replacement by enlightened views of social duty and commercial relations'.[36] These three writers all felt that what Clifford called 'English public opinion' (and behaviour) were on the side of generosity in distress rather than adherence to the laws of political economy. And for Clifford philanthropy was making itself hated by its support for those laws. It was damned on the one side for not being rigid enough in sticking to the laws of political economy, and on the other for being too much in slavery to them.

Five per cent philanthropy

If political economy, as the ideology of capitalism, was so critical of much philanthropy, was it possible that capitalism could generate its own form of philanthropy? The housing of the poor, particularly the urban poor, was universally recognised to constitute a serious problem. Free market capitalism was resulting at best in poorly built, overcrowded dwellings. Slums were spreading. In 1844 the Society for Improving the Condition of the Labouring Classes was founded. It arose out of an earlier society whose focus had been on rural housing. The aim was to build model housing as an example of what might be done. In 1850 the Society's Charter limited the annual dividend that could be paid to 4 per cent, lower than returns easily available. It was in that year that the Society completed a tenement block of family dwellings in Bloomsbury in London, an influential example. The hope was that speculative builders would follow suit, but this never happened – the financial returns were too low. So came into being a way of improving housing that was dependent on investors settling for a low dividend. It was philanthropy with a modest financial return. Prince Albert, President of the society, paid for the erection of model housing at the Great Exhibition of 1851 and this gave impetus to the movement.[37] The Metropolitan Association for Improving the Dwellings of the Industrious Classes was the other major organisation in the field. Its charter of 1845 limited dividends to 5 per cent. It erected block dwellings in London and extended its work to towns across the country. It always faced a tension between what was desirable as housing and what was possible financially. As a resolution in 1854 expressed it, 'improved dwellings can only be extensively and permanently established on terms affording a fair remuneration to the capitalist'.[38]

In 1862 the American banker George Peabody gifted £150,000 (with later additions to reach £500,000, equivalent to some £50 million in 2017) 'to ameliorate the condition and augment the comforts of the poor' in London. His trustees decided to focus on housing. Since the Peabody Trust was to be self-perpetuating, the projects engaged in had to yield a profit – this too was philanthropy with a percentage on top. Peabody estates sprang up over London in the 1860s, in Spitalfields, Islington, Shadwell, Westminster and Chelsea. Surveying them a century later, J. N. Tarn found them 'memorable primarily for their grimness and physical bulk'.[39] A year after Peabody's initial gift, a London businessman, Sydney Waterlow, formed the Improved Industrial Dwellings Company, again on a philanthropy plus 5 per cent basis. It was matched by the Artizans, Labourers and General Dwellings Company, set up in 1867. Between them these three organisations had provided over 4,000 dwellings in London by 1875, nearly 17,000 by 1895.[40] There were many other smaller enterprises, at least forty-three in total over the period 1840–1914. In London between 1856 and 1914 they provided between 11 and 15 per cent of all new working-class accommodation, a proportion that might be turned on its head: the vast majority of working-class housing was provided by speculative builders without any concern for philanthropy.[41]

The National Dwellings Society was one of the smaller organisations, set up in 1875 offering 5 per cent Preference Shares. Appealing for more investors, it set out what might be described as the ethical claims of philanthropy plus 5 per cent:

> It is a matter of great satisfaction to find that benevolence can be combined with a legitimate and safe investment ... People have said that there is no philanthropy in investing money in these companies, but surely he who helps the poor man to obtain a better home at the same price he pays for his present wretched accommodation, and at the same time obtains a fair return for capital invested, is a greater philanthropist than he who maintains him in idleness, or lodges him from charity, for the one is certain to destroy his independence, whilst the other cannot do otherwise than increase it.[42]

This was a positive view but it encountered criticisms of what was being achieved and of the sustainability of the idea that lay behind it. A major criticism was that it was not 'the poor man' who was being housed but artisans and others in regular employment with relatively high wages. For the poor the situation was getting no better. A second criticism was that the pool of potential investors willing to accept a lower dividend was too small. As it was, 5 per cent philanthropy came to rely on government for cheap loans. In the

1890s the movement reached crisis point and a new era opened: Waterlow ceased operations and the London County Council began to build what would become known as council housing. Nevertheless, it has been argued, 'the rise of council housing cannot be explained by the inadequacy of philanthropy'. The Sutton Model Dwellings Trust, set up in 1900 with £2 million left by William Sutton for housing the poor in London and other 'towns and populous places', was hampered in its operations by being placed under the control of the Court of Chancery and subject to the concern of the Local Government Board that such a large sum could disrupt local housing markets and increase pauperisation. Philanthropy on such a scale, it was felt, must be overseen by the government and the courts.[43]

Philanthropy as a profession

Philanthropy in the mid-Victorian period was widely perceived as becoming a 'profession' – and when the word was used it was often not as a compliment. Part of this was a continuing suspicion of the motives of philanthropists that dates back to Mandeville in the eighteenth century. According to Lord Hobhouse, 'love of power, ostentation, and vanity' were the principal motives driving them, along with superstition (the belief that you would benefit in the afterlife) and spite (disappointing expectant heirs).[44] Benjamin Jowett asked Florence Nightingale, rather pointedly, 'Do you ever observe how persons take refuge from family unhappiness in philanthropy?'[45] The *Saturday Review* was less than impressed by the character of philanthropists: 'Are those whose lives are passed in philanthropic undertakings', it asked, 'the best and noblest specimens of humanity supplied by our age and nation? We do not suppose that any one would seriously answer the question in the affirmative … No one expects that a person principally occupied in philanthropy will be very wise, very sympathetic, or very large-minded'.[46]

  The Times in the same year doubted whether modern philanthropists were up to the task:

> Philanthropy in former days was not an agreeable pastime. A man who devoted himself to raise the fallen, to succour the indigent, to cleanse the gaol, or transport-hulk, or slave-ship, had need of a vigorous will, a burning and yet constant enthusiasm, a strong frame, and not over-delicate nerves; for in those days men did things themselves, and not through the agency of societies, with an office, a secretary, and an organization for colossal begging. JOHN HOWARD, like an Apostle of old, went to the places and mixed with the people that he wished to reform, and he had his reward in an early grave and the admiration of the world. But modern philanthropy does not run such dangers, and will hardly excite such gratitude. The Parliamentary lover of his kind leads a by no means unpleasant life.

He converts the heathen, succours the afflicted, and civilizes the barbarian, without ever seeing a ragged garment or a tawny skin. He is the chairman of meetings and the lion of *soirées*, on account of his interest in populations which he has never visited and his knowledge of the moral state of islands which he could not point out on the map.[47]

Eighteen months later it returned to the theme:

The HOWARDS and BUXTONS, and FRYS and SARAH MARTINS of our day are not struggling martyrs sustained only by their own zeal. They rejoice in comfortable salaries and print their own good deeds at the public cost. Philanthropy has now become a profession. The glory is less, but the supply is greater.[48]

The Times was not alone in discerning what the *Saturday Review* in 1859 called 'the spread of philanthropy as a profession'. 'A considerable and conspicuous class amongst us', it declared, 'do actually pass their lives, to a very great extent, in philanthropic employments'.[49] Such people were not the rich making donations; they were the secretaries, what we might now call the chief executives, of large charitable organisations. 'Secretaryship', noted the *Theological Review* in 1866, 'is developing itself into a profession which requires a well-known type of character for its successful exercise'. It would be better, wrote Alsager Hay Hill in 1869, to have more Poor Law Guardians than people seeking to be 'secretaries of associations'. In the same year the *Westminster Review* claimed that 'many of the public institutions are kept up for the imperfectly concealed purpose of making places for people who cannot find occupations anywhere else'. Many charities, it went on, 'have degenerated into rank abuse, existing for the purpose of paying salaries to a staff of officers and servants'. Worse than that, 'No higher estimate than Dr. Johnson formed of the patriotism of his time would be formed of the philanthropy of this if its secret workings were laid bare' – philanthropy was 'the last refuge of a scoundrel'.[50]

This style of criticism peaked with an article in the *London Journal* in 1872 on 'Philanthropy as a profession'. Signed by 'J. P. H.', it was a blistering attack on those who acted as the agents of 'amateur philanthropists' (the donors), leading to the emergence of 'a class, lay and clerical, who have raised philanthropy to the dignity of a profession. Armed with authority to go about "doing good", they must be credited with a large amount of cleverness, and fairly classed among those who, convinced that "people must live", find out a way to live, and live well'. The 'professional philanthropist' made a living as 'the organizer of the cash of the well-to-do, and the trumpeter of the woes of the needy … [He] is pleasant-looking, as to facial outline, tall and plump, but not fat, and would be deemed gentlemanly were it not that his aspect is so very professional'. In fact, any pretence to being a gentleman was belied by his social origins and past life. If everyone had a skeleton in the cupboard, that of the professional philanthropists 'must be of the bony, boniest'.[51]

The idea surfacing in the 1850s that philanthropy was becoming a profession – on a par perhaps with law or medicine – put it on a quite different plane to that occupied by Howard and his contemporaries. For those who welcomed the professionalisation of philanthropy the prospect was that philanthropy, in accord with the laws of political economy, would play the most important role in tackling the problem of urban poverty. But there were others for whom to think of philanthropy as a profession, with presumably financial reward for those engaged in it, was anathema. Either way, what is notable is that the giving of money was not seen as inextricably part of being a philanthropist. Philanthropists could have 'comfortable salaries'.

There was no easy path to professional status for philanthropy. F. B. Money-Coutts in 1884 was still looking to philanthropy becoming 'a profession', but he was under no illusion that that had yet been achieved. 'Public opinion', he lamented, 'is not much educated in the science of philanthropy'; in truth, it was unlikely to see it as a science. For Money-Coutts philanthropy was 'the study of remedies for the various forms of social evil that weaken the nation'; not action, but 'study'.[52] The same message was preached fourteen years later in 1898 at a conference at King's College London on 'the relation of scientific training in economics to social and philanthropic work'. Professor Hewins was the main speaker, urging that 'scientific training' was 'as necessary to those engaged in social and philanthropic work as it was to the doctor, the manufacturer, or the merchant'.[53]

The call for philanthropy to be recognised as a profession was a bid for status in a world where there were rival claimants to expertise in the making of social policy. Chief amongst them for over thirty years from 1857 to 1886 was the National Association for the Promotion of Social Science. Arising out of a movement to extend the reformatory principle in prisons (in that way its origins similar to those of philanthropy in the eighteenth century), it grew to become a pressure group pushing for reform across the range of social policy. It secured the appointment of the Taunton Commission on education 1865–68 and the Royal Sanitary Commission 1869–71; it was largely responsible for the passage of the Married Women's Property Act of 1870 and it worked closely with trade unions.[54]

The Social Science Association was not immediately hostile to philanthropy, far from it. In January 1855 there appeared the first number of *The Philanthropist: Record of Social Amelioration, and Journal of the Charitable Institutions*. Defending its title against a potential reader who had argued that it might not be a wise one as 'people are afraid of the many errors of Philanthropy', it hoped to produce 'a "Year-book of facts" in connexion with Philanthropic effort, showing all that has been done, and pointing to what remains yet to do'. In issues up to mid-April 1855 it published accounts of the work of many charitable organisations, mainly in London, and then seems to have come to a halt, only to re-emerge in June as *The Philanthropist, and*

Prison and Reformatory Gazette: A Record of Social Amelioration and Journal of Charitable Institutions. 'Though philanthropy as it is embodied in our public charities and remedial institutions', it argued, 'is unquestionably one of the principal facts of the age, it possesses no recognized organ through which it can make its appeals, offer its earnest suggestions, and record its progress'.[55] This was interesting, both for its view that 'public charities and remedial institutions' constituted 'philanthropy' and for its claim, undoubtedly correct, that philanthropy had no outlet for publicity and discussion. Presumably not as successful as it had hoped to be, it kept casting around for an appropriate title and focus. From 1 January 1857 to 1 October 1857 it was *The Philanthropist and Prison and Reformatory Gazette*, then from 2 November 1857 to 1 March 1858 *The Philanthropist and Gazette of Charitable and Social Institutions.* In this latter guise it opened with a positive report on the opening meeting of the National Association for the Promotion of Social Science (NAPSS), and on 1 April 1858 became *The Philanthropist and Social Science Gazette*, announcing that the Council of the NAPSS had resolved that, for a limited time, each member of the Association would receive a copy of the journal and that it in turn would publish materials from the NAPSS.[56]

How long this arrangement lasted is uncertain, probably not beyond the end of the year when *The Philanthropist*, in its numerous guises, seems to have ceased publication. One reason may have been the tension between 'social science' and 'philanthropy'. Mark Pattison, attending the Association's Congress in Birmingham in 1857, picked it up when struck by how, instead of seeking to apply 'intrusive philanthropy' to the working class, the Social Science Association sought to change the middle class.[57] It was a top-down organisation, trumpeting its expertise. At the 1863 Congress, Charles Adderley, a Tory, and one of the leaders of the reformatory movement, detected 'an ebbing tide running strongly against philanthropy ... It is not practical philanthropy, but declamatory philanthropy, the dogmatic philanthropy of the platform and the press, which has somewhat exceeded the demand for it and produced a certain dulness in the market'. Two years earlier, in 1861, Benjamin Jowett, Master of Balliol College, Oxford, had voiced similar thoughts. Offering advice to Frances Power Cobbe, he warned her not to 'go to war with Political Economy because the Political Economists are a powerful and dangerous class' and also (though he acknowledged that she wouldn't agree with this), 'Because Political Economists have really done more for the labouring classes by their advocacy of Free Trade, etc, than all the philanthropists put together'. 'I wish', he went on, 'that it was possible as a matter of taste to get rid of all philanthropic expressions, "missions", etc which are distasteful to the educated. But I suppose they are necessary for the collection of money'.[58] There was something about the language of philanthropy, about its modes of address, about its assumed policies, that grated on people like Adderley and Jowett. Reforms, they felt, had more chance of success if not contaminated by mention of it or association with it. The Social Science Association seems to have shared that view, seeing philanthropy as too diffuse and open-ended to be embraced by an organisation with pretensions to guiding social policy-making. It saw itself as a science worthy of a place alongside political economy. 'The Association', wrote its secretary, G. W. Hastings, 'sprang out of the belief that many of our political economists have illogically narrowed their investigations by ignoring all view of moral duty'.[59]

A second rival to philanthropy was the COS, formed in 1869. As with the Social Science Association there was much overlap in aims. Those who wanted philanthropy to become a profession were as dismayed as the founders of the COS by the proliferation of charities and the opportunities thereby offered to charity-mongers, people living off different charities. There was overlap, too, in adherence to political economy. But the key figures behind the formation of the COS, C. S. Loch and Bernard Bosanquet, insisted that 'charity was not philanthropy'. For them 'The goal of charity was the promotion of a sense of membership in society'.[60]

There were further problems with philanthropy. The adjective 'fashionable' was often attached to it. Both the *Hampshire Telegraph and Sussex Chronicle* and *Reynolds's Newspaper* in 1852 criticised 'certain fashionable philanthropists' meeting at Stafford House under the auspices of the Duchess of Sutherland to consider an address to their 'sisters' in the United States concerning slavery. This was 'fashionable' in the sense of aristocratic. It was 'humbug philanthropy' as 'A Scotsman' put it, recalling the role of the Sutherlands in the Highland clearances. And it was costless – 'the loss of one turn round Hyde Park is all their little bit of philanthropy will have cost them'.[61] Closely linked with this exclusively aristocratic philanthropy was the fashionable philanthropy of social climbing. In Liverpool *Porcupine* in 1861 reported its belief that 'The most fashionable amusement of the present age is philanthropy … No small number of these benevolent persons are philanthropic because it is the fashion to be so; because it brings them into passing contact with this Bishop or that Earl, or even with Mr Cropper or Mr Rathbone, or any other of our leading local philanthropists'.[62] Such fashion could have the effect of there being 'social consequences of refusing to give'.[63] There might be a positive side to that but there was none at all in what the *Westminster Review* in 1869 described as 'that fashionable philanthropy which has talked so much and effected so little'.[64] The jibe dating back to the 1830s that philanthropy was all talk retained its potency.

Philanthropy and effeminacy

Perhaps more serious to philanthropy's reputation was its association with 'effeminacy'. The contributor to the *Derby Mercury* in 1855 was aware that his rosy view of philanthropy was not shared by all and that critics saw the country in decline because of 'the effeminacy of our habits'.[65] T. B. Macaulay, Whig politician and historian, must have been nursing such thoughts for he could take some comfort amidst the trials of the 1857 Indian uprising that at least it had struck a blow at 'effeminate philanthropy'.[66] The *Pall Mall Gazette* in 1865 in an article headed 'Masculine philanthropy', regretted 'the very general association which has been produced of late years between philanthropy and effeminacy'. It did not doubt that

> the philanthropists are much to blame both for their sentimentalism and for the cowardly abhorrence of inflicting, or even permitting pain, which is one of the great evils of modern society ... It would be highly important, if possible, to break the association between philanthropy and weakness, and to show how and on what principles a man might be philanthropic and that effectually, in a prosaic way, as a matter of business, and without being bothered with many of the associations which usually cling about such pursuits.

'Many women', it went on, 'and some men are by nature, and without any affectation at all, cast in the pathetic mould'. Their work could be valuable, but 'Still it is highly important that philanthropy should not be left altogether in their hands, and that the sterner and more businesslike sides of practical philanthropy – theoretical philanthropy has in general been only too stern – should be adequately represented'. By 'theoretical philanthropy' the *Pall Mall Gazette* almost certainly had political economy in its sights. For practical philanthropy it recommended that gentlemen (and they had to be gentlemen) should become Poor Law Guardians, the Poor Law 'the great instrument of public philanthropy'. Such work 'is essentially masculine, and requires the possession of all the masculine qualities in no common degree'.[67] Philanthropy in this perspective was a male role, 'private charity' feminine.

The male anxiety running through these comments reflected the fact that women were becoming increasingly prominent in philanthropy and in public life more generally. Writing advice for the poor (for example Hannah More) or fiction for the middle classes (for example Elizabeth Gaskell's *North and South*) could bring about improvement in the behaviour of the poor or provide a role model for middle-class women – it could in itself be philanthropic.[68] On the ground, visiting the poor in their homes and fund-raising, especially through bazaars, women were dominant. They constituted a rising percentage of subscribers to many charities and there was 'an explosion of charities managed exclusively by women'. By the 1890s about 500,000 women were estimated to be labouring 'continuously and semi-professionally' in charitable work.[69]

The roles that women were able or permitted to take in public charities were often confined to what could be safely described as domestic. In the hospital in Leeds, for example, their role was to ensure that linen was clean.[70] Increasingly, however, women were breaking out of these restrictions. Elizabeth Fry was the most notable example. She founded in 1821 the British Ladies Society for Promoting the Reformation of Female Prisoners, she criticised the solitary system that was being imposed in prisons, she argued for classification of first offenders by their character not their crime, she called, as early as 1827, for women to extend prison visiting to hospitals, lunatic asylums and workhouses, she withstood as best she could the criticism of men. Her work was largely within the state system of prisons and that necessarily gave her a public and political status. As Anne Summers concluded, 'Elizabeth Fry's career demonstrates how many meanings may be contained in the term philanthropy, and how paradoxical is its relationship to state agency'.[71] In the second half of the century many women found that the boundary between charitable or philanthropic and political work was porous. Louisa Twining, for example, had experience as Lady Superintendent of two charitable homes, but also campaigned tirelessly for improved nursing in workhouses, for women inspectors and women as Poor Law Guardians. She was president of the Women in Local Government Society.[72] Particularly in families where there was a tradition of public service, many of them Quaker or Unitarian, women were doing much more than fund-raising or, even if outside the home, attending to domestic tasks.[73] Alluding to a poet's fear that the Church was becoming 'womanized', Frank Prochaska concluded that 'organized philanthropy had become "womanized" in the nineteenth century'.[74] It was this that alarmed many men.

Josephine Butler in 1869 recognised the gendered division. She set out an agenda in a quotation from an unattributed source:

> Philanthropy and politics, now flowing apart, will unite in one stream when philanthropists become conscious of power to reach the *sources* of crime and misery, and when statesmen understand that their functions are assigned to them for none but a philanthropic end … That mankind may reach a better state, philanthropy, like religion, must be the work and duty of all, not of a select few. With a view to this, women (whose heart is our great reservoir of tenderness) must have hope of, not merely palliating, but uprooting national evil.

This vision of philanthropy and politics working in unity, and of women having an essential role, was followed by recognition of the inadequacies of the present. She wrote of 'the present pretty general realization of the futility, if not the positive harm, of many forms of private philanthropy, and the often-repeated depreciation of meddling individuals who pauperize the community by their old-fashioned, Lady-Bountiful way of dispensing alms and patronage'. No Lady Bountiful role for Josephine Butler. She then called for 'the large infusion of Home elements' into every kind of institution, and continued:

> We have had experience of what we may call the feminine form of philanthropy, and independent individual ministering, of too medieval a type to suit the present day. It has failed. We are now about to try the masculine

form of philanthropy – large and comprehensive measures, organizations and systems planned by men and sanctioned by Parliament. This also will fail if it so far prevail as to extinguish the truth to which the other method witnessed in spite of its excesses. Why should we not try at least a union of principles which are equally true?

Without this, without a larger role for women, 'The large and magnificently-ordered Institution is in danger of becoming as fatally a pauperizing influence as the Lady Bountiful'.[75]

If men were worried about effeminacy in philanthropy, women were worried about the dominance within it of masculine modes of thinking and action.

The novelists

'Novelists', F. B. Money-Coutts noted in 1884, 'generally make their philanthropists fools'.[76] It comes as something of a shock, however, to see how critical they were of charity and philanthropy. They don't simply poke fun at fund-raising bazaars.

Charles Dickens was actively engaged in a range of philanthropic or charitable projects, but he didn't disguise his feelings about the approach and attitude of some philanthropists, especially their focus on 'telescopic philanthropy'. In *Bleak House* Jo sweeps the doorstep of the Society for the Propagation of the Gospel in Foreign Parts, Mrs Jellyby is preoccupied with her project for Borrioboola-Gha on the left bank of the Niger to the neglect of her own family and the fearsome Mrs Pardiggle focuses her attention on the Tockahoopo Indians. In part this was an attack on Christianity gone wrong, but it also had in its sights a neglect of home problems in favour of those being faced by missionaries in the front line of what Alison Twells has called 'global missionary philanthropy'.[77]

In his unfinished novel, *The Mystery of Edwin Drood* (1870), Dickens broadened his attack to encompass philanthropy in all shapes and forms. The Reverend Septimus Crisparkle, a Minor Canon in a cathedral town, and his mother have agreed to take responsibility for two orphaned teenagers. News of their impending arrival comes in a letter from Luke Honeythunder (probably modelled on John Bright[78]), his letterhead 'Haven of Philanthropy, Chief Offices, London' where there is an ongoing meeting 'of our Convened Chief Composite Committee of Central and District Philanthropists'. Honeythunder takes the opportunity to write the letter while a long report is being read 'denouncing a public miscreant'. Crisparkle, a gentle and good man, a model muscular Christian, reflects how 'extraordinary' it is 'that these Philanthropists are always denouncing somebody. And it is another extraordinary thing that they are always so violently flush of miscreants!'

On arrival with the orphans, Honeythunder, a loud-mouthed bully, 'walked in the middle of the road, shouldering the natives out of his way, and loudly developing a scheme he had, for making a raid on all the unemployed persons in the United Kingdom, laying them every one by the heels in jail, and forcing them, on pain of prompt extermination, to become philanthropists'. Honeythunder's philanthropy, wrote Dickens, 'was of that gunpowderous sort that the difference between it and animosity was hard to determine':

> You were to go to the offices of the Haven of Philanthropy, and put your name down as a Member and a Professing Philanthropist. Then, you were to pay up your subscription, get your card of membership and your riband and medal, and were evermore to live upon a platform, and evermore to say what Mr Honeythunder said, and what the Treasurer said, and what the sub-Treasurer said, and what the Committee said, and what the sub-Committee said, and what the Secretary said, and what the Vice Secretary said.[79]

In a later chapter, entitled 'Philanthropy, professional and unprofessional', Dickens turned the screws on 'Professing Philanthropists', comparing them unfavourably to 'professors of the Noble Art of fisticuffs'. The Philanthropists 'were in very bad training: much too fleshy'. They lacked 'the good temper of the Pugilists, and used worse language'. And finally, 'their fighting code stood in great need of revision, as empowering them not only to bore their man to the ropes, but to bore him to the confines of distraction; also to hit him when he was down, hit him anywhere and anyhow, kick him, stamp upon him, gouge him, and maul him behind his back without mercy'. Crisparkle, at uncharacteristic length, takes Honeythunder to task for his reliance on 'platform manners or platform manoeuvres among the decent forbearances of private life', seeing it as 'detestable … an unendurable nuisance'.[80]

Dickens was not laughing at philanthropy and philanthropists, he was confronting it and them head on and with feeling. He hated the bureaucracy that had enveloped it, the committees, the officers – and the exploitation that went with it, Mr Honeythunder being served by 'a miserably shabby and underpaid stipendiary Philanthropist (who could hardly have done worse if he had taken service with a declared enemy of the human race)'. Above all, Dickens took exception to the platform style of public philanthropy.

George Eliot in *Middlemarch* (1871) was equally wide-ranging in her criticism of philanthropy. In her extended portraits of two types of philanthropist, the secular Mr Brooke and the evangelical 'philanthropic banker', Mr Bulstrode, she came close to questioning the whole of philanthropy. Brooke, for whom philanthropy was mainly about 'punishments and that kind of thing', is vague and ineffective, his deficiencies mercilessly exposed by the public and the newspapers when he makes the mistake of standing for Parliament. Bulstrode, under the guise of philanthropy, seeks to exercise

power as well as to keep the lid on his own misdemeanours. Dorothea duti-
fully surrounds herself with 'her particular little heap of books on political
economy' as a guide to action, but quickly puts them aside to follow the
dictates of her heart. She alone comes through with a clean bill of health.[81]

Godfrey Ablewhite in Wilkie Collins's *The Moonstone*, set in the late 1840s,
published in 1868,

> was a barrister by profession; a ladies' man by temperament; and a good
> Samaritan by choice. Female benevolence and female destitution could do
> nothing without him ... Wherever there was a table with a committee of
> ladies sitting round it in council, there was Mr. Godfrey at the bottom
> of the board, keeping the temper of the committee, and leading the dear
> creatures along the thorny ways of business, hat in hand. I do suppose this
> was the most accomplished philanthropist (on a small independence) that
> England ever produced.

With his 'head of lovely long flaxen hair, falling negligently over the poll of his
neck ... with his eyes, most lovely, charming the money out of your pockets',
he was a favourite at Exeter Hall and 'quite a public character'.[82] The charities with which he was connected that are highlighted in *The Moonstone* are
the 'Mothers'-Small-Clothes-Conversion-Society', its object to rescue unre-
deemed fathers' trousers from the pawnbroker and to shorten them to be
worn by the son, and the 'British-Ladies'-Servants'-Sunday-Sweetheart-
Supervision Society'.[83] This is good knock-about humour, the part of the
book that 'was most successful in amusing the public'. There is more bite to
the conversation between an eminent explorer, Mr Murthwaite, and Mathew
Bruff, a solicitor, about the theft of the moonstone:

> 'There was a story (was there not?) about Mr. Godfrey Ablewhite. I am
> told he is an eminent philanthropist – which is decidedly against him, to
> begin with.'
> I heartily agreed in this with Mr. Murthwaite.[84]

They have, of course, picked on the culprit.

The Moonstone, The Mystery of Edwin Drood and *Middlemarch* were
published in the years 1868–72. On the one hand, the focus in each on philanthropy stands as testimony to the important role it played in public life. It
is difficult to imagine major novelists making such an issue of philanthropy
in other periods. On the other hand, the message the novels conveyed was
unremittingly critical. It is difficult not to conclude that Dickens, Collins and
Eliot were not simply giving voice to their individual concerns but were also
confident that what they wrote would resonate with their readers. If that was
the case, but there is little evidence one way or the other, philanthropy and
philanthropists were in trouble.

Conclusion

Philanthropy in the mid-Victorian period could mean many different things, as could 'philanthropist'. William Arnot reflected on this in 1856, writing of philanthropy that

> No one pauses over the word when it occurs in his newspaper, or turns up his dictionary to investigate its meaning. Philanthropy looms large, although it be not very sharply outlined in the imagination of Englishmen. It is the habit of doing good to the wretched at great sacrifice to the doer, and accompanied generally with a dash of eccentricity. Your philanthropist has a gait different from other men. He is absent and harmless. He is less knowing that most men of business. There is a softness about him which everybody admires, but nobody would like to imitate.[85]

This, from a Scottish Free Church Minister, lecturing in Manchester, was hardly a ringing endorsement. It suggested that philanthropy and philanthropists were on the margins of society, all very well in their place, but out of touch with what critics might call 'the real world', the world of business and making a living. Philanthropists were odd, eccentric, recognisable by the peculiarities of the way they walked. What is also striking is that philanthropists are men – though their 'softness' suggests that they not truly masculine, a widespread view. It is worth bearing this marginality in mind when encountering those who basked in the thought of the generosity of the British and saw philanthropy as a central plank in the national identity.

The positive discourse about philanthropy was in fact consistently and powerfully challenged. There was nothing quite like the sustained attack by *The Times* in the 1830s and 1840s, but no one paying any attention to the public press or to fiction could be unaware of the level of criticism. Political economists were at the forefront of this. Five per cent philanthropy offered the hope that capitalism and philanthropy could work hand in hand, but its overall impact was marginal. The 'professional' philanthropist was pilloried in journalism and fiction.

The *Saturday Review* was founded in the 1850s with middle-of-the-road liberal Conservative views. Here are its headlines about philanthropy in the 1860s and 1870s: 'Philandering philanthropy', 'Foolish philanthropy', 'Sentiment and philanthropy', 'The limits of philanthropy', 'Incendiary philanthropy', 'Philanthropy in a passion'.[86] The first was an attack on fundraising bazaars, reliant for their success on 'the love of flirting, dress, and dissipation incident to the female bosom'. In the second the target was a proposal to open foundling hospitals in the wake of a scare about infanticide. The third warned against mistaking 'sentiment for philanthropy'. The fourth urged recognition of how difficult it was to live a life wholly philanthropic.

The final two shifted the focus to foreign policy, attacking Gladstone and Bright for their activities in the Eastern Question. These six articles were spread over fifteen years and do not amount to a consistent campaign to undermine philanthropy. What they perhaps suggest is that copy editors saw philanthropy as something that readers had an instinctive wariness about. And the *Saturday Review* had a countrywide influence, provincial papers reproducing its articles – you could, for example, read about 'Philandering philanthropy' in the *Westmoreland Gazette* and about 'Foolish philanthropy' in the *Hampshire Advertiser*.[87]

One feature of these years was the level of agreement between proponents and critics of philanthropy about its primary target. Philanthropy directed its attention towards the poor. It was judged by its achievements in relieving poverty – or in its failure to do so. There was continuing debate as to how far philanthropy should stretch outside the borders of the nation but, although Dickens did not invent the term 'telescopic philanthropy' until the 1850s, the most virulent debates about it took place in the first half of the century. The provision of a cultural infrastructure for cities and towns in the shape of museums, art galleries and parks, a prominent development in the period, featured hardly at all in public discourse about philanthropy. There was, however, one way in which the bounds of philanthropy were extending. *The Times* in the 1850s, quite positively, and the *Saturday Review* in the 1870s, much less so, both recognised that philanthropic ideas were at work in international relations. They were also playing their part in party politics, the Liberals seen as the party of philanthropy even though the political economists within it railed against it.

Notes

1 *The Times*, 24 Jan. 1859.
2 Ibid., 7 Feb. 1859.
3 Ibid., 13 July 1853.
4 Ibid., 22 Dec. 1859; 11 Mar. 1857.
5 Ibid., 10 Oct. 1879; 29 May 1848; 2 Oct. 1885.
6 *Derby Mercury*, 27 June 1855.
7 *Preston Guardian*, 1 Feb. 1862.
8 *Essex Standard*, 14 Sept. 1877.
9 J. Garnett, '"Gold and the Gospel": Systematic beneficence in mid-nineteenth-century England', in W. J. Sheils and D. Wood (eds), *The Church and Wealth* (Oxford: Basil Blackwell, 1987), pp. 347–58, quoting p. 347. See G. Best, *Mid-Victorian Britain 1851–75* (London: Weidenfeld & Nicolson, 1971), pp. 138–9 for the argument that the total of money given is 'utterly incalculable'.
10 *Examiner*, 4 Feb. 1871; *Liverpool Mercury*, 22 Dec. 1873.
11 *Good Words*, Dec. 1875, pp. 528–32; *Sunderland Daily Echo*, 24 Jan. 1879.

12 F. Prochaska, *Royal Bounty: The Making of a Welfare Monarchy* (New Haven and London: Yale University Press, 1995), pp. 67–99, quoting pp. 85, 80, 89, 77, 94–6.
13 Ibid., pp. 106–7, 124.
14 Ibid., p. 83; *Derby Mercury*, 27 June 1855.
15 Prochaska, *Royal Bounty*, pp. 118–19; *The Times*, 26 Feb. 1879.
16 *The Times*, 6 May 1879.
17 Ibid., 20 May 1879; see also 12 May 1856.
18 Ibid., 10 Sept. 1853; 27 Dec. 1881; 10 May 1886.
19 Ibid., 25 Oct. 1887; 11 Nov. 1879.
20 These adjectives come from *The Times*.
21 *The Times*, 9 Nov. 1850.
22 *Poverty in theVictorianAge*,Vol. III, *Charity* (Farnborough: Gregg International Publishers, 1973), 'Charity, noxious and beneficent', pp. 81, 88.
23 Quoted in G. R. Searle, *Morality and the Market in Victorian Britain* (Oxford: Clarendon Press, 1998), p. 188.
24 W. R. Greg, 'Political economy', *Westminster Review*, 28 (1865), 119.
25 *The Times*, 18 Feb. 1859.
26 Quoted in A. Vernon, *A Quaker Business Man: The Life of Joseph Rowntree* (London: Allen & Unwin, 1958), p. 64.
27 T. Beggs, 'Misdirected philanthropy as an economical question', quoted in *Examiner*, 16 Jan. 1869, p. 44; *Poverty in theVictorianAge*, 'The philanthropy of the age in its relation to social evils', pp. 446, 453–7; 'Charity', p. 684; Bagehot quoted in Searle, *Morality and the Market*, p. 192.
28 *The Times*, 30 Dec. 1878.
29 W. Bagehot, *Physics and Politics* (1872: London: Kegan Paul,Trench,Trübner & Co, n.d.), pp. 88–9.
30 B. Harrison, 'Philanthropy and theVictorians', in *Peaceable Kingdom: Stability and Change in Modern Britain* (Oxford: Clarendon Press, 1982), p. 246; *The Times*, 28 Feb. 1879.
31 Quoted in M. J. D. Roberts, 'Reshaping the gift relationship: The London Mendicity Society and the suppression of begging in England 1818–1869', *International Review of Social History*, 36 (1991), 229–30.
32 B. Lambert, *East End Pauperism* (London: James Parker, 1869), p. 11.
33 J. R. Green, *Stray Studies from England and Italy* (London: Macmillan, 1876), pp. 19–25. Denison quoted in K. Woodroofe, *From Charity to Social Work in England and the United States* (London: Routledge & Kegan Paul, 1962), p. 26.
34 *The Times*, 6 Dec. 1860.
35 Ibid., 22 Jan. 1879.
36 Ibid., 26 Sept. 1889.
37 J. N. Tarn, *Five Per Cent Philanthropy: An Account of Housing in Urban Areas between 1840 and 1914* (Cambridge: Cambridge University Press, 1973), pp. 15–22.
38 Ibid., pp. 22–7.
39 Ibid., pp. 44–50.

40 Ibid., pp. 50–8.
41 S. Morris, 'Market solutions for social problems: Working-class housing in nineteenth-century London', *Economic History Review*, 54 (2001), 525–45.
42 National Dwellings Society Ltd., *Philanthropy and Five Per Cent* (1887).
43 P. L. Garside, 'The impact of philanthropy: Housing provision and the Sutton Model Dwellings Trust, 1900–1939', *Economic History Review*, 53 (2000), 742–66.
44 E. Lascelles, 'Charity', in G. M. Young (ed.), *Early Victorian England*, 2 vols (Oxford: Oxford University Press, 1934), Vol. 2, p. 345.
45 Quoted in F. Prochaska, *Christianity and Social Service in Modern Britain: The Disinherited Spirit* (Oxford: Oxford University Press, 2006), p. 72.
46 *Saturday Review*, 20 Aug. 1859, 217–18.
47 *The Times*, 11 Mar. 1857.
48 Ibid., 24 July 1858.
49 *Saturday Review*, 20 Aug. 1859, 217.
50 *Theological Review*, July 1866, 'English philanthropy and English religion', 342; *Examiner*, 15 May 1869, 'Recurrent philanthropy', pp. 314–15; *Westminster Review*, April 1869, 'The philanthropy of the age in relation to social evils', pp. 445, 447, 452.
51 *London Journal*, 13 July 1872, 20–1.
52 *The Times*, 5 May 1884.
53 Ibid., 22 Nov. 1898.
54 L. Goldman, *Science, Reform, and Politics in Victorian Britain: The Social Science Association 1857–1886* (Cambridge: Cambridge University Press, 2001).
55 *The Philanthropist: Record of Social Amelioration, and Journal of the Charitable Institutions*, No. 1, 20 Jan. 1855; *The Philanthropist, and Prison and Reformatory Gazette; A Record of Social Amelioration, and Journal of Charitable Institutions*, 1 June 1855, 12–13.
56 *The Philanthropist and Social Science Gazette*, 1 Apr. 1858, 84.
57 Quoted in Goldman, *Science, Reform, and Politics*, p. 68.
58 Adderley in *The Times*, 12 Oct. 1863; E. Abbott and L. Campbell (eds), *Letters of Benjamin Jowett, MA, Master of Balliol College, Oxford* (London: John Murray, 1899), p. 173.
59 Quoted in ibid., p. 143.
60 J. Lewis, *The Voluntary Sector, the State and Social Work in Britain: The Charity Organisation Society/Family Welfare Association since 1869* (Aldershot: Edward Elgar, 1995), p. 25.
61 *Hampshire Telegraph and Sussex Chronicle*, 11 Dec. 1852; *Reynolds's Newspaper*, 19 Dec. 1852. For more on the Duchess's anti-slavery activity and the criticism it evoked, see K. D. Reynolds, *Aristocratic Women and Political Society in Victorian Britain* (Oxford: Clarendon Press, 1998), pp. 121–8.
62 Quoted in M. Simey, *Charity Rediscovered: A Study of Philanthropic Effort in Nineteenth-Century Liverpool* (Liverpool: Liverpool University Press, 1992), pp. 56–7.
63 *Theological Review*, July 1866, 343.
64 *Westminster Review*, Apr. 1869, 440–1.

65 *Derby Mercury*, 27 June 1855.
66 C. Hall, *Macaulay and Son: Architects of Imperial Britain* (New Haven and London: Yale University Press, 2012), pp. 325–6.
67 *Pall Mall Gazette*, 18 Oct. 1865.
68 D. W. Elliott, *The Angel out of the House: Philanthropy and Gender in Nineteenth-Century England* (Charlottesville: University of Virginia Press, 2002); P. Comitini, *Vocational Philanthropy and British Women's Writing 1790–1810: Wollstonecraft, More, Edgeworth, Wordsworth* (Aldershot: Ashgate, 2005).
69 F. K. Prochaska, *Women and Philanthropy in Nineteenth-Century England* (Oxford: Clarendon Press, 1980), pp. 29, 32, 224.
70 S. Morgan, *A Victorian Woman's Place: Public Culture in the Nineteenth Century* (London: Taurus, 2007), p. 94.
71 A. Summers, '"In a few years we shall none of us that now take care of them be here": Philanthropy and the state in the thinking of Elizabeth Fry', *Historical Research*, 67 (1994), 134–42.
72 T. Deane, 'Late nineteenth-century philanthropy: The case of Louisa Twining', in A. Digby and J. Stewart (eds), *Gender, Health and Welfare* (London: Routledge, 1996), pp. 122–42.
73 See, for example, M. Martin, 'Single women and philanthropy: A case study of women's associational life in Bristol, 1880–1914', *Women's History Review*, 17 (2008), 395–417.
74 Prochaska, *Women and Philanthropy*, pp. 69, 223.
75 J. E. Butler, 'Introduction', in J. E. Butler (ed.), *Women's Work and Women's Culture: A Series of Essays* (London: Macmillan, 1869), pp. xvii–xviii, xxxvi–xxxviii.
76 *The Times*, 14 Apr. 1884.
77 A. Twells, *The Civilising Mission and the English Middle Class 1792–1850: The 'Heathen' at Home and Overseas* (Basingstoke: Palgrave Macmillan, 2008), p. 211.
78 C. Dickens, *The Mystery of Edwin Drood*, ed. A. J. Cox (Harmondsworth: Penguin, 1974), p. 306.
79 Ibid., pp. 80–6.
80 Ibid., pp. 202–8.
81 G. Eliot, *Middlemarch* (1871; Oxford: Oxford University Press, 1997), *passim*, quoting pp. 82, 756.
82 W. Collins, *The Moonstone* (1868; Oxford: Oxford University Press, 1999), pp. 54–5.
83 Ibid., pp. 193–4, 226.
84 Ibid., pp. lv, 286.
85 W. Arnot, *Christian Philanthropy* (Manchester: YMCA, 1856), p. 4.
86 *Saturday Review*, 18 July 1863; 9 Sept. 1865; 3 Feb. 1865; 27 July 1867; 25 Apr. 1868; 21 Oct. 1876; 4 May 1878.
87 *Westmorland Gazette*, 25 July 1863; *Hampshire Advertiser*, 16 Sept. 1865.

9

The failure of philanthropy?
1880–1914

Discussion of philanthropy reached a peak in the late nineteenth century. The fundamental question that lay behind much of what was written was whether philanthropy was capable of coping with, far less resolving, the social problems that beset urban society: poor housing and sanitation, ill-health, unemployment; all this in a highly charged atmosphere centering around 'urban degeneration' and 'the future of the race'. Out of these discussions emerged different views of the proper role of philanthropy. Some felt that it had ceased to have any useful role at all and that the state should take over responsibilities that had hitherto been those of charity and philanthropy. In a word, it had failed. There were also three new competing versions of philanthropy. One stressed personal service to the poor as the hallmark of philanthropy. The second looked to a spread of employer philanthropy. And the third trumpeted what big money could contribute to resolving social ills and in providing an urban cultural infrastructure. These attempts to sustain or rebrand philanthropy failed to halt a striking decline in its prevalence in public discourse.

Altruism

One indicator of the difficulties that philanthropy faced was the spread from the 1880s onwards of a new word, altruism.[1] George Henry Lewes had introduced 'altruism' to Britain in 1852. He borrowed it from Auguste Comte whose writing had a profound influence in shaping a positivist movement and a Religion of Humanity. Comte set the goalposts for a good life high: you must live for others. Altruism was paired with its opposite, 'egoism'. Disowning Christianity, and arguing that altruism was in accordance with nature and evolution, the 'altruists', as some of them began to be called, posed a threat to orthodox Christianity and to the philanthropy that was so closely tied to it. Christians, the altruists argued, were at root egoists, concerned primarily for their own individual salvation. Altruists, by contrast, envisaged their own lives within an evolutionary progress.

In the 1850s, 1860s and 1870s there were intense debates about altruism but within a narrow circle. It is telling that altruism gets no mention at all in *The Times* until 1880. From then onwards, very largely through the popularity of the writings of Herbert Spencer, altruism began to be much more widely used, not only in works of philosophy but filtering through into novels and other manifestations of a wider culture.[2] In September 1884, in her mid-twenties, Beatrice Potter (the future Beatrice Webb) copied out for her own guidance a passage from Comte that included the lines, 'altruism alone can enable us to live in the highest and truest sense. To live for others is the only means of developing the whole existence of man'. Her future pattern of life, she later reflected, stemmed from 'the flight of emotion away from the service of God to the service of man, and from the current faith in the scientific method'.[3] This kind of conversion to altruism spelt danger for philanthropy. Philanthropy seemed old-fashioned, altruism modern. It was not philanthropy but altruism that a Canadian writer found to be 'the greatest force in most of the social movements of our day'. In the university settlements in East London, reported one commentator, '"altruism" and "collectivism" are the commonplaces of every would-be social reformer'. The Duke of Argyll might with some justice complain, while reviewing one of the bestsellers of the 1890s, Benjamin Kidd's *Social Evolution*, that 'Altruism is the new and very affected name for the old familiar things which we used to call Charity, Philanthropy, and Love', but he was in effect admitting that his last three belonged to the past.[4]

Altruism itself was under attack by the 1890s. Oscar Wilde in *The Soul of Man under Socialism* (1891) saw the chief advantage of socialism as being 'the fact that Socialism would relieve us from that sordid necessity of living for others'. He attacked 'the sickly cant about Duty' and 'an unhealthy and exaggerated altruism'.[5] For George Bernard Shaw in 1891 'the real slavery of today is slavery to the idea of goodness'. Ibsen was one inspiration for these comments, Nietzsche another. For Nietzsche, 'Bad conscience, the desire for self-mortification, is the wellspring of all altruistic values'. An English commentator in 1900 argued that 'The present furore over Nietzsche' should be seen as 'simply a part of the reaction against "psychological" and "romantic" literature and against foolish "altruism" and foolish "philanthropy"'. The joining of altruism and philanthropy, both 'foolish', was an indication of the challenge they jointly faced. Freud in 1917, seeing altruism as 'distinguished … by the absence of longings for sexual satisfaction', added a new note to the growing critique.[6]

'Not money, but yourselves'

Besides altruism, and not dissimilar from it in what it demanded of practitioners, a second major influence on philanthropy in the later nineteenth century stemmed from the work of T. H. Green. From Balliol College, Oxford, Green was the fountainhead of Idealist philosophy. Idealism differed from dominant utilitarianism in shifting away from the latter's emphasis on the individual moral agent to the idea that we are part of a larger society; we are citizens.[7] Green made the case that 'while the mass of men whom we call our brethren ... are left without the chance, which only the help of others can gain for them, of making themselves in act what in possibility we believe them to be', no one should 'surrender to enjoyments which are not incidental to that work of deliverance'.[8] It was a call to action that led directly to the settlement movement.

Green had a profound influence on anyone who came under his sway. He is the thinly disguised Mr Grey of Mrs Humphry Ward's novel *Robert Elsmere* (1888). Probably the bestseller of the nineteenth century with over one million copies sold in English-speaking countries by the early twentieth century, it explored Elsmere's loss of faith in a country parish where he encounters dismissal of philanthropy: an estate manager 'sneers at one for supposing any landowner has money for "philanthropy" just now', and the Squire, Roger Wendover, has contempt 'for all forms of altruistic sentiment ... He hated philanthropic cants'. Elsmere rediscovers his true self in the East End of London.[9] In 'The New Brotherhood of Christ' that he helped to set up, 'the rich devote themselves to the poor, and the poor bear with the rich'.[10]

It was against this background that Samuel Barnett, Church of England clergyman, social reformer and Warden of Toynbee Hall from 1884 to 1906, reflected on philanthropy and the new directions it might take in 1895 in an article for *Macmillan's Magazine* entitled 'The failure of philanthropy'. He was not alone in his thoughts. Five years previously, a writer in support of the Salvation Army's General Booth reflected on 'the miserable failure of so much well-meaning philanthropy'. 'What a depressing book', continued the article, 'would be candidly written "Confessions of a Philanthropist"! Chapter A, "My hopes;" Chapters B to X, "My disappointments and perplexity"'.[11] Barnett was, if more moderately, equally pessimistic. True, in London's East End where he worked, institutes and clubs had been founded, schools and better houses built, open spaces secured, a free library and public baths opened. 'Philanthropy is active', he acknowledged, 'but the prevailing feeling is one of anxiety'. The rich were nervous, the poor suspicious. 'With all its manifold activity philanthropy still fails to create peace and goodwill.' The reason for this, Barnett argued, lay in the motives that lay behind philanthropic activity: pity for the poor and 'a sort of pride in order'. For Barnett these 'motives of much modern philanthropy ... will never create a City of Friends' (a phrase he borrowed from Walt Whitman). Worse, 'A philanthropist, inspired by such motives, may, as many have been known to do, by his gifts corrupt a whole neighbourhood'. Detecting two growing 'forms of evil ... impertinence and gambling', he blamed 'the ways of philanthropy' for tending to encourage rather than check them. It was 'a matter of common talk', Barnett asserted, 'that the efforts of philanthropy are disappointing'.

To improve matters Barnett invoked 'Christian godliness', by which he meant recognition of the spark of divinity that 'lies hidden in common men and women'. Armed with this sense, the philanthropist would unite thought and action: he 'will give by quite another measure than that of a tenth or a half, and by quite another rule than that of expediency. He will give himself, and by study he will make himself worth giving. There would be a City of Friends'.[12]

Friendship was central to this vision of a new philanthropy. Samuel's wife, Henrietta, writing on 'Women as philanthropists', asserted that 'friendship is powerful enough to break down all barriers, social or educational, powerful enough to lighten cloud-darkened lives ... It is only the gift of friendship, of love, which can help the world ... It has been woman's work to teach love'. Barnett did not attempt to disguise that the friendship she advocated was one that crossed class barriers. It was the friendship offered by Octavia Hill and her rent collectors, the friendship of cross-class social occasions in ladies' drawing rooms, the friendship that brought working-class girls and women into contact with art galleries and concerts, middle-class women here acting out their role as 'pleasure-givers'. In this new philanthropy class would not disappear but would be softened by friendship and love. To describe it simply as 'service' was to ignore the emotional side to it, especially, Henrietta Barnett implies, for women.[13]

Samuel Barnett's belief that philanthropy should not be about gifting money was echoed by Sir Walter Besant in an address 'On University Settlements' in 1897. Seeing the work of Raikes, Buxton, Howard and Elizabeth Fry as 'sporadic', with 'no large organization ... in the direction of personal devotion', Besant continued:

> We have attempted other forms of philanthropic endeavour; we have created schools and opened churches; we have founded alms-houses; we have written very fine essays on philanthropy; enormous sums – millions upon millions – have been given in charity. In spite of all, there has been little improvement; the slums seem to grow only worse instead of better, until – when? where? how? – we know not; but suddenly, as it seemed, unexpected as we thought, there ran through the minds of men and women the same words, the same formula, at the same time – 'Not money, but yourselves'. These words rang out in trumpet tones in the minds of those who heard – 'Not money, but yourselves'. .... The note of the new philanthropy is personal service; not money; not a cheque; not a subscription written; not speeches on a platform; not tracts; not articles in Quarterly Reviews; none of the old methods: but personal service – 'Not money, but yourselves'.[14]

Invocation of a 'new philanthropy' was in the air. In 'New philanthropy' in 1886 the *Pall Mall Gazette* had described Toynbee Hall as 'the centre of the new philanthropy, the shrine of personal service'. A book review in 1891 of Stanton Coit's *Neighbourhood Guilds: An Instrument of Social Reform* was entitled 'The new philanthropy'.[15] The Hon. and Rev. James Adderley in 1893, claiming that 'what East London wants is not so much people's money as their "selves", their personal friendship', saw Toynbee Hall as 'the immediate product of the new philanthropy'. In language that would have resonated with Barnett and Besant, and perhaps with the readers of the *English Illustrated Magazine*, he concluded a survey of manifestations of the new philanthropy with a clarion call: 'Let the sons of the upper classes strike out courageously beyond the conventional philanthropy of their parents; let them be dissatisfied with soup tickets and get over their suspicions of "Socialism" ... let them believe that to work amongst the poor is not an occupation only for a "duffer of a parson", but the duty of everyone who is called to be a son of God and therefore to give himself for others.'[16] There is, it's worth noting, no such role advocated for the daughters of the upper classes.

Adderley, Barnett, Besant and others were setting out a prospectus for a 'new philanthropy' that would be sharply distinguished from the old ways both of thinking and action. Barnett, looking back fourteen years to when the university settlement movement started, wrote how then 'Philanthropy ... appeared to many to be a sort of mechanical figure beautifully framed by men to do their duty to their brother men – made with long arms, so as to reach all needs, and with iron frame, so as to be never tired. It saved its inventors all further care beyond that of supplying it with money'. The settlements were a protest against this 'substitution of philanthropic machinery for human hands and personal knowledge'.[17] In tune with this, Beatrice Webb, like Barnett starting off working with the COS and influenced by him, felt that 'the advisability of charity' depended on 'the moral qualities which are developed in the relationship of giver and receiver'. What was clear to her was that 'it is distinctly *advantageous to us* to go amongst the poor'. There were drawbacks. 'Perhaps the worst result for us', she wrote, 'is that our philanthropy is sometimes the cause of pharisaical self-congratulation. I have never noticed this in the real philanthropist; he is far too perplexed at the very "mixed result" (even if he can recognize any permanent result) of his work, to feel much pride over it'.[18]

Besant's reiteration, 'Not money, but yourselves', encapsulated this 'new philanthropy', so critical of old ways. To be a philanthropist you didn't need money. The one unspoken attribute that you did need was to belong to a class above those you were trying to help. There is no doubt that the university settlement movement, with Toynbee Hall as the leading beacon, inspired many within the middle classes to give themselves, at least for a time. In praising General Booth of the Salvation Army as 'a great philanthropist' *The Times* in 1905 reflected on 'the remarkable development of what we may term the social sense in the last four or five decades … ideals of social service have come to be regarded by large sections of the community as part of the mental equipment of every right-thinking man'.[19]

In the long run, perhaps more significant, the notion of service lay behind the development of social work, first voluntary and by the beginning of the twentieth century beginning to be paid. Philanthropists were beginning to be of two kinds – those noted for giving money and those engaged in what was often called 'personal service'. One person could combine both roles but they may have been becoming increasingly separate. As the twentieth century wore on the personal service side of philanthropy was more and more encapsulated within social work. Where did that leave philanthropy?

The state takes over?

In the early twentieth century, B. Kirkman Gray, who had done his stint in the East End and written a pioneering history of philanthropy, reflected at length on the role of philanthropy.[20] The title he first projected for *Philanthropy and the State; or Social Politics* (1908), unfinished at his death, was *The Failure of Philanthropy*. He came to recognise, however, according to B. Leigh Hutchins who helped prepare the text for publication, 'the importance of the philanthropic movement in the agitation for reform, in the trial of experiments, and in the infusion of zeal and enthusiasm into the practical work of administration'. Gray's thesis, however, was stark: 'private philanthropy cannot provide a remedy for wide-spread want which results from broad and general social causes; that it ought not to be expected to do so; that the provision of such remedies is the proper responsibility of the State and should be accepted as such'.[21] Gray's argument was that 'in the course of the last two generations the State has been forced again and again to take over tasks for which private philanthropy had found its resources insufficient'. On elementary education, for example, 'The philanthropic maximum was less than the State minimum'. Even the COS recognised that with regard to tuberculosis, 'The problem is one altogether beyond the capacity of private philanthropy to solve and must sooner or later be faced by the State'.[22]

Gray argued that philanthropy, by drawing attention to social problems, and to the scale of them, was contributing to its own demise. 'Philanthropy', he wrote, 'as an institution has acquired inertia … A resolute treatment of social distress on a National scale would in a short time do away with much of it'. The need for philanthropy would be reduced if not eliminated 'if a living wage should become customary'. Nevertheless, Gray was happy to celebrate 'the influence of philanthropists in re-making citizenship and re-constructing politics'.[23] A key role for a philanthropist was as 'agitator', popularising ideas and stimulating to action. He distinguished different types of agitator, not all of which would feature in most lists of philanthropic action: the Shaftesbury or Evangelic type, the Chadwick type (after Edwin Chadwick), the socialist type, the statistical type, Charles Booth the leading exemplar, and the literary type. 'Philanthropy's highest distinction', wrote Gray, 'is to produce a perfect agitator'.[24]

Philanthropy had faced criticism from its inception. Most of it came from outside the world of philanthropy, from defenders of slavery, from hard-nosed advocates of harsh penalties for crime, and so on. The novelty of the situation in the late nineteenth and early twentieth centuries was that the criticism was coming from within the world of philanthropy. Adderley, Barnett and Besant, and many others connected with the settlement movement, wanted philanthropy to recast the relationship between rich and poor, between, in Webb's words, 'giver and receiver', to make it one of friendship. If this was to happen the entire structure of old philanthropy, Barnett's 'philanthropic machinery', needed to be dismantled or bypassed. Nevertheless, in this view, philanthropy had a vital role to play in society. Gray, a decade later, was not so certain. 'Social politics', a sign of it the New Liberal advances on school meals, children's health and old age pensions, while it retained a role for voluntary organisations, was toppling philanthropy from its previous position as the prime provider.

Doubts about the ability of charity and philanthropy to solve social problems, stemming from within their own ranks, were vocal and sustained. In *Toiling Liverpool* (1886), Hugh Farrie doubted 'whether charity is doing any good at all to society'.[25] Leonard Courtney, a rising Liberal politician, presiding at a meeting of the Kyrle Society in 1889 to supply gardens in Lambeth, warned that 'At the present time there was a great philanthropic movement permeating society; but while recognizing and feeling grateful for this fact, there must sometimes be a haunting suspicion that in philanthropists' desire to do good their zeal sometimes outran their discretion; that, instead of an improvement, a deterioration in the condition of the people was the end of much labour'.[26] From York Joseph Rowntree concluded in 1904 that 'much of our present philanthropic effort is directed to remedying the more superficial manifestations of weakness or evil'.[27] George Cadbury in Birmingham agreed. Rowntree's son, B. S. Rowntree, described how the impact of charity was no more than marginal. General Booth of the Salvation Army did not doubt that remedies for the human misery of the cities were 'beyond the imagination of most of those who spend their lives in philanthropic work'. The radical Countess of Warwick agreed: with hungry children, the unemployed and the aged, all in need of help, 'of what possible use is it', she asked, 'to plaster this state of things with philanthropy?' Even the COS admitted in 1886 that there were 'permanent causes of distress which it is impossible for philanthropy alone to cope with or even in any sufficient degree to palliate by schemes of direct relief'.[28]

'Is philanthropy futile?' headed a leading article in the Hull *Daily Mail* in 1907. It argued that 'the work of philanthropy will have to be taken out of private hands and organized. At present it is responsible for a great deal of social and moral mischief'. 'As the State progresses upward', said the Bishop of Southwell in 1910, 'the private philanthropist, whose efforts are so often attended with disastrous results, lowering to the moral fibre of both giver and receiver, will find his occupation limited to its proper sphere ... [T]he people, enjoying justice and freedom, will no longer be debauched by the charity of the rich who care not how they give'.[29] It is was this type of criticism that informed socialist critiques. The Social Democratic Federation regularly denounced charity and philanthropy for their patronising attitudes as well as the inadequacy of what they offered. In 'A word to philanthropists' in 1894, Sunderland's socialist paper claimed that the attitude of philanthropists to those they set out to help was to 'treat them as things to be amused, educated, restricted, lectured, advised, to have everything except fair play'. We were working out 'our own salvation', claimed the writer, and had no need of the 'canting sympathy and foolish patronage' of philanthropists.[30] The state alone, it was asserted, could tackle the problems that beset a late nineteenth- and early twentieth-century city. In Rotherham in 1906 the Cinderella club, set up to feed school children, was nevertheless uneasy at this engagement in what might pass for philanthropy: 'Our main work as socialists is to abolish the need for charity by establishing a system of justice for the workers, and making it the duty of the State to care for the sick and the needy.'[31] In the Liberal welfare reforms before the First World War, the state made its move. It was not that charity and philanthropy lost their raison d'être, far from it. Rather they lost any claim to be the leading partner in the mixed economy of welfare.

Philanthropy and capitalism

The development of capitalism generated large amounts of money in private hands. Successful entrepreneurs in the early years of industrialism had individually often devoted some of their profits to housing, allotments, churches, chapels, dispensaries, brass bands and choirs for their workers. They would probably have rejected 'paternalism' as a description of what they were doing, but this was largely what it was, an obligation on a par with the donations made by landed proprietors on their estates.

In the second half of the century there was something of a step change: donations began to be made to the urban cultural infrastructure of cities and towns. The *Morning Post* in 1853 noted how in factory towns the third generation of owners 'gives to churches, schools and almshouses with a ready charity' and thought 'The number of this class of men is increasing'.[32] This was a civilising mission that could hardly be objected to on political economy grounds. Public parks, libraries, museums, art galleries, swimming pools and universities came to be seen as facilities a city should certainly have and many smaller towns might aspire to. Some of these came about through municipal enterprise, perhaps with the help of ratepayers by virtue of facilitating mid-century acts of parliament, but private donations were also common. The People's Park in Halifax, for example, was presented to the town in 1857 by the industrialist Sir Francis Crossley, the Albert Park in Middlesbrough, opened in 1868, owed its existence to the finance provided by the Bolckow ironworks.[33] In Bristol, 'largely through private philanthropy', the city 'was provided with parks and open spaces, with a library system and a reformed central library, with a concert hall and a university college. It acquired an art gallery rather later than most in 1908: a gift of Sir W. H. Wills to his fellow citizens'. It was characteristic of such donations that, as Helen Meller has put it, 'the provision of facilities was personal and strongly connected to particular places'. That said, it owed little to popular demand, but much to competitive rivalry between towns and cities. No self-respecting place wanted to be without these facilities for leisure and culture; when the mayor of Bristol opened the Art Gallery he expressed his 'relief' that Bristol had now got one – though with only twelve pictures on display it was hardly a facility the city could boast about.[34] The opening of facilities of this kind was lavishly presented in the local press, but precisely because it was local there was little in national public discourse to suggest that philanthropy had found a new role.

Employers continued to make provision for their own workforces. It was driven quite as much by business logic as by concern for the wellbeing of the workforce; as Edward Cadbury acknowledged, 'business efficiency and the welfare of employees are but different sides of the same problem'. And the philanthropy of paternalism had its limits: the level of wages paid were set by supply and demand, and low wages, as, for example, in Huntley and Palmers in Reading, could co-exist with provision of socials, and library and sports facilities.[35] Some of the measures employers took were on a vast scale. Titus Salt built Saltaire in an attempt to move his workforce from nearby Bradford. By 1871 there were chapels, almshouses, a club and institute complex, a school of art, a gymnasium and fourteen acres of park where cricket and croquet were played.[36] Later in the nineteenth century and into the twentieth there were other notable examples of enterprise on this scale, many of them Quaker-inspired: the Cadburys in Bourneville, the Rowntrees in New Earswick, none of these schemes were without problems. In New Earswick the cheapest rents were beyond the reach of the poorest and not every employee was willing to accept the social discipline that the new settlements attempted to impose. James Walvin concluded that 'Too often the philanthropic industrial Quaker has been cast in the role of the selfless, almost saintly character anxious to do his best for his fellow men and women. In truth, what they set in place made good business sense'. And this applied not only to Quakers: J. D. Jeremy found from his study of William Lever's Port Sunlight, that he 'utilised religion in the service of his business objectives'.[37] Put another way, philanthropy of this kind was inextricably bound up with the development of the capitalist mode of production. As the *Sunderland Daily Echo* said of a pension fund set up by the London Docks Company that forbade employees to contribute to other funds, this was 'capitalist philanthropy'.[38]

Donation of money and resources for these developments was rarely described as 'philanthropy'. Towards the end of the century, however, there was a growing interest in 'millionaires' and what they might contribute to alleviate such social problems as housing. When the *Spectator* in 1872 published a list of the largest fortunes left during the previous ten years it 'obtained more readers than the best essay on politics we ever published'. There was a market for books with titles like *Fortunes Made in Business* (1883) and *Millionaires and How They Became So* (1884).[39] Millionaires, however, or at least self-made millionaires, were not common. The data exclude the fortunes of the aristocracy derived from land ownership but, bearing that in mind, in 1858 only one person left over £1 million. Thereafter numbers grew. In the years 1895–1914 there were thirty who left over £2 million, compared with only six who did so between 1873 and 1894. Four of the 1895–1914 cohort left over £5 million. In 1910–14 the average annual number of new millionaire estates was 9.8. The majority of these non-landed rich made their fortunes in finance and commerce, not industry, and especially in the City of London.[40] There was much talk, normally critical, of a new class of 'plutocrats' living lives of ostentatious luxury. It needs, however, to be put in perspective: W. D. Rubinstein found that 'The wealthiest American multi-millionaires of the late nineteenth and early twentieth centuries were approximately *twenty times* wealthier than the richest British business millionaires of the period'.[41]

Nevertheless there was wealth and philanthropy, as distinct from charity, became closely bound up with it; a book reviewer in 1939 commented that 'Charity comes, as a rule, from someone not immeasurably better off, but philanthropy smacks of millions'.[42] In an article on 'The poetry of wealth', J. R. Green, Vicar of Stepney and the historian of the English people, commented that 'The whole field of social experiment lies open to a great capitalist'. 'What fame', he reflected, 'the mere devotion of a quarter of a million to public uses may give to a quiet merchant the recent example of Mr Peabody abundantly showed'. Green envisaged a future when the rich would fund art galleries, museums and theatres, where 'a hundred thousand' now flung away at Newmarket or Tattersall's, could 'establish in the crowded haunts of working London great "Conservatoires" where the finest music might be brought to bear without cost on the coarseness and vulgarity of the life of the poor'. For the time being, however, 'Great parks and great houses, costly studs and costly conservatories, existence relieved of every hitch and every discomfort – these are the outlets which wealth has as yet succeeded in finding. For nobler outlets we must wait for the advent of the Poet-Capitalist'.[43]

Green's Mr Peabody was George Peabody, the American who gave half a million pounds to London, especially for housing the poor. He was seen as exceptional. A statue was erected to him on his death in 1869, unveiled by the Prince of Wales: 'His name', he said, 'will go down to posterity as a great philanthropist'. 'Probably few men', said the Lord Mayor, 'had been more activated by the true spirit of philanthropy'. *The Times* thought Peabody had 'discovered ... a new motive for heaping together wealth – the pleasure of giving it away'.[44] Few people would have imagined that he was pointing the way towards what philanthropy would become.

Andrew Carnegie's 1889 essay 'The gospel of wealth' (the title suggested by W. T. Stead for the English edition which itself was backed by William Gladstone) set the tone for what was to come. For the immensely rich Scottish-American industrialist individualism and competition were what raised living standards and inevitably led to the accumulation of large fortunes. Most charitable giving was harmful, the very poor and feckless beyond the reach of help. It was the aspirational who should be provided with ladders to ascend, and it was the rich who could do that. They must do it in their own lifetimes: to die rich was to die 'disgraced'. Asked to provide guidance on what to give to, Carnegie had seven suggestions. If you were mega-rich, found a new university. After that, in rank order, came libraries, hospitals, parks, halls, for example for concerts, swimming pools and churches.[45]

George Bernard Shaw held surprisingly similar views. In 'Socialism for millionaires', first published in 1896 and then reissued in 1901 as a Fabian Tract, he highlighted what he called the 'hidden sorrow of plutocracy', that its members had nothing to spend their money on. For Shaw, 'the modern substitution of Combination for Competition as the principle of capitalism is producing a new crop of individual fortunes so monstrous as to make their possessors publicly ridiculous'. Influenced by Carnegie, wrote Shaw, 'unloading' had become 'the order of the day'. John Ruskin had, years ago, set an example by publishing 'his accounts with the public', particularly in the financing of Sheffield Art Gallery. People had come to expect that Passmore Edwards would annually make 'investments for the common good'. But what of others? 'The problem is how to unload without the waste, pauperization, and demoralization that are summed up in England under the word charity.'[46]

Shaw, like Carnegie, ridiculed almsgiving, but cautioned against endowing hospitals (which should be financed by the public), and against educational endowments other than those for technical education: 'An intelligent millionaire', he wrote, 'unless he is frankly an enemy of the human race, will do nothing to extend the method of caste initiation practiced under the mask of education at Oxford and Cambridge'. More positively, millionaires should give in tranches of at least £10,000 and should finance luxuries and not necessities: 'Never give the people anything they want: give them something they ought to want and don't.' Support for high culture came high on his list. But he warned even well-meaning philanthropists not to expect public acclaim. There was too much giving as 'conscience money', as 'political bribery, and bids for titles', too much buying of 'moral credit by signing a cheque'. Quite often money given for a public object would be better spent raising wages for employees. 'The mere disbursement of large sums of money', he concluded, 'must be counted as a distinctly suspicious circumstance in estimating personal character'.[47]

Kirkman Gray also reflected on this increase in the number of the wealthy, and had no time for the idea that any donations they made could in any way be a substitute for the role of the state. In a rough note he wrote

> *The millionaire.* Note (1) his claim on social esteem, just for being a million-aire (2) he is justified by his benefactions; (3) reject the former and criticize the latter, *i.e. qua* millionaire, he is not a social element of value (but a pest); if all millionaires were benefactors (which they are not) it is doubtful if even their benefaction is socially valuable: (a) it depends on whim and may be unintelligent (b) it is incalculable, and therefore demoralizing.[48]

The association of philanthropy and millionaires was, however, enduring. In the late twentieth century it became the default way of thinking of philanthropy.

Peabody, however, was seen as an exception. It was twenty years before *The Times* could salute a successor, and this time an 'Englishman' (or perhaps more properly Irishman), Sir Edward Guinness, who gave quarter of a million pounds for housing in London and Dublin. 'Mr Peabody', *The Times* commented, 'was an American, and though Englishmen scatter their charity broadcast to an extent unequalled by any other nation, they have not hitherto developed the gift of doing such things on the grand scale'. There were perhaps good reasons for not doing so, for *The Times* acknowledged that Peabody's housing schemes had failed to improve the housing of the poorest.[49]

Not only did the British, the Baroness Burdett-Coutts perhaps the prime example, scatter their fortunes widely, they were also, particularly in legacies, conventional and often unimaginative in their giving. David Owen summarised that 'Hospitals, orphanages, almshouses, church organizations, such eminently respectable national charities as the R.S.P.C.A, and the Royal National Life-boat Institution – these were the philanthropies that commonly figured in wills, together with an occasional public park, gift to a library or art gallery, or scholarship or university chair'. As *The Times* put it in 1899, there was a 'great lack of originality on the part of rich men in the disposition of their wealth'. There were exceptions. The will of Henry Gardner, for example, set up the Gardner Trust of £300,000 for the blind, leaving considerable discretion to the Trustees as to how it should be spent.[50]

Carnegie and the American foundations of the first decade of the twentieth century set new standards for giving away large fortunes. Britain benefitted from some of these and from other donations where the wealth originated in the Empire. The King Edward's Hospital Fund (started in Queen Victoria's Diamond Jubilee year, 1897) attracted some of the largest single sums. Lord Strathcona, Canadian railway magnate, gave it £500,000 in gifts and £815,000 in legacy. The Imperial College of Science and Technology received substantial funding from the diamond fortunes made in South Africa by Alfred Beit and Julius Wernher, 'Randlords' as they were called, both receiving baronetcies for their philanthropy. Between 1881 and 1914 about one hundred people bequeathed at least £100,000 to charitable objects.[51] But it was not until the mid-twentieth century that the British, in Lord Nuffield, thought they might have someone in the same league as the Carnegies and Rockefellers.

The standing of philanthropy

The volume of discussion about philanthropy in public discourse was near to its highest point in the 1890s but began to drop dramatically as the twentieth century dawned. It was not that the problems and issues it had addressed were no longer of importance, rather that philanthropy was less and less seen as offering a solution. But old habits died hard and there remained in being a philanthropic world with its own rituals and calendar. The May meetings, which it was said in 1914 began in March and lasted to July, continued to be the occasion for national organisations to meet in the capital, an evangelical Christianity at the heart of them. They were, thought *The Times* in 1901, testimony to 'the amount of voluntary energy, and often self-sacrifice, in good works' and 'No other country in Europe can show the like'.[52]

Much of this work was described in obituaries and was specifically local. Mr T. Sutton Timms of Liverpool was a noted 'North of England philanthropist', Miss Julia Maria Sterling of Falmouth was 'a well-known philanthropist in the district', the Rev. J. E. Walker of Cheltenham was 'for a generation one of the most active workers in religious and philanthropic movements in the district', supporting the Library, the Female Refuge, the RSPCA and the Anti-Vivisection Society. Louisa Lady Sitwell 'played a large but unostentatious part in the philanthropic work' of Scarborough, Miss E. M. Bell of Upper Tooting was 'a well-known local philanthropist', supporting a crèche.[53]

The existence of a philanthropic world, both national and local, did not mean that philanthropy, even in the early part of the century, was unscathed in reputation. It continued to be attacked for trying to bypass or ignore the laws of political economy. When municipal trading was under discussion in 1900, for example, *The Times* insisted on the need to 'distinguish between sound business and the vagaries of Socialism and philanthropy'.[54] Adjectives again tell their tale. Philanthropy that was practical continued to be praised but always carried with it the implication that there existed too much impractical philanthropy. The London County Council in 1889 sought to co-opt 'practical philanthropists who have spent not only money, but time and labour, on improving the lot of their fellow men'. 'Practical philanthropists' in 1889 were 'vehemently' in support of the clause in the 1889 Poor Law Act that made it difficult for parents to reclaim children taken into care.[55] In the first decade of the new century there was praise for philanthropy that was 'wise', 'considered', 'efficient', 'practical', 'true', 'enlightened', but equally criticism of it when 'incautious', 'pretending', 'misguided', 'sentimental', 'indiscriminate', 'well-meaning but ill-advised', 'spurious', 'shortsighted' or 'mistaken'. In short, the criticism of philanthropy did not end with the mid-Victorians. *The Times* in 1903 referred to 'the somewhat depressing annals of philanthropy'.[56]

The London Philanthropic Society was founded in 1841 by eight tradesmen in Bishopsgate, and gave out bread and coal in the winter, its annual meeting always graced by the Lord Mayor. Their world was under challenge. Members must have been surprised when in 1912 the Lord Mayor told them that 'what the English people at present needed was to be taught industry and thrift. If that were done philanthropic societies would not be needed'. The society had doubtless been hoping for praise of its work and a boost to its funds. Lloyd George's tax-funded national insurance acts provided the context for the Lord Mayor's comments.[57] The state was taking responsibility for circumstances where previously individuals or charities had done so, was itself becoming philanthropic. Many disliked this. 'So much philanthropic legislation', claimed *The Times* in 1910, 'is a shot at a venture, the arrow, may be, wounding the very person whom it was intended to pro-tect'. Even worse, such legislation might pass the responsibility properly belonging to an individual to someone else. *The Times* in 1911 had criticised 'vicarious philanthropy' in relation to Clause 51 of the Insurance Bill which allowed a tenant in receipt of sickness benefit to stay even if rent was not paid – the landlord became an unwilling philanthropist at the command of the state. Looking ahead on New Year's Day 1913 *The Times* hoped that the government with all its faults including 'its futile philanthropy' would 'be sent into retirement'.[58]

Philanthropy was criticised for being 'political'. It was political when in the South African War and its aftermath 'philanthropists of the armchair order' were 'exciting themselves about the comfort of our enemies', or when, in rela-tion to the Chinese labour question in South Africa, it was asserted that 'pol-itical philanthropists' had previously 'hardly noticed the death-rate of Kaffirs in mines', or when, after a speech by Winston Churchill in 1906 with 'plenty of that irresponsible sentiment, masquerading as philanthropy for the down-trodden races', *The Times* asserted 'That the knowledge of our Parliamentary philanthropists is inadequate there is no manner of doubt'. It was political when in 1905 there was pressure for intervention in the Balkans – 'what Mr Balfour calls an insane policy of philanthropic adventure'.[59]

John Galsworthy's jaundiced analysis of the philanthropic and charitable world in *The Man of Property* (1906) drives home many of these points. Charity, literally, began at home: the Forsytes 'were supporters of such char-itable institutions as might be beneficial to their sick domestics'. Old Jolyon, altering his will to give his fortune to his son, reflected on the pleasure to be derived from giving to one's own flesh and blood.[60] Mrs Baynes, not a Forsyte, was representative of a different world:

Her name was upon the committees of numberless charities connected with the Church – dances, theatricals, or bazaars … She believed, as she often said, in putting things on a commercial basis; the proper function of the Church, of charity, indeed, of everything, was to strengthen the fabric of 'Society'. Individual action, therefore she considered immoral. Organization was the only thing, for by organization alone could you feel sure that you were getting a return for your money … The enterprises to which she lent her name were organized so admirably that by the time the takings were handed over, they were indeed skim milk divested of all cream of human kindness. But, as she often justly remarked, sentiment was to be deprecated.

Galsworthy must have had the COS in his sights when he wrote this. For Mrs Baynes the reward for all her work was that 'She was a power in upper-middle-class society with its hundred sets and circles, all intersecting on the common battlefield of charity functions, and on that battlefield brushing skirts so pleasantly with the skirts of Society with the capital "S"'. And for her husband there was a knighthood 'when he built that public Museum of Art which has given so much employment to officials, and so little pleasure to those working classes for whom it was designed'.[61]

Galsworthy did not hide his distaste for this world, whether it was the family selfishness of the Forsytes, the social life of the upper middle classes centered round 'the common battlefield of charity functions', or the honours dished out to those who provided unwanted public amenities. He was alert, too, to changes in attitude. The shareholders of the New Colliery Company argued against the 'sentimental humanitarianism' that would provide support for a woman widowed after her husband, who had worked loyally for the company, committed suicide after witnessing dreadful scenes in a colliery accident. The narrator noted, with heavy irony, that 'the movement against generosity … had at that time [the date is precise: 1886] already commenced among the saner members of the community'.[62]

Novelists continued to hold individual philanthropists up to scorn. Miss Lant in George Gissing's *The Nether World* (1889) is thus described:

Of middle age and with very plain features, Miss Lant had devoted herself to philanthropic work; she had an income of a few hundred pounds, and lived almost as simply as the Snowdons in order to save money for charitable expenditure. Unfortunately the earlier years of her life had been joyless, and in the energy which she brought to this self-denying enterprise there was just a touch of excess, common enough in those who have been defrauded of their natural satisfactions and find a resource in altruism.[63]

Miss Lant, Gissing was saying, turned to philanthropy in an attempt to overcome personal sadness, but with a 'narrow and oppressive zeal'. Michael

Snowdon wanted to bestow a personal fortune on Jane, his granddaughter, rescued by him from dire poverty, with a commitment for her to work along-side Miss Lant and her colleagues, but for Jane to be forced 'into alliance with conscious philanthropists' would have been disastrous: Jane was happiest helping her friend Pennyloaf.[64]

Virginia Woolf painted a similar picture of Eleanor Pargiter in *The Years* (1937): a man whose toe she has stood on getting on to a bus 'sized her up; a well-known type; with a bag; philanthropic; well nourished; a spinster; a virgin; like all the women of her class, cold; her passions had never been touched; yet not unattractive'.[65] Woolf is perhaps more sympathetic to Mrs Ramsay, based on her own mother, in *To the Lighthouse* (1927), but only to draw attention to the latter's anxiety about her motivation and her skills. Mrs Ramsay

> ruminated the ... problem of rich and poor, and the things she saw with her own eyes, weekly, daily, here or in London, when she visited this widow, or that struggling wife in person with a bag on her arm, and a note-book and pencil with which she wrote down in columns carefully ruled for the pur-pose wages and spendings, employment and unemployment, in the hope that thus she would cease to be a private woman whose charity was half a sop to her own indignation, half a relief to her own curiosity, and become, what with her untrained mind she greatly admired, an investigator, eluci-dating the social problem.

She worried 'that all this desire of hers to give, to help, was vanity. For her own self-satisfaction was it that she wished so instinctively to help, to give, that people might say of her, "O Mrs Ramsay! Dear Mrs Ramsay ... Mrs Ramsay, of course!" and need her and send for her and admire her? Was it not secretly this that she wanted?'[66]

In these novels, written in the inter-war period but set in the late Victorian and Edwardian, Woolf turned a shrewd eye both on how philanthropic women appeared to those they set out to help and how some of them felt about themselves. At the very least they suggest that the road of philanthropy was not a smooth one.

Conclusion

The year 1882 saw the first number of *The Philanthropist: The Representative Journal of Social Philanthropic Movements and Institutions*. At its outset it distinguished sharply between charity and philanthropy. 'That charity', it claimed, 'is accountable for much of the misery which it relieves will be maintained by most people who have devoted themselves to the study of alleviating human distress'. 'Philanthropy, on the other hand', it continued, 'embraces that wider field of useful work best understood by the words,

Thrift and Providence. It is a great and glorious system of natural benevolence which seeks to advance the interests of mankind in matters tem-
poral and spiritual'. It was a 'science'. What was astonishing was 'that in a
country remarkable alike for its philanthropy and its newspaper enterprise,
that it has been so long without a journal devoted exclusively to the subject'.
The Philanthropist was to fill the gap, promoting the metropolis (London)
as 'Philanthropolis'. It sank to a close, much diminished in size, in 1911.
Its fortunes are indicative of the difficulties of philanthropy in the years
from 1880.[67]

Further evidence comes from the eleventh edition of the *Encyclopaedia
Britannica*, published in 1910–11. Stretching to twenty-nine volumes, it is
often taken as a landmark edition. In it there is no heading for 'philanthropy'.
'Altruism' has a half-page entry and 'Charity and charities' get thirty-one
pages, written by C. S. Loch, the long-serving secretary of the COS. Loch
was uncompromising in setting out the COS case and correspondingly dis-
missive in his rare mentions of philanthropy. Charity, by contrast, was 'a
science based on social principles and observation'. Loch was critical of the
New Liberal legislation providing for school meals and old age pensions –
both would undermine the desirable pressure for 'self-maintenance' and
independence.[68]

Loch's article is a reminder that there remained throughout this period
fierce opposition to the growth of state responsibility. Loch and those like
him constituted the majority on the Royal Commission on the Poor Laws
that reported in 1909. In the 1840s and 1850s philanthropy had been held up
as a force that would bring order to charity in accordance with the principles
of political economy. Now, for Loch, the roles were reversed: philanthropy
was indiscriminate and harmful, charity scientific and, as Loch was at pains
to argue, entirely consistent with political economy.[69]

Loch did not disguise his mistrust of philanthropy. Lady Bell, much more
sympathetic to it, and famous for her work in Middlesbrough described in
At the Works, had a different concern. Speaking as chair of a meeting at the
Women's Congress in 1910 she touched 'on the difficulty of carrying on
philanthropic work now that the word philanthropy had become specialised
and narrowed'.[70] This was a concern about the professionalisation of philanthropy, its shift towards becoming 'social work'. Bell's worry about the
change in the meaning and associations of the word 'philanthropy' was
an early indication of something that became much more prominent after
the First World War. Few any longer thought of philanthropy as a love of
humankind.

This line of criticism of philanthropy was matched by another and more
prominent one, that philanthropy was simply inadequate in scope and
resources to cope with the problems of an urban society. These problems
were primarily those of poverty, manifested in ill health, unemployment, slum
housing and low wages. The state by 1914 had made decisive interventions to
begin to alleviate these problems. If philanthropy was going to have a future it

was obvious by 1914 that it would lie outside direct responsibility for the relief of poverty. Those who, from a position on the left, began to think that millionaire philanthropists might have a role to play envisaged the interventions to be primarily in the field of culture, of raising the quality of life rather than tackling basic deficiencies. The same was true of philanthropic employers.

The one respect in which this was not true lay in the idea of a new philanthropy built on personal service. The call of Barnett and others undoubtedly met with a considerable response. From the point of view of philanthropy, however, there was a downside. People who started work in the new settlements – and also those doing casework for the COS – began to be drawn towards working for the state, either in policy formation or as paid and increasingly professional social workers. *The Times* in the decade 1900–09 made 495 mentions of philanthropist* and fifty-five of social worker*; in 1940–49 there were 136 of philanthropist* and 744 of social worker*. It was not that social work as a profession had high status. Far from it. As Kathleen Woodroofe noted in 1962, 'Social work in England, far from being an honoured profession, is a depressed occupation'.[71] But though its status might be low, 'social work' had taken the place once held by 'philanthropy'.

Notes

1 This account draws heavily on S. Collini, 'The culture of altruism: Selfishness and the decay of motive', in S. Collini, *Public Moralists: Political Thought and Intellectual Life in England 1850–1930* (Oxford: Clarendon Press, 1991), pp. 60–90, and T. Dixon, *The Invention of Altruism: Making Moral Meanings in Victorian Britain* (Oxford: Oxford University Press, 2008).

2 Dixon, *Invention of Altruism*, pp. 181–221.

3 B. Webb, *My Apprenticeship* (1926; Harmondsworth: Penguin, 1971), pp. 163–5.

4 Quotations in Dixon, *Invention of Altruism*, pp. 236, 299.

5 Quoted in ibid., p. 339.

6 Quotations in Collini, 'Culture of altruism', pp. 88–9.

7 A. Ryan, 'The philanthropic perspective after a hundred years', in J. B. Schneewind (ed.), *Giving: Western Ideas of Philanthropy* (Bloomington and Indiana: Indiana University Press, 1996), pp. 76–97.

8 Quoted in Collini, 'Culture of altruism', p. 83.

9 Mrs H. Ward, *Robert Elsmere* (1888; London: John Murray, 1911), 2 vols, Vol. I, p. 258.

10 Ibid., Vol. I, p. 284, Vol. II, pp. 455, 499, 508.

11 *The Speaker: The Liberal Review*, 2 (22 Nov. 1890), p. 569.

12 S. Barnett, 'The failure of philanthropy', *Macmillan's Magazine*, 73 (1 Nov. 1895), 390–6.

13 H. O. Barnett, 'Women as philanthropists', in T. Stanton (ed.), *The Woman Question in Europe* (New York and London: G. P. Putnam & Sons, 1884), pp. 108–38, quoting pp. 118, 137–8.

14 W. Besant, 'On university settlements', in W. Reason (ed.), *University and Social Settlements* (London: Methuen & Co. 1898), pp. 1–10.

15 *Pall Mall Gazette*, 17 Dec. 1886; *Saturday Review*, 3 Oct. 1891, pp. 395–6.

16 J. Adderley, 'Is slumming played out?', *English Illustrated Magazine*, 119 (Aug. 1893), 834–41.

17 S. Barnett, 'University settlements', in Reason (ed.), *University and Social Settlements*, pp. 11–15.

18 *The Diary of Beatrice Webb*, Vol. I 1873–1892, ed. N. and J. MacKenzie (London: Virago, 1982), p. 85.

19 *The Times*, 27 Oct. 1905.

20 *Oxford Dictionary of National Biography*; B. Kirkman Gray, *A History of English Philanthropy From the Dissolution of the Monasteries to the Taking of the First Census* (London: P. S. King & Son, 1905).

21 B. Kirkman Gray, *Philanthropy and the State; or Social Politics* (London: P. S. King & Son, 1908), pp. iv–v, x.

22 Ibid., pp. 2, 141, 247.

23 Ibid., pp. 324, 319–20.

24 Ibid., pp. 302–16.

25 Quoted in M. Simey, *Charity Rediscovered: A Study of Philanthropic Effort in Nineteenth-Century Liverpool* (Liverpool: Liverpool University Press), p. 107.

26 *The Times*, 22 Jan. 1889.

27 A. Vernon, *A Quaker Businessman: The Life of Joseph Rowntree 1836–1925* (London: George Allen & Unwin, 1958), p. 154.

28 Quotations in G. Finlayson, *Citizen, State and Social Welfare in Britain 1830–1990* (Oxford: Clarendon Press, 1994), pp. 138–40, 159–60, 171.

29 *Daily Mail* (Hull), 9 Oct. 1907; *Nottingham Evening News*, 14 Dec. 1910.

30 C. Waters, *British Socialists and the Politics of Popular Culture, 1884–1914* (Manchester: Manchester University Press, 1990), pp. 71–2.

31 Ibid., p. 88.

32 *Morning Post*, 27 Sept. 1853.

33 H. Cunningham, *Leisure in the Industrial Revolution, c. 1780-c. 1880* (London: Croom Helm, 1980), pp. 151–5.

34 H. Meller, 'Urban renewal and citizenship: The quality of life in British cities, 1890–1990', *Urban History*, 22 (1995), 67; see also H. Meller, *Leisure and the Changing City, 1870–1914* (London: Routledge and Kegan Paul, 1976), pp. 66, 97.

35 R. Fitzgerald, *British Labour Management and Industrial Welfare 1846–1939* (London: Croom Helm, 1988) provides a good overall analysis; Cadbury quoted in C. Delheim, 'The creation of a company culture: Cadburys, 1861–1931', *American Historical Review*, 92 (1987), 27.

36 W. L. Burn, *The Age of Equipoise: A Study of the Mid-Victorian Generation* (London: George Allen & Unwin, 1964), p. 242.

37 J. Walvin, *The Quakers: Money and Morals* (London: John Murray, 1997), pp. 191–4; J. D. Jeremy, 'Introduction', in J. D. Jeremy (ed.), *Religion, Business and Wealth in Modern Britain* (London: Routledge, 1998), pp. 19–20.

38 *Sunderland Daily Echo*, 10 June 1898.

39 W. D. Rubinstein, *Men of Property: The Very Wealthy in Britain since the Industrial Revolution* (London: Croom Helm, 1981), pp. 11, 20.
40 Ibid., pp. 28–30, 41–2, 70, 102–4.
41 Ibid., p. 247.
42 *The Times*, 25 May 1939.
43 J. R. Green, 'The poetry of wealth', in J. R. Green, *Stray Studies from England and Italy* (London: Macmillan, 1876), quoting pp. 98, 104–6.
44 *The Times*, 24 July 1869; 5 Nov. 1869.
45 A. Carnegie, *The Gospel of Wealth and Other Timely Essays*, ed. E. C. Kirkland (Cambridge, MA: Harvard University Press, 1965).
46 B. Shaw, *Socialism for Millionaires* (London: Fabian Society, 1901), pp. 2, 4.
47 Ibid., pp. 9–15.
48 Gray, *Philanthropy and the State*, pp. 322–3.
49 *The Times*, 20 Nov. 1889.
50 D. Owen, *English Philanthropy 1660–1960* (London: Oxford University Press, 1965), pp. 474–5, 491–2.
51 Ibid., pp. 475, 487–8; J. Pellew, 'A metropolitan university fit for Empire: The role of private benefaction in the early history of the London School of Economics and Political Science and Imperial College of Science and Technology, 1895–1930', *History of Universities*, 26 (2012), pp. 202–45.
52 *The Times*, 17 Apr. 1914; 27 May 1901.
53 Ibid., 2 July 1910; 25 Jan. 1911; 25 May 1911; 3 Nov. 1911; 6 Jan. 1914.
54 Ibid., 24 Mar. 1900; see also 17 Jan. 1901.
55 Ibid., 23 Jan. 1889; 4 Oct. 1889.
56 Ibid., 1900–09, quoting 8 Sept. 1903.
57 Ibid., 27 Apr. 1935; 20 Jan. 1912.
58 Ibid., 1 Mar. 1910; 1 July 1911; 1 Jan. 1913.
59 Ibid., 14 Dec. 1901; 21 June 1904; 2 Mar. 1906; 1 Mar. 1905.
60 J. Galsworthy, *The Man of Property* (1906; Harmondsworth: Penguin, 1967), pp. 25, 262.
61 Ibid., pp. 216–17, 257.
62 Ibid., p. 154.
63 G. Gissing, *The Nether World* (1889; Oxford: Oxford University Press, 1999), p. 229.
64 Ibid., p. 235.
65 V. Woolf, *The Years* (1937; Harmondsworth: Penguin, 1968), p. 83.
66 V. Woolf, *To the Lighthouse* (1927; Harmondsworth: Penguin, 1964), pp. 12, 49.
67 *The Philanthropist*, 1 (1882), 6.
68 *Encyclopaedia Britannica*, 9th edn (1910–11), pp. 884–6.
69 Ibid., pp. 885–6; see also *Manchester Guardian*, 11 Nov. 1904.
70 *Manchester Guardian*, 9 July 1910.
71 K. Woodroofe, *From Charity to Social Work in England and the United States* (London: Routledge & Kegan Paul, 1962), p. 212.

10

Philanthropy since 1914

The history of philanthropy in the century after the outbreak of the First World War has attracted little attention. For many years historians focused on the origins of the welfare state, on its implementation during and after the Second World War, and on how it has operated since then. In the late twentieth century an emphasis on the mixed economy of welfare regained attention. What was called 'the voluntary sector' came to be seen as often working with the state or pushing the state into action as well as striking out new ground on its own.[1] For the period from 1914 to the 1970s, however, 'philanthropy' was losing its place in public discourse; those working in the voluntary sector saw it as old-fashioned and Victorian.

From the 1970s onwards there was a rising volume of criticism of the welfare state. Building on this, 'philanthropy' towards the end of the century began to make new claims for itself. This was helped, indeed made possible, by the fact that many more people were making large fortunes. The 'new philanthropy' was built on new wealth.

The broad outlines of this narrative are unlikely to be shaken. They are confirmed by data presented in Chapter 2 that shows that in the 1940s there was less mention of philanthropy in newspapers than there had been in the 1760s. If, however, the focus was not on philanthropy but on topics close to it, such as civil society, or voluntary organisations, or the social services, or volunteering, or citizenship, or even charity, the narrative might look more positive. The history of philanthropy in the twentieth century is a history of its difficult relationship to developments in these other spheres of activity. In many ways it became marginalised, it carried too much baggage from the Victorian period to be able to adapt with any ease. Moreover, it had no organisational hub, no way of ensuring that its voice was heard.

Philanthropy, voluntary action, voluntary organisations and citizenship

The difficulties facing philanthropy, but also the possibilities perhaps open to it, were exemplified in an editorial and a report in *The Times* in May 1914. The editorial, 'On doing good', found that 'It is a strange and discouraging fact that people who go about doing good to others are not usually liked. Philanthropist is about as much a term of abuse as of praise; indeed, it has been said that, if ever there is a revolution in England, the first blood let will be that of the philanthropists'. Philanthropists, it said, were seen as friends to mankind in the abstract but not to particular men, and there was resentment of their habit of preaching moral values.[2] Philanthropists, perhaps more than philanthropy, carried a burden of public mistrust. To shed it would be difficult.

A week later, under the heading 'The new philanthropic spirit: Cooperation in social service', *The Times* reported a meeting of the Social Welfare Association addressed by Herbert Samuel, President of the Local Government Board, on the desirability of 'cooperation between all the agencies engaged in a common field of work and cooperation not only between voluntary organizations themselves, but also between voluntary organizations of all kinds and the public organizations of the State'.[3] Here was a vision of a new world of cooperation, presided over in the headline by 'the new philanthropic spirit'. Hope of a similar kind underlay a speech by Walter Milledge of the Bradford Guild of Help in 1908: 'We have to recognize that the State is assuming responsibilities which have hitherto been ... very partially undertaken by philanthropic agencies. The result, however, will be to broaden the outlook for the philanthropist and to enlarge his opportunities for constructive work.'[4] In the words of Hancock Nunn, an influential expert, the 'disastrous parallelism by which State and Voluntary Action *never met* is being rapidly superseded by a unity and cooperation in which they *never part*'.[5] The reality on the ground was of course messier than that, but what is interesting is Nunn's language: 'Voluntary Action', not philanthropy, not charity, is how he described the state's partner.

The First World War was a catalyst in the development of voluntary organisations. During it approximately 18,000 new charities were created, a 50 per cent increase on the number in existence before the war. 'Warfare no less than welfare needed volunteers' in the words of James Hinton with relation to the Second World War.[6] The wartime growth of voluntary action built on what Peter Grant has described as a huge pre-war reservoir of social capital residing in voluntary organisations.[7] In a previous war, in South Africa at the turn of the century, there had been a similar response, with £6 million raised by voluntary effort, testimony to 'the dynamism of provincial philanthropy'.[8] In the First World War the amount of money raised is estimated to have been at least £150 million.[9]

Voluntary action received organisational form with the establishment in 1919 of the National Council of Social Service (NCSS); in 1980, in order to distinguish it from the statutory social services, it became the National Council of Voluntary Organisations (NCVO). It had been preceded in 1915 by the appointment by the War Office of a Director General of Voluntary Organizations, Sir Edward Ward. The appointment was made to set up ways of coordinating voluntary effort when overlap and disorganisation were heading towards chaos, or, as Elizabeth Macadam was to recall, there was an 'orgy of sometimes even acrimonious competition in benevolence'.[10] The NCSS became the collective voice of the voluntary organisations and it could be a political player in its own right, just as the COS (which declined rapidly towards the end of the war) had been before. By contrast, and it was a serious weakness, philanthropy lacked organisation and any political agenda. 'Philanthropists', as Frank Prochaska noted, 'lacked a political dynamic, apart from the negative ones of maintaining social order and dishing socialism. They had no ideological vision'.[11]

Unpaid volunteers carried out much of the work of these voluntary organisations but the bigger ones also had salaried staff; and although in their formation and constitution they were independent of government they were increasingly dependent on government funding. There was nothing new in this. As far back as 1833 schools run by voluntary organisations received funding from government. The scale and spread of this, however, increased markedly after the First World War and continued inexorably to grow. In the 1930s it was estimated that one-third of the total income of registered charities was received from the state as payment for services.[12]

The war showed that the growth of the state need not be accompanied by a decline in 'voluntary organisations'. Far from it. They were on most counts in a stronger position post-war than pre-war.[13] Nevertheless, it had been obvious to many pre-war that the assumptions and language that had dominated thinking about welfare in the nineteenth century were becoming redundant. Signs of it were evident in the establishment of new organisations: the Sociological Society founded in 1904, the British Institute of Social Service, dating from 1906, ten departments of 'social science' established in British universities between 1904 and 1919, the Personal Service Association and the Guilds of Help, the latter two reactions against the spirit that dominated the COS. These new organisations shared a common outlook on the world. They had a vision of the qualities that would underlie a good state: individual altruism, an ethical imperative, active citizen-participation and a feeling of corporate identity. Welfare was not only a matter of relieving poverty. What was vital, it was argued, was to raise the quality of citizenship and to inculcate a feeling of belonging. These ideals were given added urgency as democracy expanded with the curtailment of the powers of the House of Lords in 1911 and the huge increase in the size of the electorate in 1918. Many who articulated these visions were inspired by Plato's emphasis on society as 'an organic spiritual community' and on the ethical nature of citizenship.[14]

'Citizenship' as a word had been spreading since the late nineteenth century. In 1897, the year of the diamond jubilee, T. H. S. Escott had written on 'Social citizenship as a moral growth of Victorian England'; what he wrote about might well have been described as 'philanthropy'. In the work of T. H. Green and his followers, it has been said, 'No word recurs more often ... than "citizenship"; no word is more difficult to define with any degree of precision or correctness'.[15] But that vagueness in the meaning of the word only added to its proliferation; there were many different and competing versions of citizenship, nearly all of which involved actions that might previously have been described as 'philanthropy'.[16]

In this new world 'charity' and 'philanthropy' were words that were rarely used. They were redolent of 'the Victorians', their inbuilt assumption of the well-off doing good to the poor outmoded and embarrassing. Citizens did not need philanthropy. Clement Attlee, future Labour prime minister, who had become a lecturer in social work at the London School of Economics in 1912, looked back in 1920 on the charitable of the nineteenth century and commented that they 'seem to us today to be smug and self-satisfied. They delighted in sermons to the poor on convenient virtues, and lacked the sharp self-criticism that is the note of society today'.[17] The social reformer Eleanor Rathbone in 1928 attempted 'A defence of philanthropy' but acknowledged that philanthropy was seen as 'old-fashioned and unpopular at present, regarded by the wage-earning classes as savouring of patronage and by the intelligentsia as unscientific'. She herself held out some hope that 'the curative methods of philanthropy and the broad constructive preventive methods of legislation' could work in harmony.[18] Madeline Rooff in the 1950s stressed how the First World War was a catalyst: 'Class distinctions', she wrote, 'became blurred, and the patronage of the rich towards the poor was no longer an acceptable attitude in an increasingly democratic society'.[19] Anyone in tune with this new way of thinking was unlikely to write about either charity or philanthropy, except to be condescending, critical, or, like Rathbone, defensive.

It was in this unpromising climate of opinion that in 1934 Elizabeth Macadam, a close associate of Eleanor Rathbone (they shared a house), made a claim for another 'new philanthropy'. Her book *The New Philanthropy* was accurately subtitled *A Study of the Relations Between the Statutory and Voluntary Social Services*. Macadam did not disown the older 'new philanthropy' of Besant and the settlement movement, but she sought to place philanthropy on a very different level. In some ways, though she was unaware of this, she was echoing ideas that had been a commonplace in the middle decades of the nineteenth century when people imagined statesmen and philanthropists jointly tackling social and political problems, the boundaries of philanthropy expanding into areas that by Macadam's time had come to be thought beyond its remit.

Macadam trained in social work at the Women's University Settlement in Southwark in 1898, was Warden of Victoria Women's Settlement in Liverpool from 1902 to 1910, and then the first lecturer in social work at Liverpool University.[20] She was alert to the slipperiness of words. 'Social services' was a 'heavily worked term', and no one quite knew what it encompassed. '"Charitable" Organizations' were 'perhaps the largest of the groups of organizations which in the past and even now have been allowed to monopolize the term "charity" or "philanthropy"'. 'Charity' was 'that overstrained word'.[21] It might be assumed that she would wish to move forward from the traps embedded in these words which her quotation marks tell us are problematic. Yet, as her title boasted, she wanted to reclaim 'philanthropy'. '[I]ntelligent modern philanthropic effort', she wrote, should aim to form federations of voluntary organisations and should identify 'in some way with the statutory authority'.[22] Although she was critical of much contemporary practice, she had to be upbeat: 'Great Britain can to-day show a system of combined statutory and voluntary social service which has grown up in the last forty years quite peculiar to itself. In no other country in the world can anything on similar lines be found; it is this unique partnership that I have called the new philanthropy.'[23] But in truth the word 'philanthropy' added nothing to the partnership; it was redundant. Macadam's whole career had been in the profession of social work. The partnership of statutory and voluntary social services was a partnership of professionals. On top of this Macadam had to admit that there was an 'absence of leadership in philanthropy today', perhaps because those who might be leaders had been too early swept into municipal or parliamentary life.[24] The prospects for a partnership of statutory and voluntary social services may have been good; for it to be widely accepted as a 'new philanthropy' was unlikely.

Towards the end of her book Macadam turned to 'the disagreeable process of money-raising'. During the First World War, she claimed, 'The class accustomed to generous giving gave place to a different class – the "new rich", not bred in the same tradition'. It had become more difficult to get regular subscriptions, leading to a proliferation of special appeals, sweepstakes, flag days and street collections. Government funding, which will 'in all probability be one of the main characteristics of the future social service', was highlighted. There were also trust funds, a 'much-coveted source of income', the best known of them the Carnegie United Kingdom Trust. Those with 'considerable sums at their disposal', thought Macadam, might give more consideration to such trusts.[25] But this method of funding voluntary organisations did not in itself constitute philanthropy; it was merely one means to the end. The millionaires, whose potential was so trumpeted in the pre-war period, did not seem, for Macadam, to have a central or hugely significant role in the development of philanthropy.

Four years later there was another attempt to promote philanthropy within the world of the social services. In *The Voluntary Citizen: An Enquiry into the Place of Philanthropy in the Community* (1938) Constance Braithwaite, in what she described as a personal statement, argued that philanthropy was 'essentially an expression of voluntary citizenship'. She included in the book a long study of District Nursing Associations as 'An Example of a Voluntarily Organized Social Service'. Braithwaite upheld an ideal citizenship as having volunteering or voluntary work as central. Philanthropic action of this kind, she recognised, had boundaries to it – it needed to focus on areas that the public authorities could not or would not enter.[26] Readers may have been impressed or moved by Braithwaite's commitment to this kind of volunteering – but, as with Macadam, they might have wondered whether it was appropriate or necessary to call it philanthropy. By the late 1930s 'citizenship' struck stronger chords than 'philanthropy'.

Rathbone, Macadam, Braithwaite and other women were at the centre of this rethinking of philanthropy because women, whether paid or unpaid, were so prominent in the activities encompassed by what were increasingly called the 'social services'. Such work was inextricably bound up with developing ideas of citizenship in a democratic society. These had their origin in the Victorian and Edwardian periods, but took on new centrality with the acquisition of the vote by women in 1918 and 1928. What was thought to be at stake was summed up by Clement Attlee when in 1920 he commented on the changed 'outlook of the social worker from the times when his [*sic*] principal object was benevolence down to the modern conception of social justice'.[27] Many involved in these debates commented on how philanthropy seemed old-fashioned. *Woman's Leader* in 1924 noted that the Joint University Council for Social Studies reported a swing amongst the young away from 'organized personal philanthropy' of the kind undertaken by the COS, in girls' and boys' clubs and university settlements towards more obviously political or educational work through the Labour Party, the Trades Union Congress, the Workers' Educational Association and both central and local government.[28] Vera Brittain, writer and feminist, spoke out in 1928 in favour of training for social work rather than 'an untutored plunge into unforeseen responsibilities, or the supposition that modern welfare work resembles old-fashioned "philanthropy" in requiring as its sole qualifications a kind heart and vaguely benevolent intentions'.[29] And from the Conservative side Stanley Baldwin, soon to be prime minister, spoke of how 'the old fields covered by benevolence … or philanthropy' had been narrowed by state action and urged his female audience to replace 'emotional benevolence' by the work of 'both heart and brain'.[30]

The essays collected together in *Voluntary Social Services: Their Place in the Modern State* (1945) drove home the fact that philanthropy had come to be seen as a thing of the past. G. D. H. Cole gave due weight to it when discussing forerunners of the social services in the eighteenth and nineteenth centuries but in the twentieth it was transforming itself 'from benevolence *de haut en bas*, often involving what seem to us nowadays detestably humiliating conditions even when the spirit of the promoters was one of real benevolence, into communal service, designed to widen and deepen the expression of the spirit of democratic co-operation'. Historically, he felt, 'many of the philanthropists have regarded charity as, among its virtues, a bulwark against subversive movements', something quite out of place in the coming welfare state.[31]

If philanthropy was in danger of dropping out of the language of the social services it received a boost in 1948 in William Beveridge's *Voluntary Action: A Report on the Methods of Social Advance*. Beveridge identified two motives for voluntary action. The first was mutual aid, exemplified in the friendly societies. The second was philanthropy. The latter 'springs from ... social conscience, the feeling which makes men who are materially comfortable, mentally uncomfortable so long as their neighbours are materially uncomfortable'. It is an odd definition and Beveridge did soften it later in the book by removing the exclusive emphasis on material wellbeing. The philanthropic motive, he wrote, is the 'desire by one's personal action to make life happier for others'.[32] Looking back to the nineteenth and early twentieth centuries he highlighted twenty-seven outstanding individuals, starting with Lord Shaftesbury and ending with Sidney and Beatrice Webb. Six of them were women, few were obviously wealthy except Charles Booth, though nearly all had family and other contacts that would enable them to raise money.[33] Most were middle-class, many acted, they would have said, out of religious motives.

This acknowledgement of a debt to be paid to eminent Victorians was a commonplace – often accompanied by a feeling that the twentieth century had less need for such figures. Prompted by the biography of Lord Shaftesbury by J. L. and Barbara Hammond in 1923, *The Times* reflected that 'Perhaps one of the best testimonies to his greatness lies in the absence at the present day of philanthropists of his build and stature. There are no Lord Shaftesburys now, for the same reason that there are no Florence Nightingales. Both set an example to their fellows, and it has borne fruit a thousandfold'.[34] What was being claimed here was that the Victorian philanthropists had set the tone for social and philanthropic life in the twentieth century. Lord Wakefield in 1930, presented with an album by the secretaries of over fifty of the leading charitable institutions, reflected that 'Some day someone would write a historical survey of philanthropy in England ... Such a study would to a large extent be a work of biography'.[35] The names and lives of great philanthropists seemed to be the key to the understanding of Victorian philanthropy. But in the twentieth century there was no need for the great figures – philanthropy was more broadly based, many of its fields of endeavour already marked out.

In all of these comments a narrative of philanthropy was being constructed. It started in early Victorian times and highlighted the role of individuals in seeking amelioration of the condition of the poor and the working class. The names that figured in this narrative became predictable: Lord Shaftesbury, Elizabeth Fry, Florence Nightingale, William Booth, Thomas Barnardo and Octavia Hill were the hardy perennials. None of them was known primarily for giving money. They could be described equally well as social reformers rather than philanthropists.

There was, however, recognition that there were new twentieth-century initiatives. Beveridge highlighted 'the Boy Scouts and Girl Guides, Women's Institutes, the Workers Educational Association, the National Council of Social Service, Training Colleges for the Disabled, Women's Voluntary Services, and Citizens' Advice Bureaux'. 'The capacity of Voluntary Action inspired by philanthropy to do new things', he concluded, 'is beyond question'.[36] There were still, however, needs that remained that were inadequately met. Writing with some passion about old age and childhood, about the physically handicapped and unmarried mothers, about discharged prisoners and parents, particularly mothers, without holidays, and about the need to elevate the ways leisure time was spent, he called for action by both the state and voluntary action. Caustic about the spread of the football pools, he demanded that 'The first call on the increased leisure of the democracy should be the fitting them for the responsibilities of democracy in choosing leaders and deciding on public issues'.[37] This was a far cry from the meeting of material needs that had at first seemed to constitute the motive for philanthropy.

Beveridge had a kind of utopia in mind. Mutual Aid had to change. In 'the more equal society of the future', it 'must broaden into Philanthropy, into the promotion of social advancement, not simply each for himself, but for the whole of society'.[38] Society might become one big Friendly Society. *The Companion Volume on the Evidence for Voluntary Action* cast some doubt on the realism of this agenda. Drawing on a Mass Observation Panel survey of written responses as well as on interviews, there was a feeling, especially from the panel, 'that the word "charity" has decayed in its meaning, that once it meant any sort of generous or kindly action but that now it simply means giving money'. 'The word "charity"', wrote one housewife, 'has a dreary sound these days'. Among those interviewed one-third disapproved of charity.[39] The respondents were asked specifically about 'charity'. Herbert Morrison, Home Secretary, strongly in favour of voluntary organisations, could also talk about 'cold charity'; the word carried baggage.[40] But it is unlikely that 'philanthropy' would have fared better.

There was a follow-up to Beveridge. He had suggested that there needed to be a Royal Commission to look into charitable trusts. Money that could be used for better purposes was often tied up in charitable trusts founded to meet the needs of previous centuries. To carry forward the issue, Beveridge prompted a House of Lords debate on 'Voluntary Action for Social Progress'. It was said later of it that it 'may justifiably be described as historic'.[41] That was primarily because Lord Pakenham, speaking for the Labour government, emphasised in the strongest terms the government's commitment to supporting voluntary action and its belief that, as he put it, 'the voluntary spirit is the very lifeblood of democracy'.[42] Beveridge himself reflected on 'the philanthropic motive'. It was, he said, essentially a crusading spirit, a crusade envisaged as embodied in one individual, but leading to the 'immense variety … of philanthropic agencies in this country'. 'Philanthropy', he said, 'will still be needed. It will be needed to pioneer ahead of the State'.[43]

The outcome was not a Royal Commission but a committee on Charitable Trusts under the chairmanship of Lord Nathan. It reported in December 1952. Although much of what it reported was necessarily technical, it opened with a chapter on 'The value of charity in the modern social structure'. Taking a broad view, it claimed that 'in one respect, the growth of civilization may be judged by the extent to which the obligations of philanthropy have spread to include those whose fate was previously a matter of indifference – the slave, the poor, the barbarian, the enemy'. This set the target high. Nevertheless, philanthropy was not enough. The efforts in the late eighteenth and nineteenth centuries 'to provide by private effort universal services of schools, hospitals, dispensaries, almshouses, orphanages, pensions for the aged and relief for other categories of the "deserving poor"' constituted 'One of the magnificent failures of our history'.[44] The state had to step in. Turning to Beveridge's 'philanthropic motive', the report saw it manifesting itself in three ways: 'by the giving of money, by the giving of personal service, and by the giving of both together'. It then set out its belief that

That manifestation of the philanthropic motive which consists in the giving of personal service is the most valuable element in it. It is the true heart of voluntary action and indeed of democracy itself. The giving of time and effort without personal reward, the willingness even to court misunderstanding and contumely in order to promote the wellbeing of one's fellow men, the freedom to pioneer and the will to pay the price – these are the characteristics of the philanthropic motive at its best. They are manifest in such pioneer philanthropists as, for instance, Captain Coram, John Howard, Elizabeth Fry, Lord Shaftesbury, Florence Nightingale, Octavia Hill. In others also, who, like Sir Frederick Eden, Charles Booth and the Webbs, gave their energies and some substantial part of their personal fortunes to further social research. In numberless people who give a professional service *con amore* to the needy. As well as in those innumerable voluntary workers who serve on the committees of voluntary organisations or local authorities, on advisory committees, on hospital boards and management committees, on appeals tribunals, visiting committees of various institutions, as magistrates, as voluntary leaders of youth clubs and play centres, as helpers in community centres, old peoples' homes, hospitals, maternity and child welfare centres, citizens' advice bureaux, as 'uncles' and 'aunts' to children in Homes, as active members of their religious denominations, as visitors of the old, the lonely, the sick, the handicapped, in fund raising, in office chores, in 'baby-sitting', in good neighbourliness in general, and in every other sphere in which the great mass of voluntary service in this country is manifest.[45]

The report went on to stress that voluntary service acts 'as a nursery school of democracy' and that it should come to be seen 'as a normal part of citizenship in the modern democratic state'.[46] This moving catalogue of what was being done under the umbrella of personal service or voluntary work might have philanthropy as its motive but probably few of these volunteers would have given recognition to it: they had moved beyond the world of philanthropy. The language of philanthropy was that of a generation that was passing. Moreover, the giving of money aspect of the 'philanthropic motive' was passed over in silence.

In 1953 Mary Stocks delivered the Eleanor Rathbone Memorial Lecture in Liverpool on *The Philanthropist in a Changing World*. She opened with recollections of her own well-to-do childhood in Kensington, commenting how

> The years which cover the turn of the century offered incomparable oppor-
> tunities for the active exercise of philanthropy by legions of middle-class
> women ... into the arena of active philanthropy they came: full-time, half-
> time, three evenings a week, one afternoon a week as the case might be. The
> wives and mothers did quite a lot – thanks to the supporting ministrations
> of nurses, cooks, parlour-maids and house-maids. But the crack regiment,
> the brigade of guards in this philanthropic army was the glorious company
> of maiden aunts.

Maiden aunts of this kind were much less prominent from the First World War onwards. Stocks ascribed this partly to higher taxation that made it difficult for middle-class fathers to support their unmarried daughters, making it necessary for them to find paid work. But equally important, and linked to it, was the 'expansive integration of voluntary and statutory ser- vices' and new ways of thinking which 'turned philanthropists into social reformers – on occasions even socialists'. 'You will find often', she wrote, 'that social reformers dislike being described as philanthropists because, they say, they aim at changes in the structure of society which will render philanthropy unnecessary and that philanthropists are merely attempting to palliate results while they, the social reformers are out to eliminate causes'.[47]

Turning to 'the salaried service of non-statutory bodies' Stocks noted that at the beginning of the century 'this was a negligible force – mainly secre- tarial. Today it is a vast great army'. One consequence was that 'it has made havoc of our accustomed phraseology'. Stocks recounted how before the Second World War as the salaried general secretary of the London Council of Social Service she would frequently preside over meetings where the salaried representatives of 'the voluntary movement' sat alongside unsal- aried representatives of statutory bodies. Who were the volunteers? Stocks concluded that 'The statutory machinery of the Welfare State could not operate without this prodigious application to the statutory administrative machinery of voluntary (in the sense of unpaid) social service'.[48] It was the same point that the Nathan Committee had made.

Stocks ended with a plea for a re-emphasis on 'charity' as one-to-one help. It was an odd conclusion given her title, perhaps an unstated acknowledgement that the 'havoc of our accustomed phraseology' had in effect made philanthropy redundant: in its wake there were the voluntary services and there was charity. And, like the Nathan Committee, Stocks made no reference at all to the possibility that philanthropy might re-define itself as giving by the rich.

The philanthropic world

If 'philanthropy' was losing out to 'voluntary organisations', 'citizenship' and 'volunteers', were there other fields it which it was holding its own or advancing? How did those engaged in philanthropy see themselves?

Obituaries in *The Times* provide one way of charting developments. Mention of philanthrop★ (i.e. philanthropy, philanthropist and its plural) in obituaries came to some prominence in the 1890s and reached a peak as a percentage of all obituaries in the 1900s. As a total number the peak was in the 1930s but as a percentage of all obituaries the trend was downwards from the 1900s to the 1970s. Compared with mentions of charity, philanthrop★ held the lead through to the 1920s, but had markedly fewer mentions from the 1970s onwards.

The changing place of philanthropy in obituaries in *The Times* can be interpreted in a number of ways. Editorial policy and decisions may provide an explanation, though it is likely that they will in some way have reflected what readers wanted. It could also be that for the generation dying in the 1890s and 1900s philanthropic activity during their lifetimes was actually at a higher level than before or after, that the reputation of the Victorian age as a golden age for philanthropy is accurate. The trend of decline both in numbers and percentages from the 1930s to the 1970s is some endorsement of the concern, evident in other sources, that both the reputation of philanthropy and engagement in it was hit by the rise of the welfare state. The slight upward turn from the 1980s may reflect the beginning of a lack of confidence in the ability of the welfare state to deliver services.

An alternative approach is to suggest that the changes in the place of philanthropy in obituaries, whether as a number or a percentage of all obituaries, are the least interesting fact about them. What is much more remarkable is that both numbers and percentages were so low. From the 1880s through to 2009 in only 1 per cent of all obituaries was there a mention of philanthropy★. In only 104 out of 165,438 did philanthropy★ appear in an obituary title. The overwhelming majority of people thought worthy of an obituary in *The Times* were not in any way known for their philanthropy.

The philanthropic work highlighted in obituaries was always written of in a positive way, though philanthropy was normally only one of the claims to a *Times* obituary. Typical headlines were 'Assurance and philanthropy',

Table 2 Philanthropy, charity and obituaries in *The Times*

Date	Total obituaries	philanthrop* in obituaries	charity in obituaries	philanthrop* as% of total
1880s	5,193	69	39	1.3
1890s	4,625	140	70	3
1900s	6,016	238	106	4
1910s	8,944	193	101	2.2
1920s	10,455	194	155	1.9
1930s	20,785	260	276	1.3
1940s	16,097	104	96	0.7
1950s	22,601	126	132	0.6
1960s	19,019	90	103	0.5
1970s	13,889	35	74	0.25
1980s	11,864	40	101	0.3
1990s	11,577	66	309	0.6
2000s	14,372	147	509	1
Total	165,438	1,702	2,070	1

'Law and philanthropy', 'Indian business and philanthropy', 'Industrialist and philanthropy', 'Philanthropist and sportsman' (these from 1938–44).[49] The philanthropy of such people usually included the donation of sums of money, but there were also almost always descriptions of the organisations with which the donor was involved. Take Mrs E. F. Streatfield, who died in 1931. She was 'remarkable both for her intellectual powers and for her philanthropic service', especially in relation to children's homes. 'She disapproved of legacies as generosity at the expense of others, not herself, preferring to make personal gifts at her own cost and of her own free will. Hospitals, the COS, orphanages, settlements, whose methods she knew and approved, all benefited from a knowledge based on hard personal work among the poor.'[50]

The philanthropists in obituaries worked at different levels. Some were specifically local, others at national level. There were also a large number of obituaries of foreign philanthropists, especially those from the United States and India. It is as though there was a global world of philanthropy, foreign exemplars written up as an inspiration to local giving and action. The global reach and the contents of obituaries suggest that philanthropy in the first half of the century at least had a reputation that was positive, making it seem that engagement in philanthropy, whether through gifts or service or both, was part of a worthy and estimable life. For a time what might be called the philanthropic outlook on life was sustainable and could reproduce itself.

It helped that members of the Royal Family associated themselves with philanthropy. In the political and industrial turbulence of 1910–14, in the war that followed which saw crowned heads toppled across Europe, and through the economic hard times of the post-war depression, the monarchy and its advisers saw philanthropy as a survival strategy. Fear of Bolshevism and socialism was rife, revolution a rarely absent threat. Patronage of existing organisations was the simplest way to engage though much of it went little beyond allowing the royal name to appear on letterheads – Edward VIII had 776 institutions on his patronage list. Visiting and supporting the voluntary hospitals, even campaigning on their behalf, was much favoured. More risky was asking the Prince of Wales to deliver a speech on unemployment in 1932. It was written for him by the secretaries of the National Council of Social Service and of the Pilgrim Trust. The Prince drove home 'the need, the duty, of personal service', the 'readiness to give which is the only justification for the privileges of citizenship'. It met with an immediate response, with 2,300 projects started within a year to help the unemployed. Visits to working-class areas, to factories and mines, were, however, the most significant royal philanthropy, a well-planned strategy to tie the working class to the monarchy. The reward for George V and Queen Mary came at the Silver Jubilee of 1935 when they drove through the East End and the docks to be greeted enthusiastically, the decorations in the streets, as the King noted, 'all put up by the poor'.[51]

Both at royal level and lower down the social scale networks sustained the philanthropic world. An obituary of Lady Biddulph of Ledbury in 1916, for example, spoke of her as 'a prominent figure in the social and philanthropic world', concerning herself especially with the promotion of temperance in London. In 1948 Dame Beatrix Lyall was remembered as being 'widely known for her social and philanthropic activities'.[52] In such instances the social and the philanthropic worlds overlapped and mutually reinforced one another. In 1931 Alexander Glegg, writing to *The Times* on behalf of the Royal Hospital and Home for Incurables at Putney, described how he had 'hoped to secure, as chairman for the festival dinner, some outstanding personality in the philanthropic world, whose very name and influence would buttonhole the charitable public and induce them to give generously', but he had failed.[53] The letter, however, was testimony to the existence of a 'philanthropic world'. How big it was is difficult to determine. Probably there was a core of the committed, surrounded by circles of diminishing enthusiasm, whose money skillful fund-raisers could tap. It seems likely that this world of philanthropy was much less evident after the 1940s.

The existence of a philanthropic world, however, did not mean that philanthropy was unscathed in reputation. It is here that the element of continuity from the nineteenth century is most prominent. Pleas for increased borrowing in 1920 were 'reckless philanthropy on a large scale'. In the General Strike in 1926 the Bishop of Gloucester at a diocesan conference asserted that 'the greatest enemies of the working-classes were those philanthropic persons who persisted in ignoring economic laws ... The idea that there was a Christian economics as opposed to ordinary teaching was a mistake'. In the same year, under the heading 'Dangers of state philanthropy', *The Times* reported Lady Selborne addressing the National Council of Women on 'philanthropic legislation' being a cause of housing shortages. When the National Playing Fields Association was appealing for funds in 1927, *The Times* warned that 'even in this matter of playing fields there is at least a danger that too much philanthropy may weaken the qualities of energy, self help, and personal and corporate initiative'. In 1931, it was claimed, 'British industry is handicapped by philanthropic policies that are throttling the means of financing them', especially with regard to wage rates.[54]

There is, looking at these comments from a nineteenth-century perspective, a sense of déjà vu. Yet there were other signs that people were distinguishing philanthropy in the new century from its Victorian forebears. Any invocation of philanthropy as a good was normally linked to an assertion that it was different from the old philanthropy. A new spirit infused philanthropy, it was argued, one that ministered to what people wanted rather than to what was thought good for them. At a Whitsun 'camp of understanding' for public school boys and for those whose schooling ended at fourteen, held in the immediate aftermath of the General Strike, 'the patronizing ways of the old philanthropy are gone'. In 1932, celebrating fifty years of the Metropolitan Public Gardens Association, it was said that 'The Association is not the kind of philanthropic body which forces upon people what it thinks would be good for them, but one which helps people to get what they truly enjoy and want'. In 1937 when the King and Queen visited the People's Palace in the East End, *The Times* commented that 'Even casual observers of social change may perceive ... the difference between the Victorian conception of philanthropy and that of our own day. The operative desire now is not to improve; it is to give happiness through opportunity and equipment hitherto denied to vast numbers of our fellow-countrymen. Let them be happy and fully occupied, and the improvement will follow'. A Youth Centre for exercise and play was opened.[55] As A. F. C. Bourdillon put it in 1945, modern social services tend 'to provide clubs to keep young people happy instead of homes in which they may repent'.[56]

Methods of fund-raising also attracted attention as new. Looking at the calendar for the London Season in May 1931 *The Times* was struck that 'nearly all the bigger entertainments are got up in aid of charity', giving the calendar 'so loftily philanthropic an air'. Three years later, returning to the topic under the heading 'Charity and pleasure', it noted how 'the most effective and masterly kind of philanthropic organizer – those who bring in the wisdom of the serpent to temper the assiduity of the daughters of the horse-leech – make good use of the London season'. Fifty years ago, it claimed, 'A dinner was the only recognized method of raising money for charity. Nowadays a glance over the list of the season's fixtures will show that a very great many of them have charitable ends'.[57] This did scant justice to the variety of fund-raising methods, not least bazaars, fifty years previously, but is some evidence of a sense people had of being in a new era of fund-raising where the social enjoyments of the London Season could be used for philanthropic purposes.

Mid-century hopes and fears

There were two visions of philanthropy, with roots in the nineteenth century, which co-existed in some tension through much of the twentieth century. The simplest was the giving of funds on a large scale. Carnegie and the American foundations of the first decade of the twentieth century set new standards for giving away large fortunes, but it was some time before the British thought they might have someone in the same league. That man was Lord Nuffield, 'the greatest philanthropist of the age', 'the outstanding British philanthropist of his generation'. The £10 million that launched the Nuffield Foundation in 1943 put him on a par, it was said, with Carnegie, Rhodes and Rockefeller. On its fifth birthday *The Times* lauded 'this newest of the great trusts for intelligent private philanthropy'.[58] There were few rivals. Promoting research as most of them did, in 1950 the Leverhulme Trust (founded in 1925), the Wellcome Trust (founded in 1936) and the Nuffield Foundation disbursed £0.61 million (£11.59 million at 1997 prices) of which £0.51 million came from Nuffield. By 1970, together with the Wolfson Foundation (founded in 1955), and the Joseph Rowntree Foundation (founded in 1904 and its mission substantially expanded in 1959), they distributed £59.03 million at 1997 prices. By 1997 that figure had risen to £273.54 million, the Wellcome Trust contributing £227 million of this total.[59] There remained, however, some scepticism about large-scale philanthropy. In 1965, noting the dependence of research in British universities on funding from the United States, *The Times* asked why this should be so: 'the British system and the British economy have not permitted the huge accumulations of private wealth that exist in the United States', and tax laws in Britain were less favourable to giving. Even so, it would be wrong to expect that 'the entire social system of the country be altered to foster the emergence of philanthropic millionaires'.[60] Moreover this kind of philanthropy was beginning to look as if it belonged to the past. Sheila Gould, in the *Guardian* in 1970, referred to 'these days when heavy taxation and death duties make old-fashioned philanthropy increasingly rare'.[61] It was only late in the century and into the twenty-first century that the formation of foundations began to proliferate. When the Association of Charitable Foundations was formed in 1989 it had sixty-two members, by the turn of the century 300 and by 2017 600.[62]

The other vision of philanthropy, set out by Walter Besant in 1898, was of 'personal service'.[63] In mid-century *The Times* commented on the transformation of the COS into the Family Welfare Association in 1946. In encouraging hospital almoners, in developing Citizen Advice Bureaux, the association, wrote *The Times*, 'has shown itself fully aware of the possibilities of the new philanthropy of personal service'.[64] Ideally the two visions might meet. When the Prince of Wales visited Boys' Clubs in Yorkshire in 1933 it was noted that though the government gave some help that 'will still leave a large sphere for the philanthropy which is so much greater than charity because a man "gives himself with his gift"'.[65]

Concern about the young was one common theme that seemed to run through the century. It was not new, but it was sometimes seen as new. Reflecting on youth and criminality in 1901, *The Times* argued that in the treatment of the young lies 'the hope of the wise philanthropist'. This picked up on an old theme, that the young could still be brought to better ways of life, something that was much more difficult to achieve with older people set in their ways and in their (bad) habits. In 1938 work with those who had come before JPs under the terms of the 1933 Children and Young Persons Act was seen as 'one of the most inspiring and hopeful of all philanthropic enterprises'. In 1949 it was felt that 'If there is one large branch of philanthropy which above all has captured the imagination of the present age, it is that which devotes itself to the welfare of the young'. Organisation was needed and the coordination was to be undertaken by King George's Jubilee Trust, set up on George V's death.[66]

The increasing role of government pervaded discussion as the century wore on. It was not simply a case of the state growing at the expense of the voluntary sector. As Brian Harrison and Josephine Webb put it, 'in the twentieth century both have advanced together. Volunteers extended the state's frontiers at many points, exposing new needs and devising new remedies'.[67] Numerous campaigning and advocacy organisations admirably met Kirkman Gray's early twentieth-century belief that the true role of philanthropy was as agitator.[68] Oxfam (1942), the National Association for Mental Health, now Mind (1946), War on Want (1951), the Samaritans (1953), Amnesty International (1961), the Child Poverty Action Group (1965), Shelter (1966) and many others were testimony to the vibrancy of civil society in highlighting issues that demanded attention and in action to relieve them. They put pressure on government to respond to their findings. They could in many ways be described as manifesting a love of humankind as understood in the eighteenth century. None of them, however, would have been happy to be seen as philanthropic as the word had come to be understood in the mid-twentieth century. They were, on the contrary, usually seen as 'pressure groups'.

There was widespread agreement that some tasks were beyond the capacity of voluntary organisations. The 1,000 voluntary hospitals in the interwar period, most of them very small but including the prestigious teaching hospitals, struggled to raise funds and became increasingly reliant on fees paid by patients. So too did municipal hospitals. There were also, however, forms of fund-raising through contributory or insurance schemes and

Hospital Saturdays or Sundays that gave local populations a sense of at least partial ownership of hospitals. George Campbell Gosling has argued that this was 'philanthropy reformulated' and 'maintained', with the Lady Almoner now the person who negotiated the terms on which a potential patient would enter hospital. Put positively, to contribute to your own hospital costs was an act of citizenship within a philanthropic relationship. Probably no one at the time, however, would have put it in those terms. It came to an abrupt end with the inauguration of the National Health Service in 1948.[69]

The immediate post-war period was one of difficulty and uncertainty for voluntary organisations. In the hospitals world in particular there was sense of something like betrayal of what volunteers had done and could do. The newly formed Leagues of Friends of hospitals met with scarcely veiled hostility from civil servants. The King's Fund thought the Labour Party to be 'fiercely anti-voluntary' and that it was trying to prevent hospitals from having any voluntary support. In the 1950s histories of individual voluntary hospitals were published, their texts 'deeply imbued with a sense of loss'.[70]

More broadly, however, writes Rodney Lowe, 'welfare expenditure was seen not as a rival to philanthropy and self-help, but as a means of freeing charities to concentrate on other challenges and of providing the poor with a basic independence'.[71] New lines began to be drawn in what Beveridge called 'the moving frontier' between the state and voluntary organisations. *The Times* in 1943, discussing the termination of Lord Nuffield's 1936 grant of £2 million to ease unemployment, was clear that 'The responsibility for ensuring that there is no renewal of the national disgrace of mass unemployment rests squarely on the shoulders of Parliament and people, and is not to be shifted to those of the private philanthropist, however princely'. On the other hand, the state's activity, it was claimed, might be harmful. In 1952 a leader referred to 'the two qualities which the Welfare State is said to be killing, philanthropy and financial enterprise'.[72] In 1960 it was thought that there were too many 'philanthropic societies' that were 'safe resting places of small vested interests created to fulfill social needs now largely anachronistic or met by public departments'. Such societies should become 'pathfinders and pacemakers'. Two years later *The Times* commented that there was a difficulty for philanthropists in knowing whether 'the real beneficiary does not turn out to be the taxpayer', that philanthropy was doing something which government should. 'The ubiquity of organized public help has a damaging effect on voluntary service and philanthropy, and it complicates any estimate of their probable usefulness.'[73]

Later in the same year it was claimed that 'Many citizens, local politicians among them ... regard private charity as something which the social services have made wholly anachronistic'. Regretting the 'failure to recruit all classes of the welfare state into active local welfare', *The Times* commented that 'Voluntary service had previously been the prerogative of the middle and upper classes, and it has usually continued that way'. The Seebohm

Committee on Local Authority and Allied Personal Social Services in 1968, writing of voluntary organisations, similarly regretted that 'the day when they could act as vehicles for upper and middle class philanthropy appropriate to the social structure of Victorian Britain is not past. Remnants of old practices and attitudes remain in the condescension and social exclusiveness of a few voluntary organisations, and in a suspicion and mistrust of some local authorities'. On the same theme in 1971, *The Times* argued that a 'charitable system based on a small philanthropic middle class' was no longer fit for purpose.[74] Philanthropy of a 'Victorian' kind might linger on, went the message, but its day was past.

What lay ahead was something that few could have predicted. Government began increasingly to look to voluntary organisations to carry out tasks on its behalf. The establishment by the Heath government in 1973 of a Voluntary Services Unit within the Home Office was a sign of change. Between the mid-1970s and mid-1980s government funding of charities rose sixfold. Many, for example the Spastics Society, began to receive more from government than from voluntary donations.[75] In 1998 the relationship between government and not-for-profit voluntary and community organisations was set out in a Compact that has been periodically renewed. Volunteering was to become a regular part of life, the Treasury issuing a target that by 2010 three-quarters of all adults should be spending at least two hours a week as a volunteer.[76] In the twenty-first century there was a move from government issuing grants to voluntary organisations to a system of bidding for contracts to carry out specific services, a reform that put voluntary and business organisations in direct rivalry, often to the disadvantage of the former.

A focus on the relationship between government and voluntary organisations can easily lead to neglect of what through the nineteenth century had been recognised as the most important resource that poorer people turned to in times of difficulty, namely their friends and neighbours. This in no way diminished in the twentieth century. In the late 1980s total annual expenditure by government on personal social services was approximately £4,300 million. Charities contributed a further £400 million. These were dwarfed by the estimated £24,000 million value of informal care, with six million people, 14 per cent of the adult population, acting as 'carers', the majority of them women.[77]

'Progressive people in the 1930s', it has been noted, 'dismissed the "do-gooder" as amateur, inefficient and probably also class-prejudiced'. Labour supporters were particularly liable to nurse such feelings. In the 1960s, however, attitudes began to change, in large part because many campaigning groups were on the left of the political spectrum. R. H. S. Crossman in 1973 urged the labour movement to rethink its dislike of 'do-good volunteering'. If for different reasons, Conservative politicians also began to laud the work of volunteers as the embodiment of active citizenship and as a counterweight to state bureaucracy.[78] By 1975 there were some 140 volunteer bureaux acting as recruiting and training hubs for unpaid volunteers in the social services. After a low point in the 1950s 'By the mid-1970s ... formal voluntary care was almost wholly rehabilitated'.[79]

New philanthropy

By the end of the century the tone of comments on philanthropy was changing. In a foretaste of what was to become another 'new philanthropy', in 1985, on the anniversary of Carnegie's birth, *The Times* commented that 'With the evolution of capitalism since Carnegie's day, the face of philanthropy has changed'. *The Times* did not spell out what it considered to mark 'the evolution of capitalism', but it felt that philanthropy had become 'safer' and 'blander'. Looking for change, and invoking Adam Smith, it argued that the spirits of enterprise and of benevolence were not at odds but complemented one another. In 1992, noting the association between the donation of money and the granting of honorary degrees, it was in no doubt that 'Higher education will be in dire need of more such philanthropy in the 1990s'. By 1996 'the demands upon [philanthropy] are growing fast'.[80] And then, in 1999, *The Times* was able to welcome 'signs of a new philanthropy', though they were more in evidence in the United States than in Britain. 'Philanthropy's renaissance', it went one, 'has been sparked in part by failures in the welfare state'. What marked the new era was that benefactors 'apply an entrepreneurial culture to philanthropy'. 'Philanthropy', it announced, 'fundamentally depends on the creation of wealth, wealth creation on enterprise, and enterprise on small government'.[81]

Wealth was undoubtedly increasing, the amount of it set out in 'The *Sunday Times* Rich List', published annually from 1988. It was supplemented from 2005 with a Giving Index or Giving List, recording the 'proportion of residual wealth given away or generated for charity in the most recent year for which data are available'. In the 2018 Giving List the top 300 on this measurement gifted £3.207 billion, a record. It is noticeable, however, that many of those in the Rich List failed to feature in the Giving List and that of the top 200 in the Giving List 166 gave 1 per cent or less of their residual wealth. Nevertheless, 'High net-worth individuals' (HNWIs) with the equivalent of over US$1 million and 'Ultra high net-worth individuals' (UHNWIs), with an equivalent of over US$30 million, were targeted for their potential gifting to philanthropic causes. In the United Kingdom in 2016 there were 9,470 UHNWIs. In an attempt to tap their wealth the Beacon Collaborative, a network of 'wealth holders', launched a Manifesto in 2019 that sought 'to encourage our peers to increase our annual charitable giving collectively by £2billion'. Or, as the *Financial Times* reported, 'to discuss the pitiful state of philanthropy in the country': of those earning £10 million or more per year the median level of giving in 2016/17 was £240 per year.[82]

In the first decade of the new century 'new philanthropy' was much in the news, its links to new wealth prominent. In the *Financial Times*, philanthrop★ as a keyword rose dramatically. For the first nine decades of the twentieth century, from 1900 to 1989, the average number of mentions per decade was thirty-seven. In 1990–99 it was ninety-four, and then from 2000 to 2010 an astonishing 608. The newspaper that represented City interests was promoting philanthropy. Institutions for the encouragement of philanthropy proliferated. The Institute for Philanthropy was founded in 2000, Philanthropy UK in 2001, New Philanthropy Capital in 2002, the latter founded by two men whose earlier careers had been in Goldman Sachs. In an indication that New Labour was looking to an enhanced role for philanthropy, Gordon Brown in 2009 appointed Dame Stephanie Shirley, who had made a £150 million fortune in IT software consultancy and given most of it away, as the first Ambassador for Philanthropy. Shirley aimed to promote a global network of wealthy philanthropists. When Charles Handy celebrated *The New Philanthropists: The New Generosity* in 2007 he was confident that 'Philanthropy is becoming fashionable', and that new philanthropists 'provide a social justification for the free enterprise system that it has often lacked'. In 2007 the chief executive of HSBC Private Bank attributed 'the burgeoning interest in philanthropy to the boom in new wealth in Britain over the past decade from an entrepreneurial class that has moved from becoming asset-rich to cash-rich'.[83] In 2008 Matthew Bishop and Michael Green coined a new word for what was happening, entitling their book *Philanthrocapitalism: How the Rich Can Save the World and Why We Should Let Them*. They envisaged a social contract between the rich and everyone else: the rich would earn money honestly, pay their taxes 'and give generously and effectively', and in return everyone else would stop sniping at them. With 'populist anti-rich policies on the rise', it was 'enlightened self-interest' for the rich to be philanthropic. In the same year *The Times* provided a new definition of philanthropy: 'Philanthropy is the alchemy to transform philistine profits from tobacco, sugar or steel into a cultural complex, a hospital or a new municipal stadium and earn the gratitude of millions.'[84] It seemed a win-win situation.

In fact most of the new rich were as conservative as their Victorian predecessors in their giving. Studies of million pound donations showed a consistent trend: the major beneficiaries were the more prestigious universities and the arts and culture sector.[85] Moreover, a study of the media coverage of philanthropy and philanthropists showed that suspicion of motives remained almost as strong as they had been in the 1840s.[86] New philanthropy has had many vocal advocates, but it has also been subjected to criticisms in much the same way as was the fate of Victorian philanthropy: that it is inadequate to the task, that it is the outcome of a form of capitalism that itself creates many of the ills that philanthropy seeks to remedy, that it does little to promote social justice.[87]

Conclusion

In the early twenty-first century the primary definition of philanthropy in the *Oxford English Dictionary* online read: 'Love of mankind; the disposition or active effort to promote the happiness and well-being of others; practical benevolence, now esp. as expressed by the generous donation of money to good causes.' The last phrase, starting 'now esp.', was new. Only in the twenty-first century, with 'new philanthropy' well established, did it become necessary to link philanthropy with the giving of money. There was no mention of it when the relevant volume of the *OED* was first published in 1909, nor in a revised version in 1989.[88] Confirmation that this was how philanthropy was now seen came when the Marshall Institute for Philanthropy and Social Entrepreneurship at the London School of Economics, founded in 2015, defined philanthropy as 'the desire to promote the welfare of others, expressed especially by the generous donation of money to good causes'.[89]

The first three-quarters of the twentieth century saw a marked decline in the place of philanthropy in public discourse. This did not mean that charitable and philanthropic endeavour declined. There was a significant increase in the First World War. What the nineteenth century had identified as the 'machinery' of voluntary organisations held up and, as Lord Nathan and William Beveridge noted, there were notable newcomers in the field. It might be thought that with all this continuing activity the fact that there was less appeal to or discussion of philanthropy in the media was of little importance. The decline of an old language and the adoption of a new one was, however, an indicator of significant political and social change. The adoption of the phrase 'voluntary action', as distinct from 'charity' or 'philanthropy', was closely aligned with the spread of democracy. Voluntary action was democratic action; on top of this it was a training ground for democracy on the explicitly political scene. It was intrinsic to the development of citizenship. The political activities of women and the rapid growth of the Labour Party were central to these changes.[90] Labour spokespeople regularly attacked the patronage of charity and philanthropy, they spoke of Lady Bountifuls who exuded superiority and in return for their gifts expected deference and gratitude. It did not really matter whether or not this was evident on the ground; the rhetoric resonated. Labour's opponents, as much as their supporters, needed a new language to describe what they were doing. It was partly definition by negatives: it was not 'Victorian' charity and philanthropy, the adjective indicative of a world that had passed.

There were attempts by people inclined to Liberalism or Labour to reclaim philanthropy – by Rathbone, Macadam, Stocks, Braithwaite, Beveridge – but the tide was running against them. The future lay with a new vocabulary of voluntary action, and with talk of 'the voluntary sector'. In charting the ups and downs of the relationship between the voluntary sector and the state from 1945 to 1992 Nicholas Deakin made little reference to philanthropy. True, in Margaret Thatcher's third term of office in the later 1980s, Michael Heseltine 'set in motion whole series of business-led phil-anthropic initiatives' to revive inner cities but this 'new philanthropy proved soluble when dampened by the recession after 1989 – the "city fathers" mostly decided that their paternal responsibilities were to their own firms and jobs, not the common good'.[91] If philanthropy was making little impact, the voluntary sector itself was under challenge. As Colin Rochester has put it, there has been a process since the 1960s and 1970s whereby a voluntary sector, represented by a small number of large organisations, became tied to implementing government policy. Voluntary work became thought of as 'carrying out pre-determined tasks for a formal bureaucratic organization which employs staff to manage its volunteer labour'. Rochester was deeply critical of these developments.[92]

From the perspective of philanthropy, what was interesting about these twentieth-century developments was how far removed they were, in the minds both of those actively involved in them and those at a distance, from anything that might be called philanthropy. Robert Whelan, from a right-wing position, described 'voluntary action' in 1999 as what 'we used to call philanthropy', but much as he admired nineteenth-century philanthropy he pretended to no hope that it might be reclaimed for what, for Whelan, had declined into 'involuntary action'.[93] Other developments in the twenty-first century avoid referring to philanthropy. The policy-making people who meet to discuss or work in the 'third sector', a term that began to be used only from the beginning of the twenty-first century, boosted by a *Third Sector* journal from 2002, rarely refer to philanthropy. 'Third sector' as a term, moreover, was too academic to become popular. It was essentially negative; it was anything that was neither capitalist profit making nor politics – and it came third after these first two sectors. David Cameron's 'Big Society' ini-tiative, launched during the 2010 election campaign, lacked credibility from the outset. It seemed too obviously to be an attempt to put a positive spin on austerity and the shrinking of the state – and to suggest that ordinary people could deliver services previously done by the trained and paid. Its shelf life was short. Cameron himself mentioned it for the last time at Christmas 2013, and the think-tank Civil Exchange's report on it in early 2015 set out six reasons why it had failed.[94]

'New philanthropy' had little time for any of these developments or debates. But how new was it? Beth Breeze has powerfully argued, not very. Its claims to novelty lie in three factors: that new donors are young, richer, self-made and cosmopolitan in outlook; that it is drawn to new causes such as global health and the environment, and that it has established new foundations that have specific targets and monitored outcomes. But as Breeze points out, there are many examples of precisely these three things in previous centuries.[95]

Notes

1 P. Thane, 'The "big society" and the "big state": Creative tension or crowding out?', *Twentieth Century British History*, 23 (2012), 408–28 for an excellent overview.
2 *The Times*, 12 May 1914.
3 Ibid., 19 May 1914.
4 Quoted in M. J. Moore, 'Social work and social welfare: The organization of philanthropic resources in Britain, 1900–1914', *Journal of British Studies*, 16 (1977), 96–7.
5 Quoted in M. J. Moore, 'Social service and social legislation in Edwardian England: The beginning of a new role for philanthropy', *Albion*, 3 (1971), 36.
6 J. Hinton, 'Voluntarism and the welfare/warfare state: Women's voluntary services in the 1940s', *Twentieth Century British History*, 9 (1998), 275.
7 P. Grant, *Philanthropy and Voluntary Action in the First World War: Mobilizing Charity* (London: Routledge, 2014), pp. 3, 17–18.
8 A. Thompson, 'Publicity, philanthropy and commemoration: British society and the war', in D. Omissi and A. Thompson (eds), *The Impact of the South African War* (Basingstoke: Palgrave, 2002), pp. 106–13.
9 Grant, *Philanthropy and Voluntary Action*, pp. 132–41.
10 E. Macadam, *The New Philanthropy: A Study of the Relations Between the Statutory and Voluntary Social Services* (London: George Allen & Unwin, 1934), p. 57.
11 F. Prochaska, *Royal Bounty: The Making of a Welfare Monarchy* (New Haven and London: Yale University Press, 2005), p. 205.
12 N. Deakin and J. D. Smith, 'Labour, charity and voluntary action: The myth of hostility', in M. Hilton and J. MacKay (eds), *The Ages of Voluntarism: How We Got to the Big Society* (Oxford: Oxford University Press, 2011), p. 75.
13 See B. Harris, *The Origins of the British Welfare State: Social Welfare in England and Wales, 1800–1945* (Basingstoke: Palgrave Macmillan, 2004), pp. 184–90.
14 J. Harris, 'Political thought and the welfare state 1870–1940: An intellectual framework for British social policy', *Past & Present*, 135 (May 1992), 116–41.
15 Quotations in H. Meller, 'Urban renewal and citizenship: The quality of life in British cities, 1890–1990', *Urban History*, 22 (1995), 65–6.
16 M. Freeden, 'Civil society and the good citizen: Competing conceptions of citizenship in twentieth-century Britain', in J. Harris (ed.), *Civil Society in British History: Ideas, Identities, Institutions* (Oxford: Oxford University Press, 2003), pp. 275–91.
17 Quoted in Deakin and Smith, 'Labour, charity and voluntary action', p. 73.
18 *Manchester Guardian*, 22 Nov. 1928, 15.
19 M. Rooff, *Voluntary Societies and Social Policy* (London: Routledge & Kegan Paul, 1957), p. 254.
20 *Oxford Dictionary of National Biography*.
21 Macadam, *New Philanthropy*, pp. 24, 30, 36; see also, A. F. C. Bourdillon (ed.), *Voluntary Social Services: Their Place in the Modern State* (London: Methuen, 1945), pp. 1–2: 'There is still no general agreement in answer to the question "what are the social services?"'

22 Macadam, *New Philanthropy*, p. 183.

23 Ibid., p. 18.

24 Ibid., p. 21.

25 Ibid., pp. 244–5, 250–61.

26 C. Braithwaite, *The Voluntary Citizen: An Enquiry into the Place of Philanthropy in the Community* (London: Methuen, 1938), pp. 78–9.

27 Quoted in E. Colpus, 'Women, service and self-actualization in inter-war Britain', *Past & Present*, 238 (2018), 217.

28 Quoted in E. Colpus, *Female Philanthropy in the Interwar World: Between Self and Other* (London: Bloomsbury Academic, 2018), p. 32. Colpus, pp. 1–2, claims that the four women she studies 'had a great deal to say about what it meant to be a philanthropist and to do philanthropy', but on the evidence she presents they rarely used the words.

29 Quoted in Colpus, 'Women, service and self-actualization', 220.

30 Quoted in Colpus, *Female Philanthropy*, p. 12.

31 G. D. H. Cole, 'A retrospect of the history of voluntary social service', in Bourdillon (ed.), *Voluntary Social Services*, pp. 29, 118.

32 W. Beveridge, *Voluntary Action: A Report on Methods of Social Advance* (London: George Allen & Unwin, 1948), pp. 9, 121.

33 Ibid., pp. 153–86.

34 *The Times*, 17 Aug. 1923.

35 Ibid., 3 Apr. 1930.

36 Beveridge, *Voluntary Action*, p. 301.

37 Ibid., pp. 265–6, 286.

38 Ibid., p. 300.

39 W. Beveridge and A. F. Wells (eds), *The Evidence for Voluntary Action* (London: Allen & Unwin, 1949), pp. 55–7.

40 Quoted in Deakin and Smith, 'Labour, charity and voluntary action', pp. 83–4, 91.

41 Report of the Committee on the Law and Practice Relating to Charitable Trusts, 1952, Cmd 8710, § 13.

42 *Hansard*, House of Lords, Vol. 163 (22 June 1949), p. 119.

43 Ibid., p. 95.

44 Report on Charitable Trusts, § 33, 44.

45 Ibid., § 50–1, pp. 11–12.

46 Ibid., § 53, p. 12.

47 Mrs J. L. Stocks, *The Philanthropist in a Changing World* (Liverpool: Liverpool University Press, 1953), pp. 8, 10, 13.

48 Ibid., pp. 17–18, 21–2.

49 *The Times*, 1938–44.

50 Ibid., 15 July 1931.

51 Prochaska, *Royal Bounty*, pp. 195–210.

52 *The Times*, 17 Jan. 1916; 8 Nov. 1946.

53 Ibid., 6 June 1931.

54 Ibid., 12 Feb. 1920; 3 June 1926; 22 Oct. 1926; 1 June 1927; 13 Feb. 1931.

55 Ibid., 20 May 1926; 9 Dec. 1932; 13 Feb. 1937.

56 Bourdillon (ed.), *Voluntary Social Services*, p. 9.

57 *The Times*, 1 May 1931; 24 May 1934. 'The daughters of the horse-leech' is a reference to *Proverbs*, 30, v. 15, the daughters crying out 'give, give'.

58 Ibid., 1 Jan. 1938; 10 Oct. 1957; 13 Feb. 1943; 14 Oct. 1948.

59 B. Harrison and J. Webb, 'Volunteers and voluntarism', in A. H. Halsey with J. Webb (eds), *Twentieth-Century British Social Trends* (Basingstoke: Macmillan Press, 2000), pp. 610–11.

60 *The Times*, 15 Feb. 1965.

61 *Guardian*, 26 Mar. 1970.

62 Association of Charitable Foundations, *Annual Reports*.

63 W. Besant. 'On university settlements', in W. Reason (ed.), *University and Social Settlements* (London: Methuen, 1898), p. 4.

64 *The Times*, 25 June 1946.

65 Ibid., 15 Dec. 1933.

66 Ibid., 17 Apr. 1901; 27 Jan. 1938; 16 Mar. 1949.

67 Harrison and Webb, 'Volunteers and voluntarism', p. 614.

68 B. Kirkman Gray, *Philanthropy and the State; or Social Politics* (London: P. S. King & Son, 1908), pp. 302–16.

69 G. C. Gosling, *Payment and Philanthropy in British Healthcare, 1918–48* (Manchester: Manchester University Press, 2017).

70 F. K. Prochaska, *Philanthropy and the Hospitals of London: The King's Fund, 1897–1990* (Oxford: Clarendon Press, 1992), pp. 163–6.

71 R. Lowe, *The Welfare State in Britain since 1945*, 3rd edn (Basingstoke: Palgrave Macmillan, 2005), pp. 109, 178–85.

72 *The Times*, 17 Jan. 1943; 4 Nov. 1952.

73 Ibid., 9 Nov. 1960; 2 Mar. 1962.

74 Ibid., 13 Aug. 1962; 23 May 1971; Seebohm Committee quoted in *Guardian*, 11 Feb. 1970.

75 Harrison and Webb, 'Volunteers and voluntarism', p. 600.

76 Lowe, *Welfare State*, p. 412.

77 Ibid., p. 285.

78 Harrison and Webb, 'Volunteers and voluntarism', pp. 613–15; Lowe, *Welfare State*, pp. 285–7. The word 'do-gooder' originated in the United States and seems not to have been in use until the twentieth century. The *Oxford English Dictionary* defines it as 'a well-meaning, active, but sometimes unrealistic or misguided philanthropist or reformer', used now 'chiefly with disparaging implication'.

79 Lowe, *Welfare State*, pp. 287, 290.

80 *The Times*, 19 Aug. 1985; 17 July 1992; 2 Mar. 1996.

81 Ibid., 8 Mar. 1999.

82 *Independent*, 2 Mar. 2017; *Financial Times*, 15 Feb. 2019; www.beaconawards. org.uk/manifesto (accessed on 15 Oct. 2019).

83 C. Handy, *The New Philanthropists: The New Generosity* (London: William Heinemann, 2007), pp. 3, 10; *The Times*, 17 Feb. 2007, 56.

84 M. Bishop and M. Green, *Philanthrocapitalism: How the Rich Can Save the World and Why We Should Let Them* (London: A & C Black, 2008), p. xi; *The Times*, 28 Mar. 2008.

85 See *The Million Pound Donors Reports* published by Coutts Institute.

86 B. Breeze and T. Lloyd, *Richer Lives: Why Rich People Give* (London: Directory of Social Change, 2013), pp. 157–8.

87 See, e.g., B. Morvaridi (ed.), *New Philanthropy and Social Justice: Debating the Conceptual and Policy Discourse* (Bristol: Policy Press, 2015); L. McGoey, *No Such Thing as a Free Gift: The Gates Foundation and the Price of Philanthropy* (New York: Verso, 2015); R. Reich, *Just Giving: Why Philanthropy is Failing Democracy and How It Can Do Better* (Princeton and Oxford: Princeton University Press, 2018); E. Kolbert, 'Shaking the foundations', *The New Yorker*, 27 Aug. 2018.

88 M. Sulek, 'On the modern meaning of philanthropy', *Nonprofit and Voluntary Sector Quarterly*, 39 (2010), 200.

89 www.lse.ac.uk/Marshall-Institute (accessed on 15 Oct. 2019).

90 H. McCarthy, 'Associational voluntarism in interwar Britain', in Hilton and McKay (eds), *Ages of Voluntarism*, pp. 47–68, arguing, p. 48, that associational life was 'central to the democratization of the *political* system'; Deakin and Davis Smith, 'Labour, charity and voluntary action', pp. 69–93. On the promotion of citizenship through leisure, see R. Snape, 'Theorisations of leisure in inter-war Britain', *Leisure Studies*, 32 (2013), 1–18, and 'The new leisure, voluntarism and social reconstruction in inter-war Britain', *Contemporary British History*, 29 (2015), 51–83.

91 N. Deakin, 'The perils of partnership: The voluntary sector and the state, 1945–1992', in J. Davis Smith, C. Rochester and R. Hedley (eds), *An Introduction to the Voluntary Sector* (London: Routledge, 1995), pp. 59–60, 62.

92 C. Rochester, *Rediscovering Voluntary Action: The Beat of a Different Drum* (Basingstoke: Palgrave Macmillan, 2013), pp. 36–66.

93 R. Whelan, *Involuntary Action: How Voluntary is the Voluntary Sector?* (London: IEA Health and Welfare Unit, 1999), p. 5.

94 *Guardian*, 20 Jan. 2015; *Civil Society*, 20 Jan. 2015.

95 B. Breeze, 'Is there a new philanthropy?', in C. Rochester, G. C. Gosling, A. Penn and M. Zimmeck (eds), *The Roots of Voluntary Action: Historical Perspectives on Current Social Policy* (Brighton: Sussex Academic Press, 2011), pp. 182–95.

Conclusion

Histories of philanthropy are for the most part histories of giving or gifting. This history, by contrast, has traced the shifts in the meanings of the word 'philanthropy' and the public discourse that it elicited. The assumption underlying this approach is that when a new word like philanthropy spread as rapidly as it did in the second half of the eighteenth century it was a sign of a new way of thinking and feeling. Philanthropy was built on a new and optimistic view of human nature, that we all, like God, have inbuilt sympathy for our fellow humans. It was hardly surprising that such a view did not command universal assent. The strong feelings aroused by 'philanthropy' and by those who came to be called 'philanthropists', both in favour and in opposition, are testimony to the power embedded in these two words. Philanthropy's reputation was never secure.

Philanthropy spread through print. It did not stand alone, in isolation. It became part of a mindset that responded positively to ideas of 'humanity', of 'benevolence' as something rooted in human nature, of sensitivity and sympathy. Whereas 'charity' not only began at home but also often stayed there, philanthropy was worldwide and universal in its reach. The political implications of this were profound. All humans, by virtue of being human, had rights. Philanthropy's task was to ensure that people were able to exercise those rights, even if they were prisoners or slaves. In an age that prided itself on being 'enlightened and humane',[1] philanthropy pointed the way to a better future – and Britain, with a statue to John Howard in St Paul's Cathedral, could claim philanthropy as a component of its national identity.

The French Revolution at its outset seemed to be forwarding the progress of philanthropy. But the reaction that set in against it, culminating in 1793 in war between Britain and France that lasted but for a brief interruption to 1815, put philanthropy and its advocates on the defensive. Its universalism drew down on it the accusation that it was unpatriotic. To be called a 'citizen of the world' ceased to be a compliment. When radicals began to claim philanthropy as their own, challenging property rights as the Spenceans did, the word and its associations were further imperiled. It was rescued by the anti-slave-trade and anti-slavery campaigns. These massive mobilisations of public opinion and action came to be seen as an unprecedented triumph of philanthropy over the economic interests of slave owners. Philanthropy was powerful and those who were now identified with it were the evangelicals, headed by the man who had provided leadership, William Wilberforce.

Evangelicals were at the forefront of the formation of a mass of voluntary organisations designed to improve the morals, behaviour and life chances of the working classes. Philanthropy began to be thought of as embodied in these organisations that were themselves emblematic of England's national identity. The annual May meetings at Exeter Hall in the Strand in London were an occasion either to celebrate or to deplore the rise of evangelicalism. For the critics, led by *The Times*, evangelical philanthropy was soft on crime, neglectful of domestic problems in favour of those overseas, and bent on undermining courage, manliness and sport, qualities and customs that were core ingredients of national identity. Philanthropy, they said, was led by the unmanly; it was effeminate.

Philanthropy faced another problem, or it might be opportunity: political economy. Many leaders of philanthropy saw a consonance between their theology and political economy and welcomed the Poor Law Amendment Act of 1834 and other measures designed to entrench the principles of a market economy. Just as individuals had a responsibility for their own souls so they had for procuring their own livelihood by their own efforts. Philanthropy in this regard was going to be the broom that would sweep away the doles, the giving way to the importunities of beggars, the charities that failed to investigate how deserving were the recipients of their largesse. But philanthropy itself was in danger of forgetting or ignoring these admonitions. Political economists, W. R. Greg perhaps the most vocal, but he was echoed by many others, insisted on the harm that misplaced philanthropy could do, on the danger it posed to the national economy and to national character. The target in the nineteenth century was what was embedded in the practices of the voluntary organisations that made up the world of philanthropy. Dr Barnardo, for example, was a controversial figure and generally held up as one of the great philanthropists of the Victorian era; but he was hardly a model of political economy.

The nineteenth century spawned numerous efforts, from mendicity societies to the COS, to bring good capitalist sense to the charitable and philanthropic world but in the end philanthropy as much as charity was held up for its failures to do so. Far from doing good, said the critics, philanthropy was a source of demoralisation. Towards the end of the nineteenth century the way lay open for new initiatives. One was to see a bonding between philanthropy and capitalism as the way ahead: 5 per cent philanthropy was proclaimed as a solution to housing problems, especially in London. Yet, by the end of the century, its limitations were all too apparent. There were other ways the rich could further the cause of philanthropy: by donating land or erecting buildings for civic improvement, and, as employers, by creating leisure facilities for their workers. At the dawn of the twentieth century there was talk of 'millionaire philanthropists' but they were in fact a rare species, much less prominent than in the United States.

There were also initiatives of a different kind. There was the 'new philanthropy' of personal service of Toynbee Hall and the numerous other settlements. And there was in the growing socialist and labour movement a cultural distaste for charity and philanthropy, coupled with an assertion that they failed to provide a solution to the social problems that beset Britain.

The outcome in the first half of the twentieth century was that philanthropy as a word became one to be avoided, or, as Elizabeth Macadam hoped, reinvented as another 'new philanthropy'. Volunteers and volunteering, social work, citizenship formed a triad equivalent to the philanthropy, humanity and benevolence of the eighteenth century. In the later twentieth and early twenty-first centuries, 'civil society' as a space within which campaigning and volunteering could happen, gained traction. A revival of the word 'philanthropy' seemed unlikely.

And yet it happened. It could not have done so without conditions over which it had little control: the critique of and rolling back of the welfare state, the growth of inequality and extreme wealth. This latest 'new philanthropy' was, like its predecessors, critical of much that went before it. It was going to do what the political economists of the early nineteenth century had hoped would happen, marry together philanthropy and capitalism. Like 5 per cent philanthropy, entrepreneurs would bring to philanthropy methods that worked in the capitalist world. There would be measurable outcomes, together with a rationalisation of the organisational structure of the old charitable and philanthropic world through amalgamations and take-overs. There would be new centres of power and influence within the philanthropic world, such as New Philanthropy Capital. And eventually there would be the establishment of centres for the study of philanthropy in universities, a development doubtless encouraged by the growing dependence of these institutions on philanthropic donations – when the rich give, universities, not the poor, tend to be the major beneficiaries, an outcome that would have astonished John Howard and many others.

This survey and analysis of the reputation of philanthropy raises difficult questions. It is all too common for the history of philanthropy to be written as a succession of golden ages. Yet it was in the golden ages, such as the Victorian one, that criticism was most vocal. As well as documenting the criticism, we need to ask, was it justified? Was Adam Smith right in arguing that the idea of universal philanthropy was built on a naive and unrealistic view of human nature and that it is primarily self-love that drives us? Is today's 'compassion fatigue' an indication that that is so? Did those who practised telescopic philanthropy deserve to be held up before the public for neglect of poverty nearer home and often causing harm abroad? The latter is an argument often made about the impact of aid in the twenty-first century.[2] How much substance was there to the reiterated assertion of the political economists that too much giving created a dependency class and that philanthropy did more harm than good? What was it that an East End vicar had seen that led him to think that the marvel of Christ's life was his 'repression of His powers of beneficence'? Does the identification in the nineteenth century of a class of professional philanthropists with comfortable salaries have a parallel in the spotlight shone now on the chief executives of NGOs? Was the true path of philanthropy that claimed by those who started the settlement movement, that what was wanted was 'Not money, but yourselves'? Must it always be the case, as W. R. Greg put it in the nineteenth century, that 'To the conscientious and thoughtful the path of philanthropy is one of briars and thorns'?[3]

The most fundamental change in the history of philanthropy, its monetisation, was a gradual process in Britain, but a sudden one in the United States. For most of the nineteenth century, writes Kathleen McCarthy, 'America stood at the margins of international philanthropic innovation. Almost all of the institutions that cropped up in the United States during the nineteenth century, from the antislavery movement to the modern university, were imported from Europe'. This was to change after the Civil War and with the growth of huge fortunes. 'Suddenly, philanthropy was reinterpreted as big gifts, eclipsing the historically embedded significance of collective giving and voluntarism.' Philanthropy 'was recast as an American invention'.[4]

The history of philanthropy from the turn of the twentieth century is in part a history of foundations – and the biggest foundations were in the United States. They might seem to be uncontroversial. The opposition to the setting up of the Rockefeller Foundation in the early twentieth century shows how mistaken that view is. Legally, it needed the support of Congress. One line of opposition was voiced by former US president Theodore Roosevelt: 'no amount of charities in spending such fortunes can compensate in any way for the misconduct in acquiring them'. The Rockefeller money came from Standard Oil, infamous for its monopolistic practices. The major cultural institutions in Britain in the twenty-first century face precisely the same criticism: should they accept money from corporations whose reputation is controversial, like BP or that of the Sackler family in the United States, manufacturers of the opioid that has led to the deaths of thousands of citizens? Equally challenging was the argument that such a foundation as Rockefeller 'must be repugnant to the whole idea of a democratic society'; it was 'a menace to the welfare of society', existing in perpetuity and unaccountable except to handpicked trustees. From 1909 to 1913 Rockefeller tried but failed to win the requisite support in Congress. It was eventually the New York state legislature that approved the setting up of the Foundation.[5]

For the remainder of the twentieth century and into the twenty-first the United States could proudly claim to be the most philanthropic country in the world, replacing the claims that Britain had made for itself. Critics might point to the tax advantages that American philanthropists enjoyed or to the fact that so much giving was to churches that some regarded as outside the proper boundaries of philanthropy, but the wealth that accumulated in private hands enabled Americans to do philanthropy on a scale that other countries could not match. Only in the twenty-first century did critics begin to question the role of the escalating number of foundations and of other vehicles for philanthropy. Echoing the criticism of the Rockefeller Foundation in the early twentieth century, commentators pointed to the power and influence that philanthropists could wield and how unaccountable they were. Vast sums, for example, were spent promoting the foundation of charter schools to the disadvantage of publicly controlled schools in an area of policy on which the democracy might have strong views. Philanthropy remained contentious, its reputation never as secure as its proponents might wish.[6] If philanthropy in Britain scales up as its proponents hope, exactly the same criticism will become apposite.

Tracing the paths that have led to where we are now leads to conclusions that have tended to be ignored or downplayed in existing histories of philanthropy. Broadly speaking, they are that the history of philanthropy is unintelligible without informing it with the politics, economics, ideologies and cultures of specific times. Put another way, the history of philanthropy is not only the history of a consistent practice of giving (or not giving), it is a history of fundamental changes in thinking, feeling and acting.

Notes

1 John Haygarth to John Howard, 20 May 1789, Bodleian Library, Eng Misc c. 332, fos. 22–33.
2 See, e.g., D. Moyo, *Dead Aid: Why Aid Makes Things Worse and How There is Another Way for Africa* (Harmondsworth: Allen Lane, 2009).
3 Quoted in G. R. Searle, *Morality and the Market in Victorian Britain* (Oxford: Clarendon Press, 1998), pp. 188–9.
4 K. McCarthy, 'Afterword', in F. Q. Christianson and L. Thorne-Murphy (eds), *Philanthropic Discourse in Anglo-American Literature, 1850–1920* (Bloomington: Indiana University Press, 2017), p. 241.
5 R. Reich, *Just Giving: Why Philanthropy is Failing Democracy and How It Can Do Better* (Princeton and Oxford: Princeton University Press, 2018), pp. 1–7.
6 Ibid.; D. Callahan, *The Givers: Wealth, Power and Philanthropy in a New Gilded Age* (New York: Vintage Books, 2018); A. Giridharadas, *Winners Take All: The Elite Charade of Changing the World* (New York: Alfred A. Knopf, 2018).

Select bibliography

This is a select bibliography of secondary sources, divided into books and articles. It includes some works not cited in the footnotes that contribute to the history of philanthropy.

Books

Andrew, D., *Philanthropy and Police: London Charity in the Eighteenth Century* (Princeton: Princeton University Press, 1989)

Barker-Benfield, G.-J., *The Culture of Sensibility: Sex and Society in Eighteenth-Century Britain* (Chicago: University of Chicago Press, 1992)

Beattie, J. M., *Crime and the Courts in England, 1660–1800* (Oxford: Clarendon Press, 1986)

Ben-Amos, K., *The Culture of Giving: Informal Support and Gift-Exchange in Early Modern England* (Cambridge: Cambridge University Press, 2008)

Best, G. F. A., *Mid-Victorian Britain, 1851–1875* (London: Weidenfeld & Nicolson, 1971)

Binfield, C., Ditchfield, G. M. and Wykes, D. L. (eds), *Protestant Dissent and Philanthropy in Britain, c. 1660-c. 1920* (Woodbridge: Boydell, 2019)

Bishop, M. and Green, M., *Philanthrocapitalism: How the Rich Can Save the World and Why We Should Let Them* (London: A & C Black, 2008)

Bradley, K., *Poverty, Philanthropy and the State: Charities and the Working Classes in London* (Manchester: Manchester University Press, 2008)

Braithwaite, C., *The Voluntary Citizen: An Enquiry into the Place of Philanthropy in the Community* (London: Methuen, 1938)

Brasnett, M., *Voluntary Social Action: A History of the National Council of Social Service 1919–1969* (London: NCSS, 1969)

Breeze, B. and Lloyd, T., *Richer Lives: Why Rich People Give* (London: Directory of Social Change, 2013)

Brown, F. K., *Fathers of the Victorians: The Age of Wilberforce* (Cambridge: Cambridge University Press, 1961)

Brown, L. B., *Moral Capital: Foundations of British Abolitionism* (University of North Carolina Press, 2006)

Burn, W. L., *The Age of Equipoise: A Study of the Mid-Victorian Generation* (London: George Allen & Unwin, 1964)

Carnegie, A., *The Gospel of Wealth and Other Timely Essays*, ed. E. C. Kirkland (Cambridge, MA: Harvard University Press, 1965)

Checkland, O., *Philanthropy in Scotland: SocialWelfare and theVoluntary Principle* (Edinburgh: John Donald, 1980)

Christianson, F., *Philanthropy in British and American Fiction: Dickens, Hawthorne, Eliot and Howell* (Edinburgh: Edinburgh University Press, 2007)

Christianson, F. Q. and Thorne-Murphy, L. (eds), *Philanthropic Discourse in Anglo-American Literature, 1850–1920* (Bloomington: Indiana University Press, 2017)

Collini, S., *Public Moralists: PoliticalThought and Intellectual Life in Britain, 1850–1930* (Oxford: Clarendon Press, 2006)

Colpus, E., *Female Philanthropy in the Interwar World: Between Self and Other* (London: Bloomsbury, 2018)

Comitini, P., *Vocational Philanthropy and British Women's Writing, 1790–1810: Wollstonecraft, More, Edgeworth, Wordsworth* (Aldershot: Ashgate, 2005)

Crowson, N., Hilton, M. and McKay, J. (eds), *NGOs in Contemporary Britain: Non-State Actors in Society and Politics since 1945* (Basingstoke: Palgrave, 2009)

Cunningham, H. and Innes, J. (eds), *Charity, Philanthropy and Reform: From the 1690s to 1850* (Basingstoke: Macmillan, 1998)

Daunton, M. (ed.), *Charity, Self-Interest and Welfare in the English Past* (London: UCL Press, 1996)

Davies, R., *Public Good By Private Means: How Philanthropy Shapes Britain* (London: Alliance Publishing Trust, 2015)

Deakin, N., *In Search of Civil Society* (Basingstoke: Palgrave, 2001)

DeLacy, M., *Prison Reform in Lancashire, 1700–1850* (Manchester: Chetham Society, 1986)

Dixon, T., *The Invention of Altruism: Making Moral Meanings inVictorian Britain* (Oxford: Oxford University Press, 2008)

Elliott, Dorice Williams, *The Angel out of the House: Philanthropy and Gender in Nineteenth-Century England* (Charlottesville: University of Virginia Press, 2002)

Evans, R., *The Fabrication of Virtue: English Prison Architecture, 1750–1840* (Cambridge: Cambridge University Press, 1982)

Finlayson, G., *Citizen, State and Social Welfare: Britain 1830–1990* (Oxford: Clarendon Press, 1994)

Ginn, G. A. C., *Culture, Philanthropy and the Poor in Late-Victorian London* (London: Routledge, 2017)

Goldman, L., *Science, Reform, and Politics inVictorian Britain: The Social Science Association 1857–1886* (Cambridge: Cambridge University Press, 2007)

Gorsky, M., *Patterns of Philanthropy: Charity and Society in Nineteenth-Century Bristol* (London: Royal Historical Society, 1999)

Gosling, G. C., *Payment and Philanthropy in British Healthcare 1918–48* (Manchester: Manchester University Press, 2017)

Grant, P., *Philanthropy and Voluntary Action in the First World War: Mobilizing Charity* (London: Routledge, 2014)

Gray, B. K., *A History of English Philanthropy from the Dissolution of the Monasteries to the Taking of the First Census* (London: P. S. King & Son, 1905)

Gray, B. K., *Philanthropy and the State; or Social Politics* (London: P. S. King & Son, 1908)

Harris, B., *The Origins of the British Welfare State: Social Welfare in England and Wales, 1800–1945* (Basingstoke: Palgrave Macmillan, 2004)

Harris, J. (ed.), *Civil Society in British History: Ideas, Identities, Institutions* (Oxford: Oxford University Press, 2003)

Hilton, B., *The Age of Atonement: The Influence of Evangelicalism on Social and Economic Thought, 1795–1865* (Oxford: Clarendon Press, 1988)

Hilton, M. and McKay, J. (eds), *The Ages of Voluntarism: How We Got to the Big Society* (Oxford: Oxford University Press, 2011)

Himmelfarb, G., *Poverty and Compassion: The Moral Imagination of the Late Victorians* (New York: Alfred A. Knopf, 1991)

Hindle, S., *On the Parish? The Micro-Politics of Poor Relief in Rural England c. 1550–1750* (Oxford: Clarendon Press, 2004)

Houghton, W. E., *The Victorian Frame of Mind, 1830–1870* (New Haven and London: Yale University Press, 1957)

Howse, E. M., *Saints in Politics: The 'Clapham Sect' and the Growth of Freedom* (Toronto: University of Toronto Press, 1952)

Humphreys, R., *Sin, Organized Charity and the Poor Law in Victorian England* (Basingstoke: Macmillan Press, 1995)

Hunt, L., *Inventing Human Rights: A History* (New York and London: W. W. Norton & Company, 2007)

Ignatieff, M., *A Just Measure of Pain: The Penitentiary in the Industrial Revolution, 1750–1850* (London: Macmillan, 1978)

Innes, J., *Inferior Politics: Social Problems and Social Policies in Eighteenth-Century Britain* (Oxford: Oxford University Press, 2009)

Jeremy, J. D., *Capitalists and Christians* (Oxford: Oxford University Press, 1990)

Jones, G. S., *History of the Law of Charity 1532–1837* (Cambridge: Cambridge University Press, 1969)

Jordan, W. K., *Philanthropy in England 1480–1660: A Study of the Changing Pattern of English Social Aspirations* (London: Allen & Unwin, 1959)

Kidd, A. J., *State, Society and the Poor in Nineteenth Century England* (Basingstoke: Macmillan Press, 1999)

Laybourn, K., *The Guild of Help Movement and the Changing Face of Edwardian Philanthropy* (Lampeter: Edwin Mellen, 1994)

Lewis, J., *The Voluntary Sector. The State and Social Work in Britain: The Charity Organisation Society/Family Welfare Association since 1869* (Aldershot: Edward Elgar, 1995)

Lloyd, S., *Charity and Poverty in England, c. 1680–1820: Wild and Visionary Schemes* (Manchester: Manchester University Press, 2009)

Lowe, R., *The Welfare State in Britain since 1945*, 3rd edn (Basingstoke: Palgrave Macmillan, 2005)

Mandler, P. (ed.), *The Uses of Charity: The Poor in the Nineteenth-Century Metropolis* (Philadelphia: University of Pennsylvania Press, 1990)

Moniz, A. B., *From Empire to Humanity: The American Revolution and the Origins of Humanitarianism* (New York: Oxford University Press, 2016)

Morgan, S., *A Victorian Woman's Place: Public Culture in the Nineteenth Century* (London: Taurus, 2007)

Oldfield, J. R., *Popular Politics and British Anti-Slavery: The Mobilisation of Public Opinion against the Slave Trade, 1787–1807* (Manchester: Manchester University Press, 1995)

Oppenheimer, M. and Deakin, N., *Beveridge and Voluntary Action in Britain and the Wider British World* (Manchester: Manchester University Press, 2010)

Owen, D., *English Philanthropy 1660–1960* (London: Oxford University Press, 1965)

Prochaska, F., *Women and Philanthropy in Nineteenth-Century England* (Oxford: Clarendon Press, 1980)

Prochaska, F., *The Voluntary Impulse: Philanthropy in Modern Britain* (London: Faber & Faber, 1988)

Prochaska, F., *Royal Bounty: The Making of a Welfare Monarchy* (New Haven and London: Yale University Press, 1995)

Prochaska, F., *Schools of Citizenship: Charity and Civic Virtue* (London: Institute for the Study of Civil Society, 2002)

Prochaska, F., *Christianity and Social Service in Modern Britain: The Disinherited Spirit* (Oxford: Oxford University Press, 2006)

Reich, R., *Just Giving: Why Philanthropy Is Failing Democracy and How It Can Do Better* (Princeton: Princeton University Press, 2018)

Richardson, S., *The Political Worlds of Women: Gender and Politics in Nineteenth-Century Britain* (Abingdon: Routledge, 2013)

Roberts, D., *Paternalism in Early Victorian England* (London: Croom Helm, 1979)

Roberts, M. J. D., *Making English Morals: Voluntary Association and Moral Reform in England, 1787–1886* (Cambridge: Cambridge University Press, 2004)

Rochester, C., *Rediscovering Voluntary Action: The Beat of a Different Drum* (Basingstoke: Palgrave Macmillan, 2013)

Rochester, C., Gosling, G. C., Penn, A. and Zimmeck, M. (eds), *The Roots of Voluntary Action: Historical Perspectives on Current Social Policy* (Brighton: Sussex Academic Press, 2011)

Rodgers, B., *The Cloak of Charity: Studies in Eighteenth-Century Philanthropy* (London: Methuen, 1949)

Rose, G., *The Struggle for Penal Reform* (London: Stevens, 1961)

Rozin, M., *The Rich and the Poor: Jewish Philanthropy and Social Control in Nineteenth-Century London* (Brighton: Sussex Academic Press, 1999)

Schneewind, J. B. (ed.), *Giving: Western Ideas of Philanthropy* (Bloomington and Indianapolis: Indiana University Press, 1996)

Searle, G. R., *Morality and the Market in Victorian Britain* (Oxford: Clarendon Press, 1998)

Shapely, P., *Charity and Power in Victorian Manchester* (Manchester: Chetham Society, 2000)

Simey, M., *Charity Rediscovered: A Study of Philanthropic Effort in Nineteenth-Century Liverpool* (Liverpool: Liverpool University Press, 1992)

Slack, P., *Poverty and Policy in Tudor and Stuart England* (London: Longman, 1988)

Smitley, M., *The Feminine Public Sphere: Middle-Class Women in Civic Life in Scotland, c. 1870–1914* (Manchester: Manchester University Press, 2009)

Tarn, J. N., *Five Per Cent Philanthropy: An Account of Housing in Urban Areas between 1840 and 1914* (Cambridge: Cambridge University Press, 1973)

Temperley, H., *White Dreams, Black Africa: The Antislavery Expedition to the River Niger 1841–1842* (New Haven and London: Yale University Press, 1991)

Todd, J., *Sensibility: An Introduction* (London: Methuen, 1986)

Tompson, R., *The Charity Commission and the Age of Reform* (London: Routledge & Kegan Paul, 1979)

Turley, D., *The Culture of English Antislavery, 1780–1860* (London: Routledge, 1991)

Twells, A., *The Civilising Mission and the English Middle Class: The 'Heathen' at Home and Abroad* (Basingstoke: Palgrave Macmillan, 2009)

Waddington, K., *Charity and the London Hospitals, 1850–1898* (London: Royal Historical Society, 2000)

Walvin, J., *The Quakers, Money and Morals* (London: John Murray, 1997)

West, T., *The Curious Mr Howard: Legendary Prison Reformer* (Hook: Waterside Press, 2011)

Whelan, R., *Involuntary Action: How Voluntary is the 'Voluntary' Sector?* (London: IEA Health and Welfare Unit, 1999)

Whitten, M., *Nipping Crime in the Bud: How the Philanthropic Quest was put into Law* (Hook: Waterside Press, 2011)

Woodroofe, Kathleen, *From Charity to Social Work in England and the United States* (London: Routledge & Kegan Paul, 1968)

Articles and contributions to books

Andrew, D., 'On reading charity sermons: Eighteenth-century solicitation and exhortation', *Journal of Ecclesiastical History*, 43 (1992), 581–91

Archer, J. W., 'The charity of early modern Londoners', *Transactions of the Royal Historical Society*, 12 (2002), 223–44

Brown, M., 'Medicine, reform and the "end" of charity in early nineteenth-century England', *English Historical Review*, 124 (2009), 1353–88

Cahill, M. and Jowitt, T., 'The new philanthropy: The emergence of the Bradford Guild of Help', *Journal of Social Policy*, 9 (1980), 359–82

Deane, T., 'Late nineteenth-century philanthropy: The case of Louisa Twining', in A. Digby and J. Stewart (eds), *Gender, Health and Welfare* (London: Routledge, 1996), 122–42

Drescher, S., 'The shocking birth of British abolitionism', *Slavery and Abolition*, 33 (2012), 571–93

Duthille, R., 'Richard Price on patriotism and universal benevolence', *Enlightenment and Dissent*, 28 (2012), 24–41

Evans, N., 'Urbanisation, elite attitudes and philanthropy: Cardiff, 1850–1914', *International Review of Social History*, 27 (1982), 290–323

Garnett, J., '"Gold and the Gospel": Systematic beneficence in mid-nineteenth-century England', in W. J. Sheils and D. Wood (eds), *The Church and Wealth* (Oxford: Basil Blackwell, 1987), 347–58

Garrioch, D., 'Making a better world: Enlightenment and philanthropy', in M. Fitzpatrick, P. Jones, C. Knellwolf and I. McCalman (eds), *The Enlightenment World* (Abingdon: Routledge, 2007), 486–501

Garside, P. L., 'The impact of philanthropy: Housing provision and the Sutton Model Dwellings Trust, 1900–1939', *Economic History Review*, 53 (2000), 742–66

Gautier, A., 'Historically contested concepts: A conceptual history of philanthropy in France, 1712–1914', *Theory & Society*, 48 (2019), 95–129

Gerard, J., 'Lady Bountiful: Women of the landed classes and rural philanthropy', *Victorian Studies*, 30 (1987), 183–210

Grenby, M. O., '"Real charity makes distinctions": Schooling the charitable impulse in early British children's literature', *British Journal of Eighteenth-Century Studies*, 27 (2002), 185–202

Gunn, S., 'The ministry, the middle class and the "civilizing mission" in Manchester, c. 1850–1880', *Social History*, 21 (1996), 22–36

Harrison, B., 'Philanthropy and the Victorians', in B. Harrison, *Peaceable Kingdom: Stability and Change in Modern Britain* (Oxford: Clarendon Press, 1982), 217–59

Harrison, B. and Webb, J., 'Volunteers and voluntarism', in A. H. Halsey and J. Webb (eds), *Twentieth-Century British Social Trends* (Basingstoke: Macmillan Press, 2000), 587–619

Harvey, C., Maclean, M., Gordon, J. and Shaw, E., 'Andrew Carnegie and the foundations of contemporary entrepreneurial philanthropy', *Business History*, 53 (2011), 425–50

Hewitt, M., 'The travails of domestic visiting: Manchester 1830–70', *Historical Research*, 71 (1998), 196–227

Humphreys, A. R., '"The Friend of Mankind" (1710–60): An aspect of eighteenth-century sensibility', *Review of English Studies*, 24 (1948), 203–18

Huzzey, R., 'The moral geography of British anti-slavery responsibilities', *Transactions of the Royal Historical Society*, 22 (2012), 111–39

Kanazawa, S., 'To vote or not to vote: Charity voting and the other side of subscriber democracy in Victorian England', *English Historical Review*, 131 (2016), 353–83

Kidd, A. J., 'Charity organisation and the unemployed in Manchester, 1870–1914', *Social History*, 9 (1984), 45–66

Kidd, A. J., 'Outcast Manchester: Voluntary charity, poor relief and the casual poor, 1860–1905', in A. J. Kidd and K. W. Roberts (eds), *City, Class and Culture* (Manchester: Manchester University Press, 1985), 48–73

Kidd, A. J., 'Philanthropy and the "social history paradigm"', *Social History*, 21 (1992), 180–92

Lloyd, S., 'Pleasing spectacles and elegant dinners: Conviviality, benevolence and charity anniversaries in eighteenth-century London', *Journal of British Studies*, 41 (2002), 23–57

Martin, M., 'Single women and philanthropy: A case study of women's associational life in Bristol, 1880–1914', *Women's History Review*, 17 (2008), 395–417

Martin, M. C., 'Women and philanthropy in Walthamstow and Leyton 1740–1870', *London Journal*, 19 (1994), 119–50

Moore, M. J., 'Social service and social legislation in Edwardian England: The beginning of a new role for philanthropy', *Albion*, 3 (1971), 33–43

Moore, M. J., 'Social work and social welfare: The organisation of philanthropic resources in Britain, 1900–1914', *Journal of British Studies*, 16 (1977), 85–104

Morgan, R., 'Divine philanthropy: John Howard reconsidered', *History*, 62 (1977), 388–410

Morris, S., 'Market solutions for social problems: Working-class housing in nineteenth-century London', *Economic History Review*, 54 (2001), 524–45

Morris, S., 'Changing perceptions of philanthropy in the voluntary housing field in nineteenth- and early twentieth-century London', in T. Adam (ed.), *Philanthropy, Patronage, and Civil Society: Experiences from Germany, Great Britain, and North America* (Bloomington: Indiana University Press, 2004), 138–60

Oishi, K., 'Coleridge's philanthropy: Poverty, Dissenting radicalism, and the language of benevolence', *Coleridge Bulletin*, 15 (2000), 56–70

Pellew, J., 'A metropolitan university fit for Empire: The role of private benefaction in the early history of the London School of Economics and Imperial College of Science and Technology, 1895–1930', *History of Universities*, 26 (2012), 202–45

Prochaska, F., 'Philanthropy', in F. M. L. Thompson (ed.), *The Cambridge Social History of Britain 1750–1950*, 3 vols (Cambridge: Cambridge University Press, 1990), vol. 3, 357–93

Radcliffe, E., 'Revolutionary writing, moral philosophy, and universal benevolence in the eighteenth century', *Journal of the History of Ideas*, 54 (1993), 221–40

Roberts, M. J. D., 'Reshaping the gift relationship: The London Mendicity Society and the suppression of begging in England 1818–1869', *International Review of Social History*, 36 (1991), 201–31

Sulek, M., 'On the modern meaning of philanthropy', *Nonprofit and Voluntary Sector Quarterly*, 39 (2010), 193–212

Summers, A., '"In a few years we shall none of us that now take care of them be here": Philanthropy and the state in the thinking of Elizabeth Fry', *Historical Research*, 67 (1994), 134–42

Tarr, R. L., 'The "Foreign Philanthropy Question" in "Bleak House": A Carlylean influence', *Studies in the Novel*, 3 (1971), 275–83

Webber, M. C., 'Troubling agency: Agency and charity in early nineteenth-century London', *Historical Research*, 91 (2018), 116–36

Weinbren, D., 'Supporting self-help: Charity, mutuality and reciprocity in nineteenth-century Britain', in B. Harris and P. Bridgen (eds), *Historical Perspectives on Charity and Mutual Aid: European and American Experiences since 1800* (Abingdon: Routledge, 2007), 67–88

Williams, C. D., '"The luxury of doing good": Benevolence, sensibility and the Royal Humane Society', in R. Porter and M. M. Roberts (eds), *Pleasure in the Eighteenth Century* (Basingstoke: Macmillan Press, 1996), 77–107

Index